# Cleveland CEMETERIES

## Stones, Symbols & Stories

### VICKI BLUM VIGIL

**PHOTOGRAPHS BY GALE V. FLAMENT**
(EXCEPT AS NOTED)

GRAY & COMPANY, PUBLISHERS
CLEVELAND

Gray & Company, Publishers
1588 E. 40th Street
Cleveland, Ohio 44103
www.grayco.com


Library of Congress Cataloging-in-Publication Data
Vigil, Vicki Blum, 1945-
Cleveland cemeteries / by Vicki Blum Vigil.
Includes bibliographical references and index.
1. Cemeteries—Ohio—Cleveland—History Anecdotes. 2. Cleve-
land
(Ohio)—History Anecdotes. 3. Cleveland (Ohio) Biography
Anecdotes.  4. Cleveland (Ohio) Guidebooks.
I. Title.
F499.C692 A2 1999
977.1'32--dc21          99-6709     CIP

ISBN 1-886228-25-6

Printed in the United States of America
10 9 8 7 6 5 4 3 2

This guide was prepared on the basis of the author's best knowledge
at the time of publication. However, because of constantly changing
conditions beyond the author's control, the author disclaims any
responsibility for the accuracy and completeness of the information
in this guide. Users of this guide are cautioned not to place undue
reliance upon the validity of the information contained herein and
to use this guide at their own risk.

# CONTENTS

# Acknowledgments

I would like to thank the many people who contributed to this endeavor and helped me get through it: My personal advisory committee—Judy Eigenfeld, Sharon Goelman, and Elaine Hersch. My co-workers who shared my enthusiasm. Cynthia Dettelbach and the *Cleveland Jewish News,* who gave me my first breaks as a writer. Ted Schwarz—for encouragement tempered with harsh reality. Antioch Writers' Workshop—for strong doses of refuge and rejuvenation. The Cemetery Walkers—Marcie Anderson, Irene and Nicole Mihevic, Jim and Sandy Mackemull, Sandy Sajner, Michael Flament, Margie Wilk, Sharon Goelman, and Les Meritsky, who "tested" the text. The cemetery sextons, superintendents, and workers who offered their time, assistance, and expertise. The many well-stocked and well-staffed libraries in Greater Cleveland, but most especially the staff at Euclid Public Library and Mayfield Regional Library. The Monday night writers' group—for all the support and attention to detail. Christine Krosel, archivist for the Catholic Diocese. Drew Rolik—for assistance in research and for helping find those elusive stones. Mark Hersch—for researching sports questions. Gale Flament, whose photographs enliven this book. My mom for passing on her appreciation of the written word. My dad, Emerick Blum, who accompanied me to more cemeteries then he'll ever remember. My daughters Rachel and Ariana, who offered constructive criticism and computer assistance. My son Kiva—for his long-distance support and encouragement. And finally, loving appreciation to my husband David, for insights, encouragement, and all that time spent listening. Also, I gratefully acknowledge the assistance of these people in the preparation of entries for the following cemeteries: Brookmere Cemetery—Portions of the information included in this entry are from the book *Old Brooklyn New, Book II,* by permission of Kathryn Gasior Wilmer. Butternut Ridge Cemetery—Helen A. Shaw. Fir Street Cemetery—The Cleveland Jewish Genealogical Society and, in particular, Arlene Rich. Harvard Grove Cemetery—Dennis Block, James Skidmore, and Velma Skidmore. Highland Drive Cemetery—Kathryn Gasior Wilmer. Lake Side Cemetery—Cathy Flament. Lutheran Cemetery—Kathryn Gasior Wilmer. Nelaview/First Presbyterian Cemetery—Melinda Grohol. St. Mary Cemetery—Lynette Filips Zieminski. Evergreen Cemetery—Bonnie Walker. Glendale Cemetery—John P. Gurnish. Johnson's Island Confederate Cemetery—Donald J. Breen and Roger Long. Mt. Peace Cemetery—John P. Gurnish. Westwood Cemetery—The book *Westwood: An Interpretive Guide,* and the Oberlin Historical and Improvement Organization.

# Introduction

"Why is a nice girl like you writing a book like this?"—or some other version of that question—has been asked of me many times in the past two years. The simple answer is, of course, because I want to. But it's a little more complicated than that. As I approached my fifties, I found myself reading the obituary page more often. I was attracted to reading about the lives of people I did not even know because I was interested in some particular aspect of their lives—longevity, an unusual profession, even a unique name. Then one day I saw a story about a woman whose family put "Gone to Wal-Mart" on her grave. I was hooked. I knew that cemeteries held a lot of stories, and I'm here to tell them.

And so began a journey that has taken me to more than 120 local cemeteries and to meetings with some of the nicest people in the business, the caretakers of those cemeteries and the caretakers of our local, regional, and family histories—our libraries and historical societies.

Cemetery aficionados, and they do exist, try to come up with new monikers for their haunts—silent city, outdoor museum, open-air museum—to entice more people to join in visiting and appreciating these historic sites. I applaud their motives, but I don't think we need to change the name to fool people into coming. I think they will come if we give them a reason to, an artistic sight to behold, a person to learn about. I am drawn to the cemetery because it's a quiet place, an outdoor history lesson, a place where I can see the struggles of those who went before me and get strength from them. I marvel at the pride displayed by a placed picture for all to see, or the pain revealed in a listing of the tragedies endured. I admire the nerve it took for immigrants to leave the known and come to the unknown, to arrive with a dollar in their pockets, not knowing the language, and to somehow "make it." And I like the cemetery for what it is not: it's not a place I have to go; it's not formal, with particular paths I must go down; it's not somebody else's idea to be here, it's mine.

And the show doesn't end; it goes on forever. I think that's the part that appeals to all of us—we'd all like to go on forever. Call it vanity, ego, or the wish for a legacy: we would all like to think that what we've done, or who we are, has made a difference to someone. And I'm here to tell you that it has.

Shed that false bravado and step back in time. You'll be visiting the dead, but you will come to appreciate the living.

**DISCLAIMER:** This book is meant as a guide to take you into and around the cemeteries listed. Since all but one are outdoors, please remember that the forces of nature may cause some changes. Therefore the author cannot be responsible for conditions at the cemeteries, any occurrences that take place therein, or the accuracy of the descriptions. The information given was the best available at the time.

**BE PREPARED:** Dress appropriately for the weather, wear comfortable shoes, and bring a camera. Watch out for uneven ground, and bring along your own drinking water. (Even if available, cemetery water is usually not potable.) Bring a small bag for litter. When you leave the cemetery, don't leave any visible signs of your visit—scraps of paper, gum wrappers, etc.

**ARM-CHAIR TRAVELERS WELCOME:** Not everyone is able to spend time walking through cemeteries. If you can't or don't want to walk through the cemeteries yourself, you can visit them here in words and pictures.

**AUTHOR'S NOTES:** Ethnic affiliation is meant only to describe those ethnic groups known to be buried in a particular cemetery. It does not mean other ethnic groups are not found there, only that they are not known to the author or not mentioned in literature about the cemetery. Descriptions mentioning height and width of gravestones are only approximations.

# Genealogical Resources

Perhaps because baby boomers are reaching middle age, interest in personal genealogy has grown tremendously in recent years. For those interested in family research, we offer these resources:

City of Cleveland, Division of Health,
Bureau of Vital Statistics
601 Lakeside Ave., City Hall Room 122
Cleveland, OH 44114
(216) 664-2315

City of Cleveland, Division of Parks
Maintenance and Cemetery Properties
21400 Chagrin Blvd.
Cleveland, OH 44122
(216) 348-7210

Cleveland Public Library
325 Superior Ave.
Cleveland, OH 44114
(216) 623-2800

Of particular interest will be the newspaper room, history and geography departments, and government documents.

Church of Jesus Christ of Latter-day Saints
Family History Centers & Libraries, Genealogy
Cleveland (440) 777-1518
Kirtland (440) 256-8808

These folks have been keeping family history records for a long time.

Cuyahoga County Archives
2905 Franklin Blvd.
Cleveland, OH 44113
(216) 443-7250

The county archives has a map of all the cemeteries in the county and some birth records, as well as naturalization records from 1818 to 1971; Civil War bounty record, 1862; city directories, 1823–1939 (not all), and much more.

Cuyahoga County Public Library,
Fairview Branch
21255 Lorain Rd.
Cleveland, OH 44126
(440) 333-4700

While all the county libraries have helpful information, this is the designated genealogy center—for example, they maintain necrology files, which the other branches do not have.

Diocese of Cleveland, Archives Department
1027 Superior Ave.
Cleveland, OH 44114
(216) 696-6525

Lakeland Community College,
Community Education Division
7700 Clock Tower Dr.
Kirtland, OH 44094
(800) 589-8520

Lakeland has an annual genealogy and family history conference, usually held in June.

Morley Library
184 Phelps St.
Painesville, OH 44077
(440) 352-3383

While the emphasis here is on Lake County genealogy resources, they also have county histories, land atlases, and many other documents helpful for doing family history research.

Ohio Department of Health
P.O. Box 15098
Columbus, OH 43215-0098
(614) 644-8595

Birth certificates from December 1908–present; death certificates from 1944–present

Ohio Genealogical Society
713 S. Main St.
Mansfield, OH 44907-1644
(419) 756-7294

The Ohio Genealogical Society is the largest state genealogical society in the United States. The cost is $27 for an individual and $32 for a joint membership.

Ohio Historical Society
1982 Velma Ave.
Columbus, OH 43211-2497
(614) 297-2510

Ohio Society of Military History
316 Lincoln Way East
Massillon, OH 44646
(330) 832-5553

This nonprofit military museum maintains
a research library.

Western Reserve Historical Society Library
10825 East Blvd.
Cleveland, OH 44106
(216) 721-5722

The historical society library contains necrology
files, census records, maps, and other documents that can assist in research, particularly
as it relates to the Western Reserve. The library
offers, for a fee, a series of seminars on genealogy and other hands-on programs in family
history research for both beginners and experienced researchers.

**AREA GENEALOGY
GROUPS/MEETINGS:**

African-American Genealogy Society
of Cleveland
P.O. Box 201476
Cleveland, OH 44122

Cleveland Jewish Genealogy Society
c/o Menorah Park
27100 Cedar Road
Cleveland, OH 44122

Cuyahoga Valley Genealogy Society
(216) 526-8442

East Cuyahoga County Genealogical Society
P.O. Box 24182
Lyndhurst, OH 44124

Greater Cleveland Genealogical Society
P.O. Box 40234
Cleveland, OH 44140-0254

Lake County Genealogical Society
184 Phelps St.
Painesville, OH 44077

Cuyahoga West Chapter of Ohio Genealogical
Society
P.O. Box 26196
Fairview Park, OH 44126-0196

**NOTE:**

Log on to www.grayco.com/updates for
updates to the information provided about
these organizations.

# GRAVESTONE RUBBING

Photographing a gravestone is one way to record what you have seen. Another way is to do a rubbing of the stone. This provides a more tangible souvenir, as well as a more personal remembrance. By getting personally involved, you can gain a greater appreciation for the work of the stonemason as well as the end product itself.

**MATERIALS NEEDED:**

1. Towel to kneel on

2. Paper and pencil to record details from and about the stone, including its location (city, cemetery, etc.)

3. Polaroid camera (for the perfectionist) so that if you forget where some of the interesting details are, you are easily reminded

4. A stiff brush (not wire) to clean bird droppings, lichen, and other matter off the stones

5. Scissors

6. Masking tape

7. Paper. Start with newsprint—you can use the fancy papers (rice paper, aquba) after you're more experienced.

8. Crayon, charcoal, or carpenter's crayon

9. Cardboard tube or portfolio to store finished rubbings

10. Towelettes or water-free hand cleanser

11. A soft brush, such as a paint brush, to get the gunk out of crevices

12. A spray bottle of water, to clean off the stone if necessary

13. A tote bag to carry everything

**FIND A STONE YOU'D LIKE TO RUB.** For your first time, you might want to choose something small and simple. In the interest of preservation, do not choose a deteriorating stone.

1. Gently clean off the stone with towel, brush, or water if needed; cut away any grass around the base if you will be rubbing there.

2. Get a few pieces of masking tape ready, center your paper on the front of the stone and tape paper securely to stone.

3. With the crayon, rub gently across the paper in large sweeping motions. Rub in the direction of the slant of the letters; you are finished when it is clear and dark enough for you (it will appear lighter indoors than in the sunlight.)

4. Do not remove the tape until you've looked at the rubbing from a few feet away. Check to see if you missed any spots or if there are streaks. If so, go over it very lightly using vertical strokes only. Then take off the tape.

5. If you used charcoal or graphite, you will probably need to spray on a fixative as soon as you finish. The purpose of the fixative is to bond the charcoal or graphite particles and hold them to the paper.

6. If you used crayon, after you get home buff the rubbing with a scrap of leather or an old brown paper bag. This just brings out the color a bit more.

7. You're done. Store your rubbing in a safe place or get it framed. If you are rubbing stones of family members, make copies at the local office-supply store and send them to out-of-town relatives—they are often very appreciative.

# SYMBOLS

Symbols as well as words are carved on many of the gravestones you will visit. Most of these images have a meaning beyond the figure they represent. A brief list of these symbols and their meanings follows. However, remember that some people may have chosen a symbol for personal reasons that go beyond its standard meaning, and others use it solely to create a mood.

Acorn—strength

Anchor—hope, seafaring profession

Angel—emissary between heaven and earth

Angel with bible—devotion to faith

Arches—victory over death, mortality

Arrows—mortality, death's dart

Birds—soul

Birds flying—soul in flight

Broken column—loss of head of family

Broken ring—family circle cut

Buds/rosebud—morning of life or renewal of life

Bugles—resurrection, the military

Butterfly—short life, human soul

Candle snuffed out—time, mortality

Cannons—gift of love

Coffin—mortality, death of the flesh

Corn—ripe old age

Cross—faith

Crossed swords—high military rank

Crown—victory of the soul, righteousness

Daisy—innocence

Discarded clothing—laying down life's burden

Dove—innocence, gentleness, purity, devotion, messenger of God

Eagle—soul's ascent after death

Fern and anchor—hope

Flame—arising triumphant

Floral wreath—victory over death

Flowers/bouquets—life both beautiful and brief, grief, sorrow

Fruit—eternal plenty

Garlands—victory in death

Grapevine—associated with Christianity ("I am the vine")

Half the sun—end of earthly life, beginning of heavenly life

Hand, index finger pointing up—deliverance from evil, way to salvation

Hand of God chopping—sudden death

Handshake—farewell

Harp—praise to God

Hearts—bliss/love of Christ

Horns—resurrection

Hourglass—swiftness of time

Hourglass with wings—time flying, short life, urgency of life

Imps—immortality

Ivy—friendship and immortality

Lamb—innocence

Laurel—fame, victory

Left hand—evil

Lily/Lily of the valley—innocence and purity

Linked, shaking hands—welcomed by the hand of God

Moon, stars, and sun—rising of the soul to heaven

Oak leaves—maturity, ripe old age

Open book—bible, deceased teacher or minister

Owl—messenger

Palm branch—victory, rejoicing

Poppy—sleep

Right hand—the hand of god, power, strength, righteousness

Roses—perfection, love

Rose in full bloom—prime of life

Sheaf of wheat—ripe for harvest

Shells—pilgrimage of life

Snake—evil

Shovels/picks—mortality

Sphere—gift of rest

Spilled flowerpot—hopes dashed

Stars and stripes around eagle—eternal vigilance, liberty

Thistles—remembrance

Tombs—mortality

Torch inverted—life extinct

Tree stump with ivy—head of family, immortality

Trees—life

Trumpeter—heralds the Resurrection

Urn—death, fate, mourning

Urn with blaze—undying friendship

Urn with lid—triumph over birth and death, total enlightenment

Urn with wreath or crepe—mourning

Weeping willow—sorrow

Willow and urn—life in the hereafter

Wreath—mourning and resurrection

# Cleveland CEMETERIES

## Stones, Symbols & Stories

Map by Rustbelt Cartography

# LOCATION OF CEMETERIES IN THIS BOOK

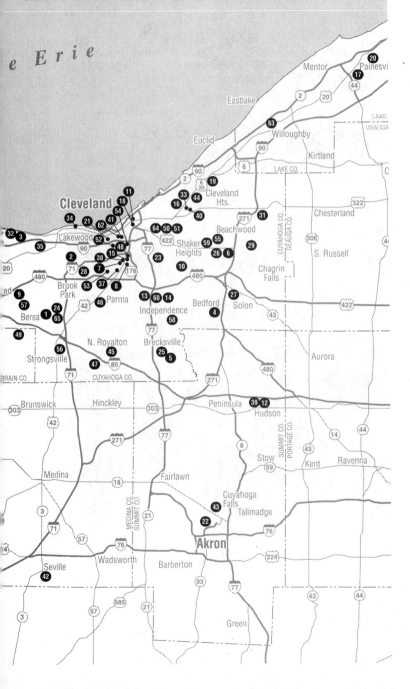

## Alger Cemetery

ADDRESS: 16710 Bradgate ~ LOCATION: Cleveland ~ PHONE: (216) 348-7216

ACREAGE: 12 acres ~ CARETAKER: City of Cleveland; No office or restrooms on site

ACCESS: Grounds open Mon–Sat 9 a.m.–3 p.m. Records at Highland Park Cemetery (216-348-7210), and Western Reserve Historical Society (216-721-5722)

NUMBER OF BURIALS: 5,500 ~ OLDEST/FIRST GRAVE: Oldest: Nathan Alger, January 21, 1813; first: Nathan Alger, January 21, 1813

RELIGIOUS AFFILIATION: Episcopalian, Roman Catholic ~ ETHNIC AFFILIATION: German, but according to legend several Native Americans are also buried here.

DIRECTIONS: I-90 to Exit 164 for McKinley Ave.; south on McKinley; left (south) on SR 237 (Rocky River Dr.); left (east) on Bradgate Ave, after Lorain Ave.; on left.

**HISTORY AND SURROUNDINGS:** This cemetery originally consisted of a one-acre plot conveyed to the village of Rockport (now part of Cleveland) in 1828 by Priscilla Woodworth. Unmarked and unrecorded graves in the original acre are estimated at no fewer than 500. Additional land was added between 1859 and 1912, bringing the total to almost 12 acres. No records are available prior to 1900, but we do know that by 1939 there were 3,000 burials here.

## LIGHTNING STRIKES

**YOUR VISIT:** Turn left into the cemetery then take the first right, take another left and then right again. Look for the Kamms stone. Behind and to the left of Kamms is a large flat marble stone for Rande Hulec (1961–1990). He was Ohio's first casualty of the Persian Gulf War. Air Force Sergeant Hulec was a meteorologist on board a C5A plane that blew up on take-off leaving Kaiser Schlauten AFB.

Continue around this section, turning right to go toward the back of the cemetery. Look for a flagpole on the left. Walk toward the fence and look for Nathan Alger's five-foot-tall aging white stone.

The Alger family (from Litchfield County, Connecticut) settled in a log cabin near Warren Road south of Detroit Avenue. The area was known as Rockport Township. Nathan Alger arrived June 12 (some say June 7), 1812 with his wife Prescilla, four sons, and three daughters. His death less than a year later was the township's first. On Nathan Alger's gravestone is written:

My friends I'm here the first that's come
and in this place for you there's room.

Records left by Nathan's son, Henry, give us a vivid picture of the tremendous hardships the pioneers endured and the strength and determination needed then just to maintain life. Once Henry traveled to

> **NOTABLE:**
>
> *Part of the charm of this cemetery is its rather large size— it takes up one end of a residential street.*

Ebenezer Merry's farm in Painesville to thresh wheat. As payment he got to keep every tenth bushel (and had to carry it home). In 1813 he walked to Cleveland to get salt—a scarce commodity the pioneers needed for preserving food. After working nine days for S. Baldwin, Henry was paid 56 pounds of salt, which he carried home on his back. He traded some of the salt for flour. According to another account, he went to Columbia township to chop trees for Captain Hoadley (see Riverside Golf Course entry) and was paid 100 pounds of flour, which he also carried home—a distance of 10 miles.

About 30 feet from Nathan is another of his sons, Thaddeus. His stone lies flat, close to a pine tree. Thaddeus P. Alger was killed by lightning on July 14, 1828 at the age of 27. It was common for gravestones to mention the cause of death, and Thaddeus's offers a fitting adaptation of the "Prepare to Meet Your God" epitaph:

> My sudden death proclaims aloud
> to you my dying friends
> to be prepared to meet your god
> When he the summons sends

As you exit, stop by the Paulick mausoleum, the only mausoleum at Alger. The story is told that because Catherine Paulick, a Catholic, married out of her religion, she could not be buried in a Catholic cemetery. So her husband had this mausoleum built for the family—however, he was not buried here. Catherine died in 1951.

OTHER CEMETERIES NEARBY: Lakewood Park, *p. 151*

~ SUPERSTITIONS ~

# Funerals on Friday portend another death in the family during the year.

*Upper portion of Nathan Alger's stone*

*Cause of death is indicated on
marker of Thaddeus P. Alger*

# Calvary Cemetery

ADDRESS: 10000 Miles Ave.  ~  LOCATION: Cleveland  ~  PHONE: (216) 641-7575

ACREAGE: 305 acres  ~  CARETAKER: Several on staff; restrooms available at the office and in sections 8 and 61

ACCESS: Grounds open daily 7 a.m.–dusk; office open Mon–Fri 8:30 a.m.–4:30 p.m., Sat 8:30 a.m.–noon. Records at cemetery office (216-641-7575), and Diocese of Cleveland (216-696-6525)

NUMBER OF BURIALS: 297,000+  ~  OLDEST/FIRST GRAVE: First: John and Catherine Hogan, died December 1, 1893

RELIGIOUS AFFILIATION: Roman Catholic  ~  ETHNIC AFFILIATION: Irish, French, English, Slovak, Slovenian

DIRECTIONS: I-480 to Exit 23 for Broadway Ave.; right (north) on Broadway Ave.; right (north) on E. 93rd St.; right (east) on Miles Ave.; on right.

OR I-71 to Exit 159A for Harvard Rd.; east on Harvard; right (south) on Broadway Ave.; left (east) on Miles Ave.; on right.

**HISTORY AND SURROUNDINGS:** As the city of Cleveland grew in the late 19th century, it soon became apparent that the two Catholic cemeteries on the East Side (St. John's and St. Joseph's) and the one on the West Side (St. Mary's) would eventually run out of burial space. In 1893, the Leland Farm property was purchased and preparations were begun to turn it into a cemetery. Several more acres were added later that year, and in November 1893 Calvary Cemetery opened. Acquisition of land continued until 1936, when the total included over 300 acres. The huge tract of land has many hilly sections, is filled with large trees, and is the only cemetery in the county with a tunnel.

## THE ACCORDION PLAYS ON

Since its opening more than 297,500 burials have taken place here. The flu epidemic at the end of World War I was responsible for the largest number of interments in a single day, November 4, 1918, when 81 people were buried. November was a record month as well—985 interments.

When Gilbert O'Neill was buried here July 12, 1920, many believed he was the first American soldier to die in action in World War I. This was later disproved.

**YOUR VISIT:** The large size of Calvary makes giving concise and accurate directions to each of the sites mentioned here impossible. As you enter from Miles, bear right and go to the office, where you can get directions and maps for specific sections you wish to see. You might want to locate graves in sections 9 through 13 first before going through the tunnel and looking at those on the other side. You may find it best simply to drive through the hundreds of acres and to get a sense of the expanse of this cemetery and appreciate it for its size and organization—a testament to good planning.

Rev. James Hanley (?–1920) was a chaplain during World War I with the 69th Regiment of New York. He is one of 325 priests buried in Calvary. His stone is gray, about four feet tall with a lot of text on one side. It is below "Griffin," which has a cross with a chalice in the center. Hanley's monument is near the large triple cross. (section 9, lot 1254)

**NOTABLE:**
This is one of the largest Catholic cemeteries in Ohio. Many of the persons buried here were important in the early life of Cleveland's Catholic community.

Anton Grdina (1874–1957) was a community activist, particularly in the Slovenian-American community. After witnessing the death and destruction resulting from the East Ohio Gas explosion on October 20, 1944, he led the community first in mourning and then in rebuilding the Norwood-St.Clair neighborhood. He was the first American to receive the Third Order of the Crown, Yugoslavia's highest civil honor, and was Knighted in the Order of St. Gregory by Pope Pius XII in 1954. His grave is very close to Hanley's. (section 9, lot 43)

Johnny Kilbane (1889–1957) won the world featherweight boxing championship in 1912. The Kilbane family monument is gray and about four feet by two feet with the last name written in large letters across the front of the stone. (However, Johnny's name is not on it.) It is behind "Gemesy." (section 9, lot 840)

The Losteiner family stones, for Daniel (1856–1929) and Julia (1863–1946), are about five rows from the road, and four markers to the right of a large evergreen bush. (section 40, lot 234)

There is no marker for George "Jiggs" Losteiner (1886–1937), one of Cleveland's most dangerous criminals. His unlawful activities began with purse snatching as a teen and escalated to include a rash of payroll and bank robberies and even murder. Losteiner was finally apprehended during a bank robbery in Bedford in 1920. He was tried for the murder of East Cleveland policeman Patrick Gaffney and sent to the Ohio Penitentiary, where he died.

President Kennedy appointed Frank Battisti (1922–1994) a U.S. federal judge in 1961, making him the youngest person to hold that position. On August 31, 1976, Battisti ruled, in *Reed v. Rhodes*, that the Cleveland Public Schools were practicing racial segregation. This led to many changes in the schools, including the controversial cross-town busing. Judge Battisti also presided at the trial of the eight national guardsmen charged in the Kent State shootings. His grave, only about a foot away from the road, is near a taller monument, labeled "O'Brien." (section 30, lot 711)

Edward Delahanty (1867–1903) played baseball for the Washington Senators and the Philadelphia Phillies. He died in Niagara Falls—the result of either an accident or suicide. He is buried about three rows from the street near the "Rush" monument, a tall angel with a wreath in hand. (section 10, lot 135B)

William Wambsganss (1894–1985) was a second baseman for the Cleveland Indians. In the 1920 World Series against Brooklyn, he made the only unassisted triple play in professional baseball. Don't look for the name Wambsganss on the stone; instead look for "Mulholland" on top of a gray two-tone marker: on the base it reads "Wambsganss." (section 30, lot 218 A)

Frank Lausche (1895–1990) was mayor of Cleveland, the only five-term governor of Ohio, and a U.S. senator. In 1954, Governor Lausche signed a bill into law that integrated the Ohio National Guard. (section 70, lot 1232)

Stella Walsh (1911–1980) won two Olympic gold medals in track in 1932. She was killed in a robbery near a discount store. Her flat marker is black and has the Olympic rings on it. (section 90)

Mary Hughes (1881–1908) was one of seven people to die in a fire while shopping at Kresge's department store on Ontario Street. The fire started after a store clerk lit a sizzling sparkler—one of the many fireworks on display for the Fourth of July holiday. (section 9, lot 897)

Stanley J. Klonowski (1883–1973) was a Polish-born businessman and banker. In 1931 he wrote to President Herbert Hoover proposing a way to handle the Depression-era bank crisis. Klonowski, a bank president, suggested creating a separate government agency to offer credit for banks and businesses in distress. Hoover took his advice and initiated a plan providing $500 million in credit for banks. (section 57, lot 765, grave 6)

Stanley J. Radwan (1908–1998) served in the Polish navy and was a prisoner at Bergen-Belsen concentration camp in 1939. He was known locally as the

*Olympic rings commemorate*
*gold medalist Stella Walsh*

Polish Strong Man who bent quarters to entertain neighborhood children and once bit a piece of steel ⁵⁄₈ inch thick in half. Stories about his strength abound. One tale tells of his escape from the concentration camp (only to be caught later) by pushing away a brick wall with his bare hands. Another depicts Radwan as an angry eight-year-old, furious for being spanked, lifting his father up high above his head, averting the meting out of future spankings. In the U. S., Radwan wrestled for 20 years, never losing a match. Ewa's Restaurant, at 4069 East 71st St., displays newspaper clippings attesting to his strength. (section 70, lot 3754, grave 1)

Frankie Yankovic (1915–1998) was the first person to win a Grammy for polka music (1983) and was nominated three times after that. His favorite polka songs were "Blue Skirt Waltz" and "Just Because." Yankovic, known as the Polka King, developed his Slovenian-style polka and attracted people of all ages to his music. His Cleveland television show, *The Frank Yankovic Show* ran on Channel Five for 27 years. Eight hundred people attended the funeral service, while outside an impromptu group of accordionists assembled to play Yankovic's music. As his funeral ended, the area outside the church was filled with his music, his accordion-playing friends, and fans from all over the country. A crew from TV-Slovenia came to cover the funeral. (section 114)

*Top: Christmas wreath with musical notes on Yankovic family marker*

*Bottom: Carving of John the Baptist depicted on Kotecki monument*

Don't miss the Kotecki monument, built by the family whose business is making monuments for others. It is a reproduction of the only painting Michelangelo did on wood. Someone once called Kotecki Monuments and asked about the reproduction, having noticed a person in the background looking rather sad. It must have been someone left out of the will, conjectured the caller. Not so, answered the family. It is John the Baptist, who was in the original painting. The monument is beautifully understated and simple. (section 18)

OTHER CEMETERIES NEARBY: Harvard Grove Cemetery, *p. 191*
Bedford Cemetery, *p. 177*

# Cathedral of St. John the Evangelist

ADDRESS: 1007 Superior Ave.  ~  LOCATION: Cleveland  ~  PHONE: (216) 771-6666

ACREAGE: Unknown  ~  CARETAKER: Catholic Diocese

ACCESS: Call to schedule your visit around masses and special events. Records at Diocese of Cleveland (216-696-6525), and Western Reserve Historical Society (216-721-5722)

NUMBER OF BURIALS: Unknown

OLDEST/FIRST GRAVE: Oldest: St. Christine; first: Bishop Rappe, 1877

RELIGIOUS AFFILIATION: Roman Catholic

ETHNIC AFFILIATION: French, German, Irish, Italian, Scottish

DIRECTIONS: West: I-90 to Exit 172A for East 9th St.; north on East 9th St.; right (east) on Superior Ave.; on left.

East: I-90 to SR 2; west on SR 2 to E. 9th St.; south on E. 9th; left (east) on Superior Ave.; on left.

**HISTORY AND SURROUNDINGS:** The Cleveland Catholic Diocese consists of an eight-county area that was established as a separate diocese in 1847. The following year Bishop Rappe chose this site for the cathedral and construction began. Financial difficulties delayed completion until 1852.

The impressive French Gothic architecture and beautiful wood interior create a place for individual spiritual repose as well as communal devotion. The 26-inch-thick walls provide insulation from the hustle and bustle of the busy downtown area. The mensa, or altar top, is a solid piece of Botticino marble weighing 1,400 pounds.

**CRYPT AVAILABLE**

Major reconstruction between 1946 and 1948 increased seating capacity to 1,200 and brought the addition of a specially built Holtkamp pipe organ. A 185-foot bell tower was added as well.

Burials in the churchyard were once common in Europe and the United States. Often, higher-status individuals were honored with placement closest to the church entrance. Burial inside the church itself is less common.

Situated as the cathedral is, in the center of town near one of the busiest intersections, it is surprising how once inside the cathedral, you feel shielded from the chaos of the outside world.

Some might argue that this does not qualify as a cemetery but, in fact, it is one.

**YOUR VISIT:** Enter the cathedral and take time to notice its many architectural and artistic features. Walk toward the front of the church. To the left of the altar is the mortuary chapel. An ornamental wrought-iron gate, usually locked, separates this from the rest of the church. If it is locked, look through the gates. A good time to visit is the last Sunday of the month (except December) when tours are held after the 12:15 mass.

Above the gate is the phrase "Requiescat in Pace" (may they rest in peace). The marble-covered crypts of the former bishops and an auxiliary bishop of the diocese rest here. In the center is a marble altar with a statue of the Risen Christ above it. Prior to the renovations made in 1948, these remains were kept in a chapel in the basement.

Bishop Louis Amadeus Rappe (1801–1877) was the first bishop of the Cleveland Diocese and served from 1847 to 1870. Born in France, he came to America in 1840. He organized the Sisters of Charity of St. Augustine, who then opened Cleveland's first general hospital, St. Vincent Charity. Rappe was a supporter of the total abstinence movement and as such was unpopular among some of the immigrant communities. Some thought he was too strict, and in the 1860s the Irish parishes requested he be relieved of his duties. Others claimed he favored the German and French priests. Rather than cause a split in the community, Bishop Rappe resigned in 1870.

Bishop Richard Gilmour (1824–1891) served as bishop from 1872 to 1891. Converted to Catholicism in 1842, Gilmour was ordained in 1852. While in Cincinnati he won papal commendation for a popular translation of Bible history. He is credited with founding the *Catholic Universe* in 1874 as a way to combat prejudice.

Bishop Ignatius Frederick Horstmann (1840–1908) was a founding member of the American Catholic Historical Society. He served as bishop from 1892 to 1909, a period when many European immigrants came to Cleveland but did not always coexist peacefully. Thirty new parishes began in Cleveland during his tenure, 22 of which were organized around nationality interests.

*Casket being removed from basement to mortuary chapel in 1948*

Courtesy of Catholic Universe Bulletin

Archbishop Joseph Schrembs (1866–1945) served the Cleveland Diocese from 1921 to 1945. Born in Germany, he was the second youngest in a family of 16 children. During World War I he was a member of the National Catholic War Council. Archbishop Schrembs was instrumental in establishing Parmadale orphanage as well as starting the Rosemary Home for handicapped children. He supported unions and was an early advocate of using radio broadcasting for preaching and instruction. He received the title of Archbishop in 1939.

Edward Francis Hoban (1878–1966) was in charge of the cathedral's renovation in 1946, one year after he became bishop. Other projects he actively supported or initiated were reorganization of Parmadale, expansion of St. John's College, retreats for lay people within the church, and the construction of Holy Family Cancer Home.

John Raphael Hagan (1890–1946) received special permission to be ordained one year before his 25th birthday. He was superintendent of diocesan schools in Cleveland for 23 years and active in many education-oriented groups; he founded the Catholic PTA movement, supported the National Education Association, and was one of the founders of the Experimental School at Catholic University. Hagan died four months after his consecration as a bishop.

*Bishop Edward Hoban consecrating the altar at mortuary chapel on September 7, 1948*

Bishop Clarence B. Issenmann (1907–1982) was born in southern Ohio and received his doctorate in theology from the University of Freiburg in Germany. After serving the Cincinnati community he was appointed coadjutor bishop of Cleveland in 1966 (the coadjutor bishop assumed the major administrative duties while the senior bishop retained the title). While bishop, he reorganized the school board of the diocese and supervised construction of Villa Angela, Lake Catholic, and Lorain Catholic high schools, and St. Vincent-St. Mary High School in Akron. He also began the apostolate for the Spanish-speaking community and set up the Commission on Catholic Community Action.

**NOTABLE:**

St. Christine's relics are under the altar of Mortuary Chapel. She was a third-century martyr. Pope Pius XI gave these relics to Bishop Schrembs in 1928.

OTHER CEMETERIES NEARBY: Erie Street Cemetery, p. 38

~ SUPERSTITIONS ~

# A bird in the house is a sign of a death.

# If a robin flies into a room through a window,

# death will shortly follow.

# Denison Cemetery

**ADDRESS:** 2300 Ellen Alley  ~  **LOCATION:** Cleveland  ~  **PHONE:** (216) 348-7210
**ACREAGE:** 1.5 acres  ~  **CARETAKER:** City of Cleveland; no restrooms on site
**ACCESS:** Grounds open daily dawn–dusk. Records at Highland Park Cemetery (216-348-7210)
**NUMBER OF BURIALS:** 706  ~  **OLDEST/FIRST GRAVE:** Oldest: 1823
**RELIGIOUS AFFILIATION:** Nondenominational  ~  **ETHNIC AFFILIATION:** N/A
**DIRECTIONS:** I-71 to Exit 246 for US 42 (Pearl Rd.); south on US 42 (Pearl Rd.); left on Garden St.; on left.

**HISTORY AND SURROUNDINGS:** A marker to the left of the entrance notes that this was originally Brooklyn Centre burial ground. The Denison Cemetery was opened in 1844 and so named because of the street it is near. Very little is known about Denison except that it was taken over by the city of Cleveland sometime after 1894. This cemetery is so small that the gate permits entrance by pedestrians only. How does the city manage to get lawn mowers and other equipment inside in order to maintain the area?

**L.O.V.E. CHILD BURIED HERE**

**YOUR VISIT:** Read the dedicatory plaque as you enter. Then turn right and look toward the center of the cemetery for the white stone marked "Love." The stone has an acrostic on it:

> Laurice
> Olive
> Vera
> Ensign born July 24, 1893, died June 15, 1908.

This stone is all that's left to tell about this child who died as a teen.

Stay in the center section and look for a monument for John B. Denison. He was born November 15, 1799, and died March 16, 1857.

Look in the area near the apartments for the marker of Newton J. Doolittle, who died September 8, 1870. The GAR (Grand Army of the Republic) marker tells us he served in the Civil War.

Back toward the Denison marker, by the 23rd Place fence, is a stone for Alexander Ingham (1763–1858). Ingham served in the Revolutionary War, though it appears he was quite young at the time.

Another Revolutionary War veteran lies closer to the fence and near the entrance gate. Ebenezer Fish (1757–1827) was born in Groton, Connecticut, and made the entire journey from there to Brooklyn on foot. While in the army, Fish was taken prisoner while defending Fort Griswold. Ebenezer and Moses Fish were cousins of James Fish (see Scranton Road Cemetery). During the War of 1812, Moses was drafted, but Ebenezer took his place, knowing Moses was not very strong. Ebenezer fought in a battle on Mackinaw Island in Michigan.

Next, look for the Foote markers back toward the gate but in the center of the plot. These are black rolled stones with information on the underside of the markers. There are several graves from the Foote family. Edwin T. Foote was a surveyor with Moses Cleaveland's Connecticut Land Company, and these are believed to be his relatives. There is a marker with the name Edwin T. Foote and a partially legible date of (perhaps) 1835. Next to his marker is that of Margaret Foote, possibly dated 1899. This family goes back to Cleveland's first settlers.

**NOTABLE:**

*Two soldiers of the Revolutionary War are buried here. Both graves have SAR markers. It is also easy to find graves of Civil War veterans. The stone of Sergeant Henry Young notes that he and his daughter died within one month of each other.*

Stone of L.O.V.E.

Ebenezer Fish served in the Revolutionary Army

Surveyor Foote was offered land in what is now downtown Cleveland, but instead he chose property on Schaaf Road. He was looking for good soil on which to set up his farm. He chose well; the area became for a time the greenhouse capital of the United States, and several active greenhouses can still be found there.

Harriet Beecher Stowe, author of *Uncle Tom's Cabin*, was also a Foote (see Nelaview/First Presbyterian cemetery). Her father was Asa Foote. According to Foote family records, Asa was a common name, so it is unlikely that the Asa buried here is the author's father.

Further over toward Pearl Road are the markers for the Young family. Note that Henry Young died just a month before his daughter Nettie. There are several Civil War soldiers buried here. You will recognize their stones as the white government-issue markers with a crest in the center. The one for Captain Peter G. Schneider says "KIA age 28" (killed in action). Other Civil War veterans buried here are Sergeant Edward Sawtell, Simeon Wallace, and Corporal Crawford Brainard.

OTHER CEMETERIES NEARBY: Riverside Cemetery, *p. 54*
Brookmere Cemetery, *p. 134*
The memorial to Foote and Wolf, *p. 83*

~ SUPERSTITIONS ~

You must hold your breath
while going past a cemetery or you
will breathe in the spirit of
someone who has recently died.

# East Cleveland Cemetery

ADDRESS: East 118th St.  ~  LOCATION: Cleveland  ~  PHONE: None

ACREAGE: 12 acres  ~  CARETAKER: Cleveland Heights and East Cleveland; no rest-rooms on site

ACCESS: Grounds open daily dawn–dusk. Records at East Cleveland Service Depart-ment (216-681-2419), and Western Reserve Historical Society (216-721-5722)

NUMBER OF BURIALS: approx. 1,100  ~  OLDEST/FIRST GRAVE: Oldest and first: 1851

RELIGIOUS AFFILIATION: Nondenominational  ~  ETHNIC AFFILIATION: German, Irish

DIRECTIONS: I-90 to Exit 177 for Martin Luther King Blvd.; south on MLK; left (east) on Euclid Ave.; left (north) on E. 118th St.; on right.

**HISTORY AND SURROUNDINGS:** In 1849, the trustees of the township of East Cleveland bought land from the Oumick family and another fami-ly for use as a community cemetery. The land is actually now in the city of Cleveland. But at that time, Cleveland's boundary was East 55th Street, and Cleveland has never assumed responsibility for the site. It has also been known as Wade Park Cemetery.

About 70 years ago, Cleveland Heights and East Cleveland agreed to share in the upkeep of the site. In 1988, they agreed to maintain the cemetery in alter-nate years. However, as East Cleveland's financial problems grew, that arrangement proved difficult. The cemetery often goes neglected and then will sud-denly be cleaned up after some newspaper or televi-sion journalist rediscovers it. Trees that seem to have been here forever include oak, willow, sycamore, sweet gum, and horse chestnut. The train tracks are just beyond the back wall.

**CLEVELAND CONNECTIONS TO CUSTER AND CODY**

As you walk through the cemetery you may see debris left by oth-ers—the residents here do not disturb the land, only the uninvited and careless do so.

**YOUR VISIT:** Find "Custer" on the right side after the first right onto the cemetery access road. Banks Custer (1882–1935) died of surgical shock. He was the second cousin of General George Custer and lived at 782 East 150th Street. (section 10)

Philip Cody, grandfather of Buffalo Bill Cody, is buried in this same section.

Philip's second son, Isaac, moved to Davenport, Kansas, in 1855 and became active in keeping Kansas a free state. Isaac visited Cleveland several times to give speeches promoting the cause. Seriously injured by a provocateur during one of his anti-slavery talks, Isaac died from his wounds within a year. He is buried in Pilot Knob Township Cemetery in Kansas.

William F., Isaac's son, about ten years old and living in Kansas at the time of his father's death, was sent to Cleveland for an education. By then his grandparents were no longer alive, so it is likely he stayed with other relatives on the Cody property near East 83rd Street. He didn't stay long, and by age 14 he was working in the Colorado gold mines. Shortly thereafter he joined the Pony Express. William earned his nickname "Buffalo Bill" after the Civil War from his job supplying railroad construction crews with Buffalo meat (see Evergreen Cemetery) The *Cleveland Press* published columns written by Buffalo Bill in 1908. (section 10)

Continue on the cemetery drive as it curves left. Before the mausoleum is the gray "Ford" marker, on the right side of the road, about

10–15 feet after "Cozad." Hezekiah Ford (1750–1848), born in Abbington, Massachusetts, was a private with the Connecticut Line in the Revolutionary War. Ford served in Captain William Ward's Hampshire Company when they repelled Benedict Arnold's attack.

Continue around the next bend (right) and just as the drive bends left again look for "Edwards." The six-foot-high, blackened marker looks like a flat-topped obelisk on a pedestal. It is behind the tall "Hallenbeck" stone. Adonijah Edwards (1741–1831) fought in the Revolution as a private with the Vermont Line.

*Top: Tree lined vista of tombstones in East Cleveland Cemetery circa 1950*

*Bottom: Marker for Philip Cody, grandfather of Buffalo Bill Cody*

Throughout the cemetery you will see names such as Dille, Doan, Eddy, and Quilliams. All are names of nearby streets—indicating the importance of the person for whom they were named.

William Quilliams's parents emigrated from the Isle of Man and moved to Painesville, where he was born. The family then came to Cleveland and owned a farm on what is now Quilliams Road in Cleveland Heights. William, a carpenter, enlisted in the Civil War. He was a sergeant in Battery B, First Ohio Light Artillery and served for three years. In 1876, he lost his right hand in an accident and had to give up carpentry. He served as an officer of the Court of Appeals of Cuyahoga County and made many friends through that position. Frederick Quilliams, William's son, was a doctor and surgeon. His home and office were both located at 1618 East 118th Street.

**NOTABLE:**

*Charles Maynard Chambers (1889–1948) served in both World War I and World War II. His government marker states "hero of Wars I and II."*

**MORE TO KNOW:** Samuel Cozad came to East Cleveland in 1808. He and his sons owned the land where Case Western Reserve University now stands, as well as land currently within Lake View Cemetery. The Cozad House, still standing at East 115th and Mayfield Road in University Circle, is believed to have been a stop on the Underground Railroad.

**STORY BUT NO STONE FOUND:** Percy Benjamin Day (1896-1908), son of Hiram and Catherine Day died in the Collinwood School fire March 5, 1908. Records indicate he is buried here, but I could not locate the grave and the cemetery office has no record of it. However, friends tell me they have seen the marker near others of the Day family.

There is also supposed to be a mass grave of 12 Civil War veterans who died in a box-car fire.

A 1956 *Cleveland Press* story pictured a stone dog guarding the grave of its creator, Charles E. Reader, who died in 1909. It could not be found.

OTHER CEMETERIES NEARBY: Nelaview/First Presbyterian Cemetery, *p. 51*
Lake View Cemetery, *p. 105*

~ SUPERSTITIONS ~

# A white moth inside or trying to enter the house means death.

# Erie Street Cemetery

ADDRESS: 2291 East 9th St.  ~  LOCATION: Cleveland  ~  PHONE: (216) 348-7210
ACREAGE: 8.8 acres  ~  CARETAKER: City of Cleveland; no restrooms on site.

ACCESS: Grounds open Mon–Sat 9 a.m.–3 p.m. Records at Highland Park Cemetery
(216-348-7210), and Western Reserve Historical Society (216-721-5722)

NUMBER OF BURIALS: 17,900+

OLDEST/FIRST GRAVE: Oldest: Rebecca Carter, daughter of Lorenzo Carter, died in 1803;
first: Minerva White, daughter of Deacon Moses White, died in 1827

RELIGIOUS AFFILIATION: Persons of all faiths were buried at Erie Street Cemetery until
1840, when different religious groups formed their own burial grounds.

ETHNIC AFFILIATION: African-American, English, Native American, Romanian

DIRECTIONS: West: I-90 to Exit 172A for E. 9th St.; north on E. 9th; on right. East:
I-90 to Exit 173A for Prospect Ave.; west on Prospect; left on E. 9th St.; on left.

**HISTORY AND SURROUNDINGS:** Chosen for location, not landscape, Erie is Cleveland's oldest existing cemetery. (The city's first burial plot was located at Ontario and Prospect near the old Bailey Company, later the May Company's garage.) Many of those buried here were Cleveland's original settlers who shaped the city and ensured its future. It is the city's most well-known and historically significant burial ground.

ORPHAN NEWSBOY MAKES NEWS

In 1825 Cleveland Village trustees bought this land for one dollar from Leonard Case, Sr. The council decided the eight acres was more than enough for burial purposes, so in 1836 they permitted a gunpowder magazine and a poorhouse hospital to be built on unused land. The displeased offspring of the original lot owners filed a lawsuit in federal court, alleging the cemetery land was to be used for burials only. The suit was denied.

By 1904 Highland Cemetery opened, and Mayor Tom L. Johnson's administration felt Erie Street Cemetery was no longer the city's prime burial site. Several bodies were reinterred at Highland. A public outcry arose because the move was seen as unnecessary. Next, the city attempted to reclaim some of the cemetery land to build streets. Incidents like these led to the formation of the Pioneers Memorial Association in 1915. Thanks to the Association, in 1925 City Manager William Hopkins was persuaded to build the Hope Memorial (Lorain-Carnegie) Bridge around—not through—Erie Street Cemetery. In 1940, Erie was rededicated.

In the 1920s, the cemetery was thought to be a meeting place for thieves and other unsavory types. The area behind the old vault was ostensibly used by cocaine and opium dealers. Vandals once broke into the vault of former Mayor Josiah Harris; rumor had it Mr. Harris was buried with a large diamond ring. The robbers opened the wrong casket, his mother's, and left in a hurry. The rumor about the diamond was untrue.

**YOUR VISIT:** Enter from East Ninth Street. The grave of Moses White is in the first section to the left, about halfway between the drive and the wall. White (1791–1881) moved to Cleveland with his wife Mary in 1816. He was a charter member of the First Baptist Church of Cleveland and helped organize the first religious school in Cleveland in 1833. Although they had eight children, only two survived to adulthood.

Close by are the stones for the Carter family. Lorenzo Carter (?–1814) was Cleveland's first permanent resident. In May of 1797, he built a conspicuous log cabin on the east bank of the river at the foot of St. Clair Avenue. The speedy completion of a boat allowed him to launch a ferry at the foot of Superior Street and begin trading with the Indians. Major Carter was also an excellent marksman whose downing of game helped many of the early settlers. Carter suffered from cancer of the lip, which most likely was the cause of his death. His log cabin is represented at a small park in the Flats called Settlers Landing. The inscription refers to the fact that other settlers moved away from the center of town because of the ague (fever from malaria), but the Carters stayed.

Proceed on the driveway to a large boulder on the right. A few feet further on the left is a dark monument marked "Barnett." Walk into this section (north) to find the new, flat, gray granite stone for Malvin. John Malvin (1795–1880) came to Cleveland as a freed slave and worked as a canal boat operator, eventually owning his own boat. He was the first American ship owner to come through the port of Cleveland. He and his wife were the first African-American members of the Baptist Church— but it took them 18 months to integrate the pews. He worked with white leaders to repeal laws that discriminated against blacks, such as those that prevented black men from testifying against white men in court.

Until recently Malvin's grave was unmarked. In 1997 a marker was placed here, and the dedication included a tribute by the director of the National Museum of American History of the Smithsonian Institution. The stone's inscription is the same as the headline on Malvin's obituary:

> The eventful career and noble work of a worthy man whose
> thoughts were of his people, John Malvin, accomplished
> educator, ship owner, minister and carpenter.

He is considered one of the most important African-Americans in Ohio's history.

Continue walking toward East 14th Street and find the unfinished Rouse mausoleum. Notice the number 4 at one end of the base and the number 5 at the other end. These are section markers. The unfinished vault was built for Benjamin Rouse. Construction was so slow that he became impatient, and once the underground portion was finished he brought the project to a halt. Family burials did take place there—by removing the stone over the entranceway.

Loop back and walk toward East Ninth Street. On the left, about two-thirds of the way back toward East Ninth, is the burial site of Chief Joc-O-Sot (1810–1844), a Sauk Indian chief who lived during the Black Hawk War. He was also known as Walking Bear. The chief performed in Wild West shows in the United States and Europe and supposedly sat for a portrait at the request of Queen Victoria. However, no such portrait has ever been located. During one of his trips abroad, the chief became ill, and on his way home, arrived in Cleveland too ill to continue the trip to Missouri. He remained in Cleveland, where he became a hunting and fishing companion of Dr. Horace Ackley. Joc-O-Sot died penniless and destitute at the age of 34. Ackley and others arranged for his burial at Erie Street Cemetery. Two stones mark the grave of Joc-O-Sot: The larger is a boulder with a plaque on top which displays engravings of an elk, fish, raven, and wolf; the smaller, flat slab was broken by vandals.

Next to Chief Joc-O-Sot is buried Chief Thunderwater (1865–1950), a spiritual leader from the East who conducted an annual ceremony of

*Modern replacement to nearby marker*          *Vandalized marker of Chief Joc-O-Sot*

placing maize—the Native American symbol of eternal friendship—on Joc-O-Sot's grave, which symbolized that if Joc-O-Sot were still alive, Thunderwater would raise corn, cook it, and feed it to him. Thunderwater, an Oghema-Niagra Indian, was the son of a Seneca father and an Osaki mother. He became known as Cleveland's "official Indian," serving at ceremonies and formal events. He also made regular appearances in Buffalo Bill shows.

*Peace pipe marks grave site of well known chief*

Several feet farther on the left is the newer upright stone for Fenton. Gamaliel Fenton (1763–1849) was a soldier in the Revolutionary War who fought at Horse Neck and White Plains. Fenton left New England in 1788 and later served at Plattsburg in the War of 1812. He arrived in Cleveland at the age of 70 with his wife Elizabeth. He died in a cholera epidemic, and she died four years later of apoplexy. His new stone has a reproduction of Archibald Willard's *Spirit of 76* on it.

A few feet more towards East Ninth Street are several flat stones close together, some broken, which were taken from the original Ontario Street Cemetery. Among these are the stones of Stephen Gilbert (1777–1808) and Adolphus Spafford (1792–1808), who drowned in Lake Erie on the same day. Anna Spafford was Adolphus's sister.

**STORY BUT NO STONE FOUND:** David Eldridge (?–1797) was Cleveland's first fatality. He fell off his horse and drowned while crossing the Grand River with Moses Cleaveland's first surveying party. His funeral, held days later, was presided over by Rev. Hart in accordance with Episcopal rites.

Barbara Forman (1848–1856) died following a severe whipping by her teacher. Her death shocked Cleveland residents.

James Kingsbury was originally buried at Erie Street Cemetery, only to be reinterred later at Highland Park.

Nicolae Stoica (?–1916) left his wife and nine children in Romania in search of a better life in the United State. He eventually got work building a tunnel under Lake Erie to one of the intake cribs that provided Cleveland's drinking water. While the tunnel was under construction, an explosion on July 25, 1916, killed 19 men. Stoica and four others who died during the accident were buried in a common grave. When several of Stoica's children came to Cleveland in the 1920s, they could not locate his grave. Not until 1983 did the city confirm his burial plot here. On December 12, 1983, a tombstone was laid on the grave.

Asahel Tuttle (1767–1837) was a soldier in the Revolutionary War.

Alfred Williams (1889–1900), an orphan, was brought to Cleveland from Pennsylvania by a man who put on glass-blowing exhibitions. He worked as a newsboy and had no permanent home. He was found dead from poisoning—a suspected suicide. The public learned of the tragedy and offered to help bury him. But his fellow newsboys, who wanted to do something for him themselves, pooled their money and bought a burial lot at Erie Street Cemetery.

Later, Joseph Carabelli (the founder of Lakeview Granite and Monumental Works) donated a monument for him—a seated figure of a newsboy holding papers, known as the Marble Newsboy. The inscription read: "He was a newsboy without father, mother or home and was buried by his newsboy comrades." It used to stand in a corner of the cemetery close to East 14th Street, but now cannot be found—it either sank into the ground (a common fate of old monuments) or was vandalized.

Passengers of the vessel *C.P. Griffith* that burned and sank near Willoughby in 1853 are reported to be buried in the first 20 graves in section 12.

John Willey (?–1841) was elected the first mayor of Cleveland Village April 11, 1836, and reelected the next year as well.

OTHER CEMETERIES NEARBY: Cathedral of St. John the Evangelist, *p. 28*
Scranton Road Cemetery, *p. 73*

~ SUPERSTITIONS ~

# A person who dies on Good Friday
# will go right to heaven.

# Fir Street Cemetery

ADDRESS: 6015 Fir Avenue ~ LOCATION: Cleveland ~ PHONE: (216) 961-4369

ACREAGE: 0.9 acres ~ CARETAKER: Gates are locked; call to arrange your visit

ACCESS: Records at Cleveland Jewish Genealogical Society (440-449-2326); Western Reserve Historical Society (216-721-5722) has a Jewish archivist

NUMBER OF BURIALS: approx 850 ~ OLDEST/FIRST GRAVE: Oldest: 1865 (a child's grave)

RELIGIOUS AFFILIATION: Jewish

ETHNIC AFFILIATION: Hungarian, Lithuanian, Polish, Russian

DIRECTIONS: I-90 to Exit 169 for W. 44th St.; north on W. 44th; left (west) on Lorain Ave.; right (north) on W. 65th St.; right on Fir Ave.; on right.

**HISTORY AND SURROUNDINGS:** The Liberty Aid and Hungarian Aid societies founded this, Cleveland's second-oldest Jewish cemetery. The exact date of its beginning is not known. It was also known as Peach Street Cemetery. Park Synagogue and Heights Jewish Center own the grounds and maintain the records along with the Jewish Welfare Federation. The cemetery no longer accepts burials; the last burial was in 1969. It is located in an urban area, and there is more broken glass on the outside of the cemetery than grass on the inside.

**HOW BIZARRE TO FIND A CZAR IN CLEVELAND**

**YOUR VISIT:** Even if you don't get inside, you can see a lot from the gate. Walk around outside the cemetery and try to read some of the gravestones. Many are written in Yiddish and Hebrew. Others have become illegible thanks to the stress of time and weather.

"Sampliner" is easily visible from the main gate. Herman Sampliner (1835–1899) was the founder of the B'nai Jeshurun/Temple on the Heights congregation. His goal, not achieved in his lifetime, was to have a Jewish hospital in Cleveland. Mt. Sinai Hospital was completed in 1916.

Seen from the east alley, the Bernstein stone has a double marker joined at the top with an urn on it. Harry "Czar" Bernstein (1856–1920) arrived in Cleveland from Poland at the age of 12. He opened Perry Bank, hiring tellers who spoke the languages of the immigrants they served. He was also successful as owner of the Perry Theater, which brought Yiddish drama to Cleveland in the 1890s.

Bernstein was elected to City Council and eventually invited to be part of Mark Hanna's well-heeled and highly influential group of Republicans. His nickname refers to his position as ward leader, which he performed like a dictator. The Jewish community was embarrassed by his reputation for vote-rigging—he was able to "guarantee" thousands of votes and gave away almost as much money as he made.

The Bialosky marker, more difficult to see, is further in toward the center of the cemetery. Kate Bialosky (1846–1912) and her husband owned land in the center of Cleveland that was sought after for a new project—the Terminal Tower. Thinking they could get a better price, the Bialoskys did not sell right away. They held out so long that the parcel was eventually sold for less money than was originally offered. Upset and depressed over these circumstances Mrs. Bialosky committed suicide in her daughter's home in Sharon, Pennsylvania. Jewish custom dictates that people who commit suicide be buried by the fence (an area considered unconsecrated ground), but the Bialosky family overcame this obstacle by using Kate's English name in the obituary and her Hebrew name, Gittel, on the grave marker.

**STORY BUT NO STONE FOUND:** Moses A. Adelstein (1813–1903) organized Cleveland's first Russian synagogue and the city's first free Jewish cemetery, Lansing Cemetery.

Isaac Goldman (1858–1928) was born in Poland and arrived in Cleveland in 1881. He started work in the construction field and became Cleveland's first Jewish building contractor.

Fanny Jacobs (1835–1919) was the founder of Park Synagogue's sisterhood.

Adolphe Kline (1830–1902) fought in the Hungarian Revolu-

*Top: Markers of Harry and Sarah Bernstein inscribed in Yiddish and English*

*Bottom: Nontraditional burial of Gittel Bialosky next to her husband*

tion under Louis Kossuth. Only 17 when he volunteered, Kline fought in 14 battles and was promoted to lieutenant after saving the life of a general. His political ideas continued to get him in trouble in Hungary, and he emigrated to the United States in 1864.

Rabbi Gershon Ravinson (1848–1907) followed nine previous generations of rabbis in his family. He was born in Russia, spoke several languages, and was an acknowledged leader in the study of Talmud.

Rev. Elias Rothschild (1858–1914) was a kosher butcher in Cleveland for 35 years. He was known to help the needy, sometimes letting them stay in his house or eat at his table. When the Free Loan society had financial problems, Rothschild was said to have contributed $50 of his wages to ease the burden of the association.

**NOTABLE:**

*For a Jewish cemetery Fir Street is somewhat unusual. It is not common for Jews to have symbols such as urns on their graves, but you'll see them here and at Willet Street. This may be a custom that was brought from Europe and then quickly stopped, in an effort to "fit in."*

OTHER CEMETERIES NEARBY: Alger Cemetery, *p. 21*
Willet Street Cemetery, *p. 75*

~ SUPERSTITIONS ~

# Mirrors in a house with a corpse should be covered or the person who sees himself will die next.

# Immanuel Evangelical Cemetery

ADDRESS: 4510 West 130 St.  ~  LOCATION: Cleveland  ~  PHONE: None

ACREAGE: 0.8 acres  ~  CARETAKER: none

ACCESS: Grounds always open. Records at Western Reserve Historical Society (216-721-5722)

NUMBER OF BURIALS: Unknown  ~  OLDEST/FIRST GRAVE: Unknown

RELIGIOUS AFFILIATION: Methodist  ~  ETHNIC AFFILIATION: German

DIRECTIONS: I-480 to Exit 12 for W. 130th St.; north on W. 130th; on right.
OR I-71 to Exit 242 for W. 130th St.; south on W. 130th; on left.

**HISTORY AND SURROUNDINGS:** West 130th Street was Settlement Road when this small plot of land, donated by Mr. and Mrs. John Mack, started being used as a cemetery. In 1852 it was known as the United German Settlement Cemetery and belonged to members of Rockport Methodist Church, which was bought by a congregation of the United Church of Christ in the 1960s. Known as God's Acre, Immanuel Evangelical suffers from lack of upkeep, which makes it look like a forgotten and forsaken relative. The church across the street, home to a small congregation, owns this cemetery but is hard pressed to care for it. Neighbors have complained to Cleveland officials about the site, but the city, with other financial woes, is reluctant to take on more. Sadly, this cemetery may be remembered more for what the monuments no longer say than for what they do.

### GOD'S ACRE NOT WHAT IT USED TO BE

**YOUR VISIT:** Park on one of the side streets and walk right in. You will see many broken tombstones, toppled one on top of another. Most are only partially legible and some are inscribed in German.

OTHER CEMETERIES NEARBY:
Butternut Ridge Cemetery, p. 137

*Old graveyard and aging cars are neighbors*

# Monroe Street Cemetery

ADDRESS: 3207 Monroe Ave. ~ LOCATION: Cleveland ~ PHONE: (216) 348-7216

ACREAGE: 13.63 acres ~ CARETAKER: City of Cleveland; no restrooms on site

ACCESS: Grounds open Mon–Sat 9 a.m.–3 p.m. Records at Highland Park (216-348-7210), and Western Reserve Historical Society (216-721-5722)

NUMBER OF BURIALS: 31,400+ ~ OLDEST/FIRST GRAVE: Unknown

RELIGIOUS AFFILIATION: Nondenominational ~ ETHNIC AFFILIATION: Dutch, German

DIRECTIONS: I-90 to Exit 170 for US 42 (W. 25th St.); north on US 42 (W. 25th); left on Monroe Ave.; on left.

**HISTORY AND SURROUNDINGS:** This cemetery was officially established in 1841 through the purchase of six acres of land in what was called the Barber and Lord subdivision. However, burials were known to have taken place here beginning in 1818 when this plot became known as the West Side Cemetery. During the Civil War, soldiers who died in army camps near Cleveland were often buried here.

**HORSE BREEDER GOES UNDERGROUND**

The cemetery has seen better days. The gravel road is overgrown, the office is deteriorating.

**YOUR VISIT:** As you drive in the gate, one of the first monuments on the left is the tall obelisk of the H. L. Whitman family. This marker is considered one of the more outstanding at Monroe Street Cemetery.

Continue a few feet past the office on the right and notice the gray Crowl monument with an urn on top. Alvia Crowl (1857–1880) drowned in Lake Erie on a mission to rescue the shipwrecked schooner *Jane Bell*, which he and his brother owned. The boat was traveling from Detroit to Ashtabula when a storm brewed up. About seven miles from Ashtabula the ship dropped anchor, and as the storm worsened the boat was pulled several miles southwest and then struck rock bottom. The eight crewmen passed the night calmly, and in the morning local citizens brought small boats to their rescue. The rescue mission, however, met with trouble: one of the rescue boats overturned immediately, killing a New Jersey man, forcing the captain and first mate to swim, and leaving the fourth man, Alvia Crowl, to cling to the overturned boat, and later drown.

The story of early life in Cleveland is told here—children dying at a young age (Mamie at age 5, and Marguerite as an infant at 25 days), and

*The Gothic gate at the entrance to Monroe Street Cemetery*

deaths from pneumonia (A. M. H. Crowl, 1862–1910). It was common in the 19th century to list cause of death on the gravestone.

Back up and turn down the first of three roads that run the length of the cemetery, the first one on the left as you entered. You'll pass a crypt on the right, in very poor condition with no name visible. On the left toward the Monroe Street fence is the Castle family plot—the rose-colored sandstone obelisk stands atop a gray-and-black base. We read again how sickness led to early death (one child at nine months, another at age five years).

This is a good example of how a family plot is designed: stones in a border around a large monument, indicating the entire area is for one family.

William Castle (1814–1872) was the last mayor of Ohio City and the 14th mayor of Cleveland (1855–56). The west side of Cleveland was actually a separate municipality known as Ohio City. Castle earned his post as Cleveland's mayor as part of the agreement to annex Ohio City to Cleveland. He is also mentioned as being interred at Lake View— perhaps he was removed from Monroe and reinterred.

Retrace your steps a little by staying in this section but walking a few yards in the direction of the entrance gate, and look for Thome. Jim Thome (1813–1873) was a Presbyterian minister, not a baseball player. His father was a slave owner, but young Thome had adopted abolitionist views by the time he entered Lane Seminary in Cincinnati—views that nearly got him thrown out of the seminary. After leaving Lane, he studied at Oberlin, was active in the American Anti-Slavery Society, and spent six months in the West Indies. From 1838 to 1848 Thome was lecturer in "rhetoric and belles lettres" at Oberlin College. Thome came to Ohio City and served as minister of First Presbyterian Church of Brooklyn from 1848 to 1871. He and his wife, Anna S. Allen, had three daughters.

Return to "Castle" and proceed a little farther toward West 25th Street to a marker with "Greenbrier" on it. Alfred Greenbrier (1808–1888), a mulatto, left Kentucky and arrived in Cleveland in 1827. He was a horse breeder and an active abolitionist who provided speedy transportation to fugitives. His home, complete with secret hiding places, offered help and respite to many escaping slaves. It was located on the city's outer boundaries and was a depot on the Oberlin-Richfield-Cleveland line of the Underground Railroad

Though city officials suspected him, his illegal activities were never discovered. His cause of death is listed in the cemetery records as "old age." The name "Greenbrier" can be read at the base of the monument, but no other dates or information are legible. The monument is located in the section specified as Greenbrier's burial site so we can assume, though we do not know for certain, that this is his stone.

At the end of this row, turn right and proceed across the back of the cemetery. Between the road you just turned off and the next road on your right, look to the left for a rather strange monument with a baby on it. The baby's head seems much larger than its body, and no name is visible on the stone, which is whitish-gray and rather low to the ground. Continue up the second road, turning left as it intersects with the original access road into the cemetery.

**NOTABLE:**
*The story of early life in Cleveland is told here—children dying at a young age (Mamie at age 5, and Marguerite as an infant at 25 days), and deaths from pneumonia (A. M. H. Crowl, 1862–1910). It was common in the 19th century to list cause of death on the gravestone.*

Turn left down the third road (more like an overgrown trail); on the right is a tall white obelisk commemorating the life of I. U. Masters. Irvine U. Masters (1819–1865) was a shipbuilder active in city politics who served as mayor of Cleveland. He was known for being the official greeter for Abraham Lincoln when the president visited Cleveland in February of 1861. Masters was mayor of Cleveland from 1863 to 1864.

**STORY BUT NO STONE FOUND:** Henry Adamy (1756–1835 or '36), a Revolutionary War soldier, served as a private in the New York troops. Although his grave could be found in 1967, it is now impossible to locate.

A newspaper article from 1937 mentions a grave marked "Schuftig," which means "rascal" or "shiftless" in German. Apparently friends of George Dumperth, who died in 1882, found the man's body buried in a potter's field and had him moved to Monroe Street Cemetery. The inscription on the grave was: "He had no wife, loved wine and song; had many a friend, did no man wrong."

August and Wilhelmenia Ruthenberg were the parents of Charles Emil Ruthenberg (1881–1927), one of only three Americans buried in the Kremlin. (The others are Bill Haywood, an early union organizer, and John Reed, a well-known writer and president of the American Communist Party.) Known as CER, Charles became active in the socialist party and later founded and was the first general secretary of the American Communist Party. His radical ideas, numerous speeches, and participation in many public demonstrations earned him the title "the most arrested man in America." From 1917 to 1927 there were only six months when CER was not in jail, indicted, or appealing. In the Canton workhouse he was hung by his wrists for refusing to work in the basement laundry. Ruthenberg died in Chicago from a burst appendix. Red-shirted guards watched his body for two days until his wife and son arrived from Cleveland. His cremated remains were placed in an urn inscribed: "Our Leader, Comrade Ruthenberg." After services in Carnegie Hall, CER was buried in the Kremlin Wall.

OTHER CEMETERIES NEARBY:  Willet Street Cemetery, p. 75
Scranton Road Cemetery, p. 73

~ SUPERSTITIONS ~

# Pointing at a funeral procession will cause you to die within the month

# Nelaview / First Presbyterian Cemetery

ADDRESS: 16200 Euclid Ave.  ~  LOCATION: Cleveland  ~  PHONE: (216) 851-2777

ACREAGE: 0.5 acres  ~  CARETAKER: Church staff; restrooms in church, when open

ACCESS: Grounds open daily dawn–dusk. Records at church office and Western Reserve Historical Society (216-721-5722)

NUMBER OF BURIALS: 115  ~  OLDEST/FIRST GRAVE: Oldest: Elizabeth Ruple, 1811 (stone shows 1811, but family history indicates it was really 1841); first: Susannah Barr, October 9, 1812

RELIGIOUS AFFILIATION: Presbyterian  ~  ETHNIC AFFILIATION: English, Scottish

DIRECTIONS: I-90 to Exit 182 for E. 185th St.; south on E. 185th; left (south) on Nottingham Rd. (becomes Dille Rd.); right (west) on Euclid Ave.; left on Nela Rd.; on left.

**HISTORY AND SURROUNDINGS:** Andrew McIlrath donated land for this cemetery in 1807.

Plans for a church addition in the 1960s called for moving several of the gravestones, but church officers needed permission from the Ohio Supreme Court in order to do so. The move was approved, and those markers are now located in an alcove on the eastern end of the cemetery. There is a dedicatory plaque on the alcove wall.

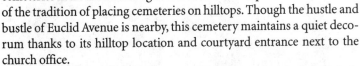

CAUGHT DANCING

This is one of the area's few remaining church cemeteries in an urban setting. It is also a fine example of the tradition of placing cemeteries on hilltops. Though the hustle and bustle of Euclid Avenue is nearby, this cemetery maintains a quiet decorum thanks to its hilltop location and courtyard entrance next to the church office.

Noteworthy pastors who have preached from this church include William H. Beecher, whose father, Lyman, was a notable New England preacher. Lyman was Rev. Henry Ward Beecher's brother as well as the brother of Harriet Beecher Stowe. William may have shared the Beecher name, but he did not share the same gift of oratory. He came to Ohio because he heard there were private funds available to establish a school. Unfortunately he was not an effective leader and soon left.

**YOUR VISIT:** If the church is open, enter through the courtyard by first going into the church from the parking lot. If it is closed, simply walk to the side of the parking lot and go around the church.

There are only 115 graves here. All of those mentioned below are easily found between the courtyard entrance and the side entrance on the eastern end of the cemetery.

John Shaw (1774–1835) married Sarah McIlrath and they moved to Cleveland in 1803. A strong advocate of education, Shaw taught for the county schools for several years. Though he and his wife had no children, their fondness for children was reflected in Shaw's will, written just two months before his death; he bequeathed 90 acres for a school— the nearby Shaw High School.

Sarah Shaw, affectionately known as Aunt Sarah, was excommunicated from the church for dancing. When she refused to repent, her excommunication was continued for one year. At her request she was buried at the foot of Susannah Barr, her lifelong friend.

Enoch Murray (?–1818) was the first Mason to settle in the Western Reserve. The Masonic symbol marks his stone. His wife, Polly, died three years earlier.

Sargent Currier (1757–1823), a Revolutionary War veteran, enlisted in New Hampshire and served three years in the Continental Army. His stone is in two pieces but is otherwise well preserved. The inscription, a version of what I call the "prepare to die" epitaph, reads:

*The weeping willow was a common motif on 19th century tombstones.*
*The depictions here have withstood the passage of time*

My glass is run, my grave you see,
prepare for death and follow me.

Andrew McIlrath (1759–1836) was a private from Connecticut who
fought in the Revolutionary War. His epitaph reads:

With heavenly weapons I have fought the
battles of the Lord,
finished my course and kept the faith, and
wait the sure reward.

Lydia Mattox (1792–1837) has a marker that
was originally upright, but now rests flat. It says:

Cal'd of God to seek his grace
She joyfully obeyed
And eager flew to Christ embrace'd
On whome her hopes were stay'd

**NOTABLE:**

*As you meander
through this church
graveyard remember
that East Cleveland was
once home to John D.
Rockefeller and is still
home to Nela Park, one of
the first corporate cam-
puses in the nation.*

OTHER CEMETERIES NEARBY:  Euclid Cemetery, *p. 87*
East Cleveland Cemetery, *p. 35*

~ SUPERSTITIONS ~

# If a woman is buried in black,
# she will return to haunt the family.

# Riverside Cemetery

ADDRESS: 3607 Pearl Rd.  ~  LOCATION: Cleveland  ~  PHONE: (216) 351-4800
ACREAGE: 90 acres  ~  CARETAKER: Bill Halley
ACCESS: Grounds open daily 7:30 a.m.–5 p.m.; office open Mon–Sat 8 a.m.–4 p.m.
Records at cemetery office and Western Reserve Historical Society (216-721-5722)
NUMBER OF BURIALS: 46,500  ~  OLDEST/FIRST GRAVE: Oldest: Josiah Barber Sr., 1842;
first: Margaret Taylor, April 14, 1876
RELIGIOUS AFFILIATION: Nondenominational
ETHNIC AFFILIATION: Byelorussian, Chinese, Estonian, and Egyptian
DIRECTIONS: I-71 to Exit 246 for US 42 (Pearl Rd.); south on US 42 (Pearl); on left.

**HISTORY AND SURROUNDINGS:** This property, once part of Titus Brainard's farm, originally had a tributary of the Cuyahoga River running through its eastern portion, giving the cemetery its name. The east/west division known to present-day Clevelanders was in existence even one hundred years ago, although at that time it made more sense, because people had to cross the river and perhaps even pay a toll to make the journey from one side to the other. Soon after Lake View Cemetery was established, West Side civic leaders thought it time for a landmark cemetery on their side of town. Trustees organized Riverside in November 1875, and development began the following March. Riverside Cemetery opened to the public on July 8, 1876.

**SOMETHING IS BREWING HERE**

On November 11, 1876, the dedication ceremony was held in a small circular area east of the chapel, where Dutch elm trees were planted as part of the dedication. Unfortunately, all of the trees were lost to Dutch elm disease. Dedication day brought a surprise visit by Ohio governor Rutherford B. Hayes, who had only the week before been elected president of the United States. From this location (memorial circle on the map), you can look straight down the road for 1,000 feet—once the longest straight road in any cemetery in the U. S.

Until the end of 1974, all of the graves at Riverside were dug by hand. The original 102.5 acres have over the years been reduced to 90 by freeway and other development. The land seems flat but has a natural slope and rise. Some sections are traditional, with stones and markers above ground; others are like a memorial park, with flat markers only.

**YOUR VISIT:** As you drive in from Pearl Road the office is on the right, a few hundred feet from the entrance. Made of Massachusetts brownstone that is actually red in color, the Romanesque-style building is on the National Register of Historic Places. Within this modest edifice are three fireplaces: two on the first floor and one that can only be reached from a narrow spiral staircase to the meeting room upstairs.

After you've had a chance to look at the outside of the building (and inside if you visit during office hours), continue down the road with section 6 on your right and 7 on your left. Behind the wide "Heffner-Miller" stone is the Gerstacker plot. Dr. Carl Gerstacker (1885–1945) once was the chairman of Dow Chemical. The artificial turf, placed on his family lot at his request, was laid to enhance its year-round appearance. (section 6)

A few feet toward the center of the section and to the left is the Astrup burial site. The name does not face the road, but a carved wreath can be seen on the side of the stone. William Jacob Astrup (1845–1915) founded the Astrup Awning Co. in 1876. By 1956, the business was the country's largest producer of sails for ships sailing on the Great Lakes. The company is still in business on West 25th Street. (section 6)

Continue down this road, looking on the left for the Newell monument. A few feet farther is the dark "Elsasser" stone. Behind that, close to the ground is Minnie Brown's stone. Minnie Brown (1845–1895) was a victim of the Central Viaduct disaster. Widowed and the mother of five children aged 15 and younger, she is buried here beneath a stone marked simply "Mama" and next to another marked "Papa." She drowned when the streetcar she was riding in plunged off a high-level bridge in Cleveland's Flats. (section 7)

Continuing in the same direction, find the marker for section 24 on

Courtesy Riverside Cemetery Association

*On the National Register of Historic Places, Riverside's office includes three fireplaces*

the left. Near the road on the right is "Flandermeyer." The Flandermeyer family owned a drugstore nearby. Family members were cremated and put in colored glass jars—the type often used in drugstores of the day. The jars were then buried in an underground vault near the family monument. (section 9)

After the Flandermeyers are five or six small stones. One is for Eastman, with "librarian" written below her name. Linda Anne Eastman (1867–1963) was born in Oberlin, Ohio, and became a teacher in the Cleveland Public Schools. After establishing a small library in her classroom, she saw the need for a larger selection of books for children. This drew her toward what would become her life's work as a librarian. Eastman worked at the Cleveland Public Library for 46 years; when she became head librarian in 1918, she was the first woman in the world to lead a library of its size. She helped establish the open shelf system and special services for children, the blind, and the hospitalized. She was also acknowledged nationally for establishing the travel and business bureaus of the library. Eastman worked on designs for the Main Library, which opened in 1925. Later she helped formulate plans for the School of Library Science at what is now Case Western Reserve University. The Eastman Reading Garden of the Cleveland Public Library was named for her in 1969. (section 9)

Continue to section 25 on your left. Behind and to the right of "Baggett" is "Richardson." The name does not face the road. John M. Richardson (1837–1902), an architect with the Cudell group, worked on the design for Franklin Circle Church, the George Worthington Hardware building, and the Perry Paine building. Mark Hanna asked Richardson to design a building to serve as the powerhouse for the streetcar system—the building we know today as the "powerhouse" in the Flats. In 1898 he designed the Jennings apartment complex, which was six stories high and one of the first apartment buildings to have an elevator. (section 25)

By the 1900s, it was said that there was one brewery for every square mile in Cleveland. The city's role in the brewery industry is well chronicled at Riverside.

On the right is "Muth," visible from the road and just before "Daykin" with the lion on top. George V. Muth (1834–1899) was a brewer who moved to Cleveland from Wisconsin. The brewery and the family home were both on Buckley Road. He sold his business, which then became known as Star Brewery. Muth had a foot amputated due to blood poisoning, which eventually led to his death. His headstone has the word "Papa" on it. (section 23)

The road bends and the D. S. Brainard mausoleum is on the left. Next to it is the Leisy family plot with stones elevated a foot off the ground.

Isaac Leisy (1838–1892) learned brewing from his father, though it was an unusual business for a Mennonite family. In his first year of business Leisy brewed more than $20,000 worth of beer. Isaac's son, Otto, took over the brewery, building it into the largest in Northeast Ohio, occupying eight acres of land.

When Prohibition brought brewing to a halt, the family switched to producing "near beer," soda pop, and ice cream. After Prohibition, theirs was one of four local breweries still in existence. There had been 28 prior to the ban.

Leisy Brewery became the most financially successful brewery in Ohio. The Leisy family even did their own malting. Leisy beer was available at the old League Park, and the company sponsored the first television broadcast of a Cleveland Indians baseball game. Leisy is remembered for saying that those brewers who could "see their trade" from the brewery did well. (The Leisy Brewery was located in the same area as its customers.)

The family's carriage house at 3400 Vega Avenue is still standing, but their mausoleum at Riverside, modeled after Monticello, was taken down in 1973 and family members were interred in the ground on the site. A bust of Isaac, originally in the mausoleum, is being restored and will be kept by the family. (section 25)

**NOTABLE:**

*E. G. Marshall, owner of Marshall Drug Stores, supposedly spent the first two days of his honeymoon riding through Riverside Cemetery in a horse-drawn carriage—with his new wife, of course.*

Look toward the right in section 23 for a boulder with "Jones" on it. Carlos Jones (1827–1897) made his fortune manufacturing farm instruments and investing in real estate. His son, John Marvin, drowned in a well on the Jones property at age 12. This, and the sudden death of his first wife, Delia, at 24, inspired Jones and his second wife, Mary, to establish the Jones Home for Children (now part of Applewood Centers) in 1887. (section 23)

Continue straight ahead until the road curves. Section 39 appears on the right. Pass "Titus Brainard" on the left and "Brewer" on the right. Stop at the "Meyer" obelisk on the left, near the stone with Chinese lettering. This is now section 28. Look for three or four small stones in a circle; in front is one for Diode (Diodate) Clark.

Diode Clark (1798–1876) arrived in Cleveland from Springfield, Massachusetts, in 1807. He began his journey on foot with his brother, Kelly, who turned back, leaving Diode to continue alone. Clark was 19 when he arrived in Cleveland with only a few items of clothing and one dollar in his pocket. By chopping wood and clearing forests, he made enough money to buy a farm in Brooklyn, where he became the first male schoolteacher. His other accomplishments include being one of the first to manufacture lime in the city, serving as county commissioner for four terms, and being a trustee in what was later known as the Hanover Street Methodist Church. Clark and his first wife, Caroline Aiken, had three children. She died in 1828 and a year later he married Sarah White Lindsley, who died in 1863. The following year, Clark married Mrs. Samuel Tyler. Nearby Clark Avenue is named for Diode Clark, and Aiken Avenue for his first wife and her family. (section 28)

Return to "Meyer" on the left and walk into section 39 on the right. This is the Weideman plot, where the families of John C. Weideman, his daughter Elsa, and son-in-law, Omar E. Mueller (1881–1946), are buried. Weideman (1829–1900), Cleveland's first elected police commissioner, was founder and president of The Weideman Co., one of the largest wholesale grocery companies in the U.S.. Mueller, a Harvard graduate, eventually was president of the Cleveland Home Brewing Co.(1932–1946), makers of Black Forest Beer. His father, Ernst Mueller, founded the company in 1907 after buying five buildings from Schmitt Brewers at East 61st and Outhwaite streets. The brewery was very successful, affording the Mueller family a summer home on Rocky River Drive. Omar's other contributions include service as U.S. consul to Toronto, Canada, and Bahia, Brazil. He was also a nationally ranked tournament bridge player. The brewery closed in 1952 and was sold in a public auction. (section 39)

On the left in section 28 is the Lamson/Sessions monument. When Samuel Sessions (1824–1902) moved his factory here from Connecticut, he brought all his employees, either because of concern for them or fear of not finding fitting replacements. Samuel joined with his cousins, Isaac Lamson (1832–1912) and Thomas Lamson (1827–1882), and the company became the Cleveland Nut Company, a leading manufacturer of fasteners. Lamson and Sessions is still listed on the New York Stock Exchange. The monument, known as the canopy monument, was built in 1877 at a cost of $10,000—a record at the time. People came from as far as Lorain to see it. The family helped found the Visiting Nurse Association and Pilgrim Congregational Church, and established the first domestic science class in the Cleveland schools. (section 28)

Next to "Lamson/Sessions" is "Pelton." Frederick Pelton (1827–1902), Cleveland's mayor from 1871 to 1873, chaired the commission that chose the site for the Superior Viaduct Bridge. He was also a captain in the Civil War. His monument was bought at the Chicago World's Fair. (section 28)

On the left as section 28 ends and 20 begins, is "Rhodes." James Ford Rhodes (1848–1927) worked at his father's successful mining company but sold it to his brother-in-law, Marcus Hanna, to pursue a more scholarly career. Later he won a Pulitzer Prize for his book, *History of the Civil War*. Cleveland's Rhodes High School is named for him. (section 20)

Turn right at first intersection after "Rhodes" and look for "Foster," a rose-colored stone. Claud Foster (1872–1965) was born and raised in this neighborhood. He was always fixing things around his home and on the family farm. Foster learned how to play wind instruments, joined a band, and by age 14 was supporting himself with his musical talents.

His interest in tools grew from his previous farm experience, and he learned the machinist's trade. As Foster watched a friend work on his clarinet, he got the idea for a car horn using reeds and tubes. After visiting an Erie organ manufacturer, Foster developed a musical car horn that used gases from the exhaust pipe. Foster's Gabriel Horn was on its way to success. Foster's horn was soon followed by another invention, the snubber shock. The Gabriel Snubber Company manufactured 75 percent of all automobile shocks, and Foster became known as the "doctor of car riding." Foster did not forget his roots and was active both financially and personally in local charities. In 1938, he set up a trust to build a new YMCA, now known as the Brooklyn YMCA. A plaque in the lobby states that the building is dedicated to Julia Williams Foster, his mother. In 1952, Foster had a party at the Statler Hotel where, in the course of minutes, he gave $4 million to Catholic, Jewish, and Protestant hospitals, children's homes, universities, and other charitable institutions. (section 22)

Proceed around section 22 and on the right at the next intersection is "Gehring." Charles Gehring (1830–1893) opened his brewery on West 25th Street in 1852 and was the first to make lager beer. The brewery, however, did not survive Prohibition. Gehring's family, like many others, lived across the street from their business. His son, Charles, committed suicide and, though buried at Riverside, is at a different site than his father. (section 22)

Directly opposite is "Coffinberry." James McClure Coffinberry (1818–1891) was a common pleas judge with a reputation for never having a decision reversed. His son, John B. Coffinberry, held public office in three different communities. He was a councilman in Cleveland, mayor of Lorain, and then mayor of Lakewood. John died in 1927 at the age of 80. (section 23)

Memorial Circle is located in the center area between sections 22 and 23. This is where Riverside's dedication ceremony took place. There was a fountain and pond here, but it was later filled in.

To the left, look for the site where Josiah Barber is buried. The rectangular "Humiston" stone with clawfeet is nearby. Several small stones surround Barber's taller one. Josiah Barber Sr. (1771–1842) was the first mayor of Ohio City and the first toll taker on the Cuyahoga River. He bought old Brooklyn's first distillery and lived at West 25th and Franklin. Barber Avenue is named for him. He was originally buried in

Monroe Street Cemetery. The white obelisk with a plaque on it notes that Barber's son, Josiah Jr., was the first president of Riverside Cemetery. Josiah Jr. died exactly 42 years after his father, also on December 12. His death was attributed to "dropsy," now known as edema. (section 23)

Return to Gehring, then turn right to Hopwood at the next corner. Avery Hopwood (1883–1928), known as "the playboy playwright," is buried with his mother, Julia, who died less than a year after his death. A prolific and popular Broadway writer, Hopwood was the Neil Simon of his day. He had four plays (*Ladies' Night, Spanish Love, The Bat,* and *Gold Diggers*) on Broadway at the same time—an unheard-of feat during the post–World War I era. He visited Gertrude Stein and Alice B. Toklas in Europe and collaborated with Mary Roberts Rhinehart on several works. While vacationing in France, he supposedly fell off a pleasure boat and drowned. Other accounts, however, mention his swimming in shallow water and suggest the possibility of a heart attack brought on by heavy drinking.

Hopwood was financially successful, leaving an estate worth over one million dollars. He set up a creative writing award at the University of Michigan, his alma mater, in his and his mother's names. Recipients of this award include John Ciardi, Lawrence Kasdan, and Arthur Miller. Hopwood's pet monkey, Peppy-Squeak, was passed on to Julia, who provided a $10,000 trust fund for his care. (section 22)

Turn around and come back up Centennial Drive, with section 9 on the right and 10 on the left. To the left are "Barstow-Moga" and "Turrington." McLaughlin's one-foot-high stone is five rows behind Turrington and near an evergreen. James McLaughlin (1860–1895) was a victim of the Central Viaduct streetcar disaster. Across the road you should

be able to see Claude Foster's stone. (section 10)

Proceed to the chapel in front of you. Built in 1876, this is the cemetery's only original building still standing. The back part of the chapel was added when coal furnaces became available. The portico was put on after 1876, together with a drop ceiling inside to keep the building warmer. From outside you can see the chapel's small, triangular-shaped blue glass windows, now hidden

*Shrubs harbor playboy playwright's granite marker*

*Only original surviving structure: the chapel, built in 1876, was restored in 1998*

inside by the drop ceiling. Under the chapel floor is a receiving vault with a hand crank that would lower coffins through an elevator shaft. As many as 30 caskets could be stored—a practice common during the winter when the ground was too frozen to hand-dig graves.

The chapel has been restored and was rededicated in 1999. Prior to 1998, the last chapel service was in 1953. Sadly, the original oak pews were given away. But century-old pews removed from a local church fit perfectly into the allotted space.

After looking at the chapel, circle around and go up A Street to section 5 and the Schlather mausoleum. Leonard Schlather (1835–1918), who moved to Cleveland in 1854, worked for and later bought Hoffman Brewery at 1903 West 28th Street. It became the Schlather Brewery and was relocated near the current Great Lakes Brewing Company.

Schlather and his wife, Catherine, had seven daughters, five of whom Schlather had buried by the time Catherine died in 1890. Two died as infants and were buried at Monroe Street; two others died as young girls.

Schlather also owned the Casino Restaurant and Café (renamed Weber's when it was sold), which featured a hanging oak staircase that was saved when the building was razed in 1978. That staircase could later be seen at the Atrium Restaurant in Westlake.

At age 62, Schlather married Anna Catherine Sophia Schwarz, age 30. She was the same age as his youngest daughter. In 1902 he sold the brewery, and the family took a world tour for a year.

Schlather was one of the founders of St. Luke's Hospital. He also contributed toward the statues of Goethe and Schiller on Martin Luther King Jr. Boulevard and the Richard Wagner statue originally located at Edgewater Park. Although Schlather's house was torn down, his second wife, Sophia, willed much of its contents to the Rocky River Library. Included in the pieces at the library are several paintings, rare crotch mahogany furniture, and an 1886 Steinway piano. Sophia also donated $100,000 to build the rear wing of the library, which was completed just before her death. All of Schlather's children except one daughter predeceased him. His home stood where the St. Ignatius football field is now. He died of tuberculosis. (section 39)

Go toward the office, take a left turn, and head down the hill toward sections 14 through 19. Pass the urn garden and two sections for babies. To the far right is section 14 and the unmarked grave of Henry Hagert. Henry William Hagert (1925–1945) was tried and convicted of the murder of twins. A Cleveland funeral director who had to drive to Columbus to bring the body back served as a witness to the execution. Hagert's grave is near the fence by Willowdale. There is no headstone, but at one time there was a sign with the initials HWH. Unfortunately that sign has disappeared. (section 14)

Straight ahead are sections 19 and 29. It is here that cadavers donated for use by Case Western Reserve University medical students are finally put to rest.

**STORY BUT NO STONE FOUND:** One cemetery superintendent remembered a man coming—rather cheerfully—to his office to make arrangements for the burial of his mother-in-law. While he was at the office, the phone rang and the man's wife said her mother was not dead after all. A telegram that should have said "Mother and dad arriving, meet train" instead read "Mother dead, arriving meet train."

Another unusual story is about a local funeral director in the 1930s whose son died suddenly at 35 years of age. The service was held in the chapel, but the funeral director requested the body not be buried immediately. The father came regularly to visit his son, often sitting in a chair in the basement and reading to his deceased child. Finally, after about 10 months, the cemetery staff insisted the body be buried.

OTHER CEMETERIES NEARBY: Denison Cemetery, p. 32
Brookmere Cemetery, p. 134
The monument for Wolf and Foote, p. 83

# St. John Cemetery

ADDRESS: 7000 Woodland Ave. ~ LOCATION: Cleveland ~ PHONE: (216) 641-7575
ACREAGE: 13 acres ~ CARETAKER: Catholic Diocese; no restrooms on site
ACCESS: Grounds open daily dawn–dusk. Records at Calvary Cemetery (216-641-7575), and Diocese of Cleveland (216-696-6525)
NUMBER OF BURIALS: 20,000 ~ OLDEST/FIRST GRAVE: First: James Scully, January 1, 1856 (age 28), and the stillborn child of Aut
RELIGIOUS AFFILIATION: Roman Catholic ~ ETHNIC AFFILIATION: French, German, Irish
DIRECTIONS: I-77 to Exit 161 for E. 55th St.; north on E. 55th; right (east) on Woodland Ave.; on right.

**HISTORY AND SURROUNDINGS:** The land for this burial site was bought from Norman and Mary Baldwin May 4, 1855, but the cemetery did not open until 1858. The cemetery is called St. John because it was first established to serve the people of St. John's parish. Since the terrain here was level, this site developed more quickly than its neighbor, St. Joseph Cemetery. Most of the pioneer priests are buried here in a plot set aside for them. Until all the land was needed, the western section was used as a vegetable garden. The iron gate and modest displays inside provide a tranquil backdrop in this now semi-industrial area.

**LOCAL MAN KILLED BY SHARK**

**YOUR VISIT:** About 15 feet to the right (west) as you enter through the Woodland Avenue gate is the priests' section. You'll see a 12-foot-tall white marker for Fathers Conlon and Dillon. Father James Conlon (?–1875) and Father John Dillon (1807–1836) are, at their request, buried in the same grave. Father Conlon was first Vicar General of the Diocese and the first resident pastor at St. Patrick's, where he served 22 years. Father Dillon was the first resident pastor of Cleveland, and it was his influence that led to the establishment of St. Mary on the Flats, Cleveland's first Catholic Church.

South of the priests' section is a monument in memory of several French pastors. Rev. Joseph S. A. Gerardin's death is attributed to smallpox, which he contracted while making sick calls. Also nearby is Rev. James Monohan, the first priest ordained in Cleveland. Born in Ireland, Monohan was ordained by Bishop Rappe on November 19, 1848, at St. Mary on the Flats.

Continue walking down the road in the center of the cemetery. Toward the back of the cemetery, the road makes a small circle. On the right, just before the road begins to curve, is an impressive monument to the Beckman family. Notice how simple the carving is, yet it exudes a feeling of importance because of its height.

About 40 feet to the left and farther from the road are the O'Reilly markers. These are low to the ground but not flat, and have "father" and "mother" written on the stones. James Kelly O'Reilly (?–1900) was refused membership in the Cleveland Grays, a private military organization, because he was Irish. Determined to help his new country, he became the first enlistee with the 8th Ohio Hibernian and served in the Battle of Gettysburg, a turning point in the war. O'Reilly had been hospitalized with sunstroke but joined his unit out on a ridge between the two armies. Later O'Reilly worked as a sculptor who made plaster "death masks" used for monuments. He met his future wife, Susan O'Brian, after the New York draft riots of July 1863.

Return to the path and continue around the circle and back toward the entrance. As you near the entrance, on the right side (east) across the road from the priests' section is the 15-foot-tall dark Garvey monument. Lieutenant John Garvey (1833–1862) of Company B of the 7th Virginia Regiment was wounded at the Battle of Antietam on September 17, 1862. He died from those wounds three months later in the Smoketown Hospital.

Nearby but farther from the path is the 20-foot-tall Smith monument. It features several children holding up a female figure. On the monument it states "Patrick Smith born at Bailyboro County, Cavan Ireland March 17, 1827, died Cleveland May 11, 1902."

Behind Smith is James Farsey, who came to Cleveland in 1827. He was known for his great strength, which caused many to fear and respect him. He was considered a "lake man": when Irish Catholics were taunted—as they often were—with an effigy of St.

*Inscription indicates John Mooney's dedication to a friend*

Patrick holding a string of potatoes, Farsey would find the perpetrator and dunk him in the Cuyahoga River.

In this same area but closer to the road than the Smith monument is the grave of John B. Mooney (1857–1912). The monument's inscription includes the fact that Mooney was eaten by sharks while trying to rescue a drowning friend off the coast of St. Augustine, Florida.

**NOTABLE:**
*The 20-foot-tall Smith monument features several children holding up a female figure (an excellent example of a cemetery as an outdoor museum).*

**STORY BUT NO STONE FOUND:** East of the receiving vault is the grave of Miss Pance, a French national who came to Cleveland with Miss Ferec to establish an orphanage for girls. They arrived here in 1851 and began their work. Shortly afterward, Pance inherited some money, which she promptly used to make the orphanage bigger and better. The first building was on East 6th Street north of St. Clair, but the orphanage then relocated across the street and was known as St. Joseph Orphanage.

Joseph Kriz (1819–1895) was a successful cooper (barrel maker) who began doing a lot of work for a man named John D. Rockefeller. Rockefeller, who needed many barrels for his oil, soon offered Kriz an interest in the oil business but Kriz refused. Like many immigrants did in those days, the family later changed its name—to Cross.

OTHER CEMETERIES NEARBY:  St. Joseph Cemetery, *p. 66*
Woodland Cemetery, *p. 79*

~ SUPERSTITIONS ~

# If three people are photographed together, the one in the middle will die first.

# St. Joseph Cemetery

ADDRESS: 7916 Woodland Ave.  ~  LOCATION: Cleveland  ~  PHONE: (216) 641-7575
ACREAGE: 12.5 acres  ~  CARETAKER: Catholic Diocese; no restrooms on site
ACCESS: Grounds open daily dawn–dusk. Records at Calvary Cemetery (216-641-7575), and Diocese of Cleveland (216-696-6525)
NUMBER OF BURIALS: 18,000
OLDEST/FIRST GRAVE: First: Michael Walsh, December 18, 1849
RELIGIOUS AFFILIATION: Roman Catholic
ETHNIC AFFILIATION: Two-thirds of the first Catholic residents of Cleveland were Irish, the rest were mostly German. The graves here attest to this fact.
DIRECTIONS: I-77 to Exit 161 for E. 55th St.; north on E. 55th; right (east) on Woodland Ave.; on right.

**HISTORY AND SURROUNDINGS:** This cemetery, the oldest Catholic cemetery in Cleveland, opened in 1850 to serve the St. Joseph parish at 21st and Woodland. That parish closed in 1985 and the church burned down in 1993. The cemetery was established through the purchase of 15 acres of land from Norman and Mary Baldwin for the fee of $1,587 on January 22, 1849. With the sale of some land to the railroad and to light industry, the parcel's size was later reduced to 12.5 acres. Most of the land was hilly and uneven, and there seems to have been a prejudice against being buried on such land. Only about four acres were level, and this was known as the Old St. Mary section. Several of the religious communities buried members of their order here, including the Sisters of Notre Dame and Sisters of the Good Shepherd.

**LOCAL FAMILY OFFERS GOLD**

The hills and open space offer a refreshing change of pace from the nearby urbanization.

**YOUR VISIT:** As you enter the gates, walk straight ahead, and about 30 feet to the left you'll find a marker for Reverend Thomas Lamb (1863–1917), the most noted clergyman here. He had a gift for homilies and was a skilled retreat master and spiritual director. His marker is about 12 feet high with a cross on the top.

Go back to the path and walk to the extreme left of the entrance (east), to the flat section. Climb the modest hill at the eastern edge of the cemetery. This is the northeast section of the property, in what is known

*A wrought iron gate was typical of many early cemeteries*

as "old St. Joseph's," and is the oldest Catholic burial ground in Cleveland. Look behind "Detmar" for "Walsh," the second-tallest monument in the area. Michael Walsh (1829–1849) was the first person buried at this cemetery.

Return to the main path, go down the hill and to the left to the 18-foot-tall granite cross. The large cross was originally in the center of the cemetery, but this is now the southern section of the cemetery. (Because of the land sale to the railroad.)

Notice the vaults to the Sisters of Notre Dame and Sisters of the Good Shepherd, built into the hillside.

Continue following the path around the back and to the west of the cemetery. As you near the Woodland entrance, "Toole" is on the right. The marker is about five feet tall, fading white, and it looks as if something has broken off the top portion. The Tooles were important to Cleveland—they gave gold for the construction of St. John's Cathedral. The other side of the "Toole" stone has the name Murphy on it; this indicates it is

*A slab covers the entry and lists the names of nuns interred within and above*

a family gravesite. One name could be the wife's maiden name or the married name of a daughter.

**NOTABLE:**

*Historians believe the first Catholics in Cleveland arrived about 1825, at the time of the building of the Ohio and Erie Canal. They apparently left when the canal was finished (more returned later, of course), and the earliest Catholic name associated with the village of Cleveland is that of William Murphy, who arrived in 1830.*

**STORY BUT NO STONE FOUND:** Originally there was a culvert at St. Joseph with a stream flowing beneath it. On September 3, 1901, heavy storms caused flooding that unearthed the grave of John Smith. His marker had the dates 1783–1813 on it, and the epitaph read: "Here lies one who loved his country better than himself, he died to preserve her liberty." But this cemetery only dates back to the 1840s. It is believed that Mr. Smith was originally buried at Erie Street Cemetery and later was reinterred here.

OTHER CEMETERIES NEARBY:   St. John Cemetery, p. 63
Woodland Cemetery, p. 77

~ SUPERSTITIONS ~

If the person buried lived a good life.
flowers will grow on the grave.
If the person was evil. weeds will grow.

# St. Mary Cemetery

ADDRESS: 2677 West 41 St. ~ LOCATION: Cleveland ~ PHONE: (216) 961-0399
ACREAGE: 6 acres ~ CARETAKER: On site
ACCESS: Grounds open Mon–Fri 8:30 a.m.–4 p.m., Sat 8:30 a.m.–noon. Records at cemetery office, and Holy Cross Cemetery (216-267-2850)
NUMBER OF BURIALS: 2,800 ~ OLDEST/FIRST GRAVE: Unknown
RELIGIOUS AFFILIATION: Roman Catholic
ETHNIC AFFILIATION: Bohemian, German, Italian
DIRECTIONS: I-90 to Exit 169 for W. 44th St.; south on W. 44th; left (east) on Clark Ave.; left on W. 41st St.; on right.

**HISTORY AND SURROUNDINGS:** The city's first Catholic Church was St. Mary on the Flats on the west side of the Cuyahoga River. Until the Diocese was established in 1847, Catholic burials took place in public cemeteries like Erie Street Cemetery. This cemetery, once known as Burton Street, was affiliated with the Carroll Avenue parish and is located in the middle of a commercial area. The book *People of Faith*, published by the Catholic Diocese of Cleveland, states that St. Mary Cemetery was established in 1861. Yet a map of the cemetery lists 1855 as its dedication date.

Though most of the graves are of settlers who came to Cleveland just after the Civil War, at least one casualty of the war is interred here.

**OLDEST CATHOLIC CEMETERY WEST OF CUYAHOGA RIVER**

*An example of the cast iron decorations found here*

**YOUR VISIT:** Enter from West 41st Street. The oldest part of the cemetery is the quadrant near Clark and West 41st. In this area you will find the flat markers of the Werz (Wurz) family. Catherina's fading white marker has a cross above her name—the family name is not visible. Next to her is Corporal Francis Werz (Wurz). A boot- and shoemaker like his father, Frank enlisted June 19, 1861. On August 9, 1862, he was wounded at Cedar Mountain near Culpeper, Virginia, in the fourth battle in which Company A of the 7th Regiment participated. He died of gangrene in the military hospital in Alexandria, Virginia, on January 5, 1863.

Straight ahead is a circle with a wooden cross in the center. Here are the graves of nine pastors:

Rev. Anthony B. Stuber (1872–1945), Pastor of St. Ignatius Church

Rev. John C. Schaefer (1892–1965)

Rt. Rev. Monsignor Nicholas Pfeil (1859–1935)

Rev. Casimer Reichlin (1843–1917), Rector of St. Stephen's Church

Rt. Rev. Joseph M. Koudelka (1852–1921), Bishop of Superior, Wisconsin

Rev. Anthony L. Bates (1870–1951)

Rev. Carl J. Anthony (1890–1942), pastor of St. Mary's Church, Berea, Ohio

Francis A. Cerwoord (?–1932)

Rev. George L. Koob (1884–1970)

Walk to the nearby veterans' section.

OTHER CEMETERIES NEARBY:  Riverside Cemetery, p. 54
Willet Street Cemetery, p. 75

*The priests' circle*

# St. Theodosius Cemetery

**ADDRESS:** 8200 Biddulph Rd. ~ **LOCATION:** Cleveland ~ **PHONE:** (216) 741-1310
**ACREAGE:** 35 acres ~ **CARETAKER:** On site; restrooms at office
**ACCESS:** Grounds open daily 7:30 a.m.–dusk; office open Mon–Fri 8:30 a.m.–4 p.m., Sat 8:30 a.m.–noon. Records at cemetery office
**NUMBER OF BURIALS:** 15,000 ~ **OLDEST/FIRST GRAVE:** First: 1902
**RELIGIOUS AFFILIATION:** Orthodox Christian
**ETHNIC AFFILIATION:** Greek, Russian, Serbian
**DIRECTIONS:** I-480 to Exit 15 for Ridge Rd.; north on Ridge ; left (west) on Biddulph Rd.; on right.

**HISTORY AND SURROUNDINGS:** The tiny brick chapel at this flat cemetery is used for services during inclement weather. Inside is a mural depicting the resurrection of Christ, painted by Andrei Bicenko.

## STRONGEST MAN IN THE WORLD

**YOUR VISIT:** As you enter the main gate from Biddulph Road, straight ahead is the veterans' memorial with a plaque nearby. After viewing the memorial turn right and park by the chapel.

Near the chapel are the graves of Father Kappanadze and his wife. Father Jason Kappanadze (1875–1962) and his wife, Matushka Maria (1875–1962), were killed in a car accident. Father Kappanadze, born in Georgia, Russia, was sent to Kodiak, Alaska, to head a parochial school in 1895. He and his wife came to Cleveland in 1902 and returned to Russia in 1908. During World War I, Kappanadze was a pastor in the Imperial Russian Army. He and his wife escaped Russia in 1921, and he returned to Cleveland as pastor at St. Theodosius, where he served from 1922 to 1957. As a protopresbyter, he held the highest office open to a married priest.

From here, walk along the drive toward section M. There is a bench near the drive of section E. Across the drive from that bench look for "Fill" in section M. Four stones down this row is Petar

*A portrait of Petar Zebic with classic handlebar moustache graces his stone*

(Peter) Zebic (1876–1947), who was born in Yugoslavia and emigrated to the U.S. in 1911. While alive, Zebic let everyone know of his astounding strength. In death, his headstone continues that tradition with the engraving "strongest man in the world" underneath his bearded picture.

Zebic was a colorful character who toured North and South America, exhibiting his great power by bearing weights of 1,600 to 2,000 pounds on his shoulders. He even tested his strength against two automobiles pulling on his arms in opposite directions.

Zebic claimed to have once found a 4,600-year-old mummy in the Bolivian city of Potosi. Risking jail, he smuggled the mummy out of Bolivia and exhibited it for a fee. Eventually the mummy was stored in a friend's garage in Pennsylvania, where police found it after a fire. When questioned by police, Zebic was indignant that the officers could not tell these were the remains of a mummy. As proof he showed them the skull (still preserved), which was four to five inches longer than normal, following the custom of the Indians who bound their children's heads to produce a desired shape.

Zebic ran the Samson Tea & Tonic Company Shop at East 79th Street, where he sold bottles of "The World's Best Liniment" and "Only Hair Tonic in the World." Calling himself "Professor Zebic" at a time when such titles were rarely challenged, he boasted of a diet of cheese and vegetables, costing a mere $.25 a day.

Take a walk through the cemetery, noting the many iron crosses, and the variety of languages used on the markers.

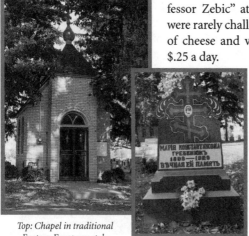

*Top: Chapel in traditional Eastern European style*

*Orthodox cross with inscription in Cyrillic alphabet*

**OTHER CEMETERIES NEARBY:**
Lutheran Cemetery, p. 197
Brainard/Broadview Cemetery, p. 132

# Scranton Road Cemetery

ADDRESS: Scranton and Wade ~ LOCATION: Cleveland ~ PHONE: (216) 348-7210
ACREAGE: 2.5 acres ~ CARETAKER: City of Cleveland (not on-site); no restrooms
ACCESS: Grounds open daily dawn–dusk. Records at Highland Park Cemetery
(216-348-7210), and Western Reserve Historical Society (216-721-5722)
NUMBER OF BURIALS: No record ~ OLDEST/FIRST GRAVE: First: Mary Wilcox, 1816
RELIGIOUS AFFILIATION: Nondenominational ~ ETHNIC AFFILIATION: German
DIRECTIONS: I-90 to Exit 170 for US 42 (W. 25th St.); south on US 42 (W. 25th);
left (east) on Wade Ave.; on right.

**HISTORY AND SURROUNDINGS:** James Fish, who arrived in 1812, was the first permanent settler in Brooklyn Township. Although he is buried here, his grave is probably underneath the street. James's mother-in-law, Mary Wilcox, was buried in 1816 on a half-acre lot on his land. Fish later deeded this land to trustees of a school district for use as a burial ground. A story about James Fish mentions him clearing his 80-acre tract of land and finding an area filled with rattlesnakes. Having narrowly escaped the rattlers, he said "What a smart idea it was in God Almighty to put bells on them things."

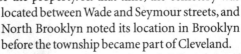

RATTLESNAKES
In BROOKLYN

Over time, the cemetery fell into neglect. In 1849 some lot owners formed the North Brooklyn Cemetery Association care for the property. At that time, the cemetery was located between Wade and Seymour streets, and North Brooklyn noted its location in Brooklyn before the township became part of Cleveland.

Scranton Road Cemetery is the alleged site of the remains of the abandoned Lorain Heights Cemetery.

**YOUR VISIT:** Carefully maneuver your car through the gate and down the well-worn path that divides the cemetery in half lengthwise. This is an easy cemetery to explore. Look for the Fish monument toward the back of the cemetery on the right, past the flagpole.

*Marker for Lydia Fish shows*
*typical damage of age and weather*

James Fish is credited with being the first permanent settler here. He arrived in 1812 with his wife, Lydia, and his mother-in-law, Mary Wilcox. The Fish family monument here states Elisha Wilcox (husband of Mary Wilcox) died in 1788. How, then, to explain this if there were no inhabitants in the area at the time of Wilcox's death? Perhaps the family brought his body with them from New England, which would have made their journey even more difficult. Or perhaps they were more practical and the monument serves as a memorial to him but does not include his remains.

Face the flagpole and look for Frederick C. Bambam (1885–1911) on the left side of the path, about 30 feet closer to Scranton Road than the flagpole.

He has a "Woodman of the World" insignia on his gravestone, referring to an insurance company whose primary benefit was a death benefit.

Walk around and notice the markers with German names as well as those written in German.

OTHER CEMETERIES NEARBY:
St. Mary Cemetery, *p. 69*
Riverside Cemetery, *p. 54*

*The Woodman of the World insignia on gravestones was an early form of advertising*

~ SUPERSTITIONS ~

## It's bad luck to meet a funeral procession head on.

# Willet Street Cemetery

ADDRESS: 2254 Fulton Rd.  ~  LOCATION: Cleveland  ~  PHONE: (216) 321-1733

ACREAGE: approx. 2 acres  ~  CARETAKER: Mr. Corrigan

ACCESS: Call first to have gate unlocked. Records at Mayfield Cemetery (216-321-1733), Cleveland Jewish Genealogical Society (440-449-2326), and Western Reserve Historical Society (216-721-5722)

NUMBER OF BURIALS: 1,500+  ~  OLDEST/FIRST GRAVE: First: Mr. Kanweiler

RELIGIOUS AFFILIATION: Jewish  ~  ETHNIC AFFILIATION: Bavarian, German, Prussian

DIRECTIONS: I-71 to Exit 170 for West 25th St.; north on West 25th; left (west) on Monroe Ave. until it ends.

**HISTORY AND SURROUNDINGS:** People of all faiths were buried at Erie Street Cemetery until 1840, when this cemetery was established for Jewish burials only. Thus, Willet became the first sectarian cemetery in Cleveland. The early Jewish settlers were immigrants from Germany and Austria-Hungary who bought this land in Ohio City in 1840. This is a small urban graveyard in a residential part of town. The Tombstone Tavern across the street knows how to take advantage of location.

**WHAT WAS THE DEED KAHN HATH DONE?**

**YOUR VISIT:** Please call to arrange your visit. The gate is locked, but they'll gladly open it for you with a day or two notice.

As you walk in the entrance, turn left until you are near a grass path that runs almost through the center of the plot. The path is directly in front of a large gate.

The Kahn monument is up two rows and on your right; the obelisk with the name E. Levy Kahn (1827–1885) has an etching of the Chevalier de la Légion d'Honneur on it. Kahn was given this medal for his role as a courier during the French intervention in Mexico in the 1860s.

Walk forward another two rows to see the marker for Civil War veteran Jacob Brown (1835–1904), who first enlisted in the 55th Regiment, OVI (Ohio Volunteer Infantry) at Norwalk, Ohio, in 1861. He was captured at Chancellorsville in May 1863 and was paroled that same month. Brown reenlisted, only to be wounded at Resaca, Virginia, in May of 1864. He received a disability discharge that same year in Cleveland.

Return to the center grass path and continue four more rows. On the left is the marker for Jacob Arnstine (1819–1879), an émigré from

Bavaria who earned his living as a peddler. He was the first Cleveland Jew documented to have served in the military. Arnstine enlisted in the

Mexican War and was discharged in July 1848. Upon discharge he was given a land grant of 160 acres.

Continue walking toward the back of the cemetery where the fence jags a little and look for the old white stone of Martha Wolfenstein (1869–1906). Born in Prussia, Wolfenstein came to the United States as an infant. Her father was a rabbi in St. Louis, and the family moved to Cleveland in 1878 when he became superintendent of the Jewish Orphan Home. Wolfenstein is recognized as the first Jewish woman to write Jewish stories for the secular press. She got her start translating German poetry, and later wrote stories that were published in the Jewish press. In 1901, *Ikylls of the Gass (The Alley)* was published by the Jewish Publication Society and serialized in the Anglo-Jewish press. In 1905 a collection of her stories, *The Renegade and Other Stories*, was published. Wolfenstein was working on a play when she died of tuberculosis.

OTHER CEMETERIES NEARBY:  Monroe Street Cemetery, *p. 47*
St. Mary Cemetery, *p. 69*

*Typical Jewish marker with very little ornamentation*

*Aging Arnstine marker*

# Woodland Cemetery

ADDRESS: 2367 E. 65th St.  ~  LOCATION: Cleveland  ~  PHONE: (216) 348-7210

ACREAGE: 55.42 acres  ~  CARETAKER: City of Cleveland

ACCESS: Grounds open Mon–Sat 9 a.m.–3 p.m. Records at Highland Park Cemetery (216-348-7210)

NUMBER OF BURIALS: 87,500  ~  OLDEST/FIRST GRAVE: First: 1853

RELIGIOUS AFFILIATION: Nondenominational

ETHNIC AFFILIATION: Bohemian, German, Greek, Hungarian, Irish, Polish, Romani, Russian, Scottish, Swedish, and Welsh

DIRECTIONS: I-77 to Exit 161 for E. 55th St.; north on E. 55th; right (east) on Woodland Ave.; on left.

**HISTORY AND SURROUNDINGS:** Cleveland purchased the land for Woodland Cemetery for $13,000 in 1849, after a cholera epidemic filled Erie Cemetery in the late 1840s. This site was so elegantly designed and maintained that courting couples often promenaded through its 68 acres. It is named for the beautiful groves of trees it contained. Bouts of vandalism damaged the trees and led the city to make plans for moving all graves to Highland Park and building a large low-income housing project on this site. But opposition from relatives of those interred as well as from veterans' groups halted the plans.

GO BY
THE BOOK

About 10 years ago, a fire gutted the office/maintenance building, and though pieces of the archway survived the building is no longer structurally sound. The pile of stones east of the Woodland entrance is what is left of the old archway. According to staff there are plans but not enough money to restore the arches. An open area near the Quincy gate marks the spot where the caretaker's house once stood.

Located in the inner city, Woodland is surrounded by light industry, some boarded-up buildings, and two Catholic cemeteries. The land is generally flat and the design is symmetrical. Some historians claim the presence of an Indian mound that might have been used for burials. Many of the pathways are overgrown. There were once more than 100 species of birds and 1,500 trees here. Sycamores still line the main trails and there are also ash, birch, maple, and oak trees throughout.

There are many beautiful carvings here. The Sprankle mausoleum is an example of Gothic revival–style architecture. Notice the exquisite details, especially on the gate. Diagonally across from Sprankle is the Breed/Burritt monument. This sarcophagus has clawed feet, and in typical Victorian style the stone roping around the top imitates wood. The Brainard/Burridge mausoleum is a mastaba—an Egyptian-style tomb with sloping sides and a flat roof. The columns on the side are also in keeping with the Egyptian architectural style. Woodland Cemetery is also home to more simple styles of grave markers, such as a pile of stones, known as a cairn, which was a simple way to denote a grave.

**YOUR VISIT:** Enter from Woodland Avenue, bearing right around section 14 with section 4 on the left. In the southeast part of section 14 lies William Creighton (1837–1863), a printer who worked at the *Cleveland Herald*. When the Civil War erupted, he formed an infantry company and reported to Camp Taylor in Cleveland. His unit, Company A, 7th OVI (Ohio Volunteer Infantry), fought at Antietam, Chancellorsville, and Gettysburg. Creighton was cited for gallantry at the Battle of Winchester and was wounded at Clear Mountain. While leading an assault on Taylor's Ridge in Georgia, Creighton ran to help Lieutenant Colonel Orrin Crane, commander of the 7th OVI. As Creighton was caring for Crane's wounds, he was shot and killed. Crane died as well. These two, the highest-ranking Clevelanders to die in battle during the Civil War, are buried next to each other.

*Civil War reenacter honors graves of Colonel Creighton and Lieutenant Colonel Crane*

Continue to section 13 and find Handerson's light-colored, two-foot-high sandstone marker. Henry E. Handerson (1837–1918) was born in Gates Mills. His father died in an accident on the Chagrin River and his brother drowned. Mr. Lewis Handerson, his mother's brother-in-law, adopted Henry and they moved to Tennessee. When war broke out, he quit his medical studies and volunteered for the Confederacy. Wounded at Rappahannock, Handerson was promoted to captain and then adjutant general.

He was taken prisoner in the Battle of the Wilderness and moved by the Union troops to Morris Island in South Carolina. The prisoners came to be known as "The Immortal 600"—high-ranking Confederate officers imprisoned under harsh circumstances and placed in the crossfire between the North and the South. Handerson had medical training and provided medical services to soldiers of both armies. After Lee's surrender, Handerson signed a loyalty oath and completed his medical studies.

His only children to reach maturity were a son and daughter from his second marriage, to Clara Corlett. Handerson was one of the founders of the Cuyahoga Medical Association (Cleveland Academy of Medicine) and was a professor at the College of Wooster. In 1915 he returned to the South to celebrate the 50th anniversary of the end of the Civil War. The bronze marker noting Handerson's part in the war was erected in 1956.

Turn right to get back on the main drive and take a quick left to section 21. Look for a white obelisk that is dedicated to the Union soldiers. Behind the obelisk is Theodore Mitchell's government marker. Mitchell (1835–1910) served in the U. S. Army and received the Congressional Medal of Honor for capturing the flag of the Tennessee Brigade CSA (Confederate States of America) while serving as a private in Company C of the 61st Pennsylvania Infantry.

Close to Mitchell, USCI (United States Colored Infantry) and USCHA (United States Colored Heavy Artillery) designate the graves of Richard Owens, Elijah Jackson, Foster Brown, Theodore Brown, and others, all buried in section 21. As with many Civil War markers, there are neither death dates nor hometowns mentioned on their stones.

In 1996, Bill Smith, a local history buff from Mentor, discovered the meaning of the letters on the stones; until then, the community had been unaware of this example of an important part of our history. It is estimated that 200,000 African-Americans joined the Union army or navy. Most were either escaped or emancipated slaves. The army units were segregated; the navy was not segregated onboard ship.

Reuben Wood (1792–1864) is memorialized by a tall obelisk about 10 feet away from these soldiers. It's difficult, but possible, to read. Wood was born in Vermont and lived in Canada as a youth. He made a hasty return to America to avoid serving on the wrong side in the War of 1812. Wood came to Cleveland in 1818 and was elected to various offices, including village president and chief justice of the Ohio Supreme Court. He became governor in 1850—the first Cleveland resident to achieve that position—and was reelected in 1851. An active abolitionist, Wood worked to change the fugitive slave laws. He came very close to receiving the nomination for president at the 1852 Democratic National Convention—it was an Ohio delegate who refused to deliver his votes to Wood. Franklin Pierce won the nomination, and the presidency.

Drive between sections 35 and 53 and walk into section 35, toward section 26. Look for a large stone book near the two mausoleums. This extraordinary example of a book monument shows in precise detail the pillow that the book rests on, and tassels hanging down from the pillow. The stonemason did an excellent job—the tassels look like soft silk, not hard stone.

**NOTABLE:**

*The most prominent monument here is for Freda Schubert (1852–1894). It has a beautiful statue of a winged lady holding a feather or quill in her left hand and a flower in her right.*

Go back to section 53 and look for Lizzie Ely (1890–1955), whose monument reads: "The True Queen of the Gypsies." Her grave used to be decorated in winter with food and wine. According to the caretaker, during Gypsy funerals attendees would hang a decapitated chicken upside down over the grave and place a bowl of pennies on the grave. They would set out fruit and sometimes clothing. During the burial, coins were thrown into the open casket, which was covered with marble to prevent grave robbing. A tent was erected as a center for music, dancing, and eating. In the past, feuds between different clans have led their members to vandalize the monuments and put curses on the graves.

In this same section is Amialea Miller; "Gypsy Queen" is written on her stone. She was married to Steve Miller, the Gypsy King. Her headstone has her picture on it; beneath the stone is a cement slab.

Back on the main drive, go to section 49, where it comes to a point. About 25 yards from the gravel road with section 53 on the left, you'll find Green on the right. John Patterson Green (1845–1940) was the son of a former slave. Green, his mother, and two sisters moved to Cleveland in 1857. He was the first African-American elected to office in Cleveland, becoming a justice of the peace in 1873.

Green was Cleveland's first African-American lawyer and was twice elected to the Ohio House of Representatives. In his second term, he sponsored House Bill 500, establishing the first Monday in September as Labor Day in Ohio. Other states followed his lead and it became a national holiday.

In 1892, Green became a state senator—the only African-American elected to a northern senate seat in the 19th century. Green's eloquence was put to use in several presidential campaigns, including William McKinley's.

In 1920, Green's autobiography, *Truth Stranger Than Fiction*, was published. Mayor Burton declared "John P. Green Day" on Green's 92nd birthday. Green was struck by a car and died on the eve of Labor Day when he was 95.

Return to the main drive and go further into the cemetery to section 72. The most prominent monument

*The marker for John P. Green, founder of Labor Day*

here is for Freda Schubert (1852– 1894). It has a beautiful statue of a winged lady holding a feather or quill in her left hand and a flower in her right.

Turn around as if to exit from Woodland, but turn left to reach section 31 for Jackson. W. E. Jackson was an African-American who was only 15 years old when he enlisted to fight for the Union.

On the way back to the main road, drive by section 12 and look for Clark's short white stone in front of the rose-colored stone for "Reverend D. C. Blood." Merwin Clark (?–1864) was known as the "boy officer" because at the age of 21 he was an officer in the Civil War. There is a bust of Clark at the Soldiers and Sailors Monument in Public Square.

**STORY BUT NO STONE FOUND:** Lucy Bagby Johnson (1841–1906) was arrested by U. S. marshals in Cleveland in 1861 as a runaway slave. Three well-known lawyers arranged for her release on a writ of habeas corpus, but it was denied.

Public outcry on her behalf was so strong and the mood so volatile that 150 deputies were called in to control the crowd. The federal commissioner, who wanted to keep the peace, donated $100 and created a fund to purchase her freedom. But her owner refused the offer and she was sent south. A train rescue attempt was unsuccessful. Finally, during the Civil War, she was rescued by a Union officer who prevented her owner from taking her farther south.

Lucy Bagby married George Johnson, a Union soldier, and they lived in Pittsburgh until she returned to Cleveland to live. In 1905 Johnson was a guest at the annual meeting of the Early Settlers Association. For many years she led the annual Independence Day Parade in Cleveland.

John Frazee (1829–1917) was a corporal in the Cleveland Grays (a private military organization) before the Civil War, when he became an officer. In 1832 he became Cleveland's first chief of police.

OTHER CEMETERIES NEARBY: St. John Cemetery, p. 63
                          St. Joseph Cemetery, p. 66

~ SUPERSTITIONS ~

Light candles on the night
after November 1. One candle should
be lit for each deceased relative
and placed in a window in
the room where death occurred.

# Single Marker

**NAME:** Mabel Foote and Louise Wolf

**LOCATION:** West 25th St. (under the "Cleveland Metroparks Zoo" sign)

**DETAILS:** These two Parma teachers were murdered on February 16, 1921, as they walked home together. Evidence at the scene indicates that either of them could have escaped the attacker alone, but they would not leave each other. At this location is a small park with an urn-like memorial to Foote and Wolf. The inscription reads: "In memory of Mabel Foote and Louise Wolf who died February 16, 1921, erected by Cuyahoga County teachers December 1, 1932."

The women are not actually buried here. Foote was buried in her family's private cemetery; information on where Wolf is buried was unavailable.

**OTHER CEMETERIES NEARBY:** Riverside Cemetery, *p. 54*
Brookmere Cemetery, *p. 134*
Brainard/Broadview Cemetery, *p. 132*

Both photos courtesy Cleveland Public Library Photograph Collection

*Mabel Foote*                          *Louise Wolf*

# EAST

## Bet Olam Cemetery

ADDRESS: 25796 Chagrin Blvd. ~ LOCATION: Beachwood ~ PHONE: (216) 831-9441

ACREAGE: 23.2 acres ~ CARETAKER: On site; restrooms at office

ACCESS: Grounds open Sun–Thurs 8 a.m.–5:30 p.m., Friday 8 a.m.–4:30 p.m.; office open Sun–Fri 8 a.m.–4:30 p.m. Records at cemetery office (not open on Saturdays or Jewish Holidays), Cleveland Jewish Genealogical Society (440-449-2326), and Western Reserve Historical Society (216-721-5722)

NUMBER OF BURIALS: 10,000 ~ OLDEST/FIRST GRAVE: First: December 1, 1910

RELIGIOUS AFFILIATION: Jewish

ETHNIC AFFILIATION: German, Lithuanian, Polish, Russian

DIRECTIONS: I-271 to Exit 29 for US 422 (Chagrin Blvd.); west on US 422 (Chagrin); on left before Richmond Rd.

**HISTORY AND SURROUNDINGS:** In 1910, because Anshe Emeth/Park Synagogue on East 37th Street was beginning to outgrow Fir Street Cemetery, the synagogue sent Sam Newman to find a suitable plot of land for expansion. Newman ended up getting stuck in a snowstorm, and the Reindfleisch family put him up overnight. After an evening's conversation, Reindfleisch offered to sell his land to the synagogue for a deposit of $100. Newman accepted. When Newman returned and reported his actions to the board of directors, angry board members thought he had exceeded his authority and removed him from the board. But after visiting the site they realized what a good deal he had made and reinstated him.

## THREE AND A HALF HUSBANDS

Once area farmers heard what Reindfleisch had done, they petitioned to nullify the deed because they did not want a Jewish cemetery nearby. A little-known law saved the day: once a cemetery has been dedicated, it cannot be undedicated. The congregation responded by dedicating the land and having a burial on the site.

Mr. Reindfleisch became the caretaker of the cemetery, and his son was caretaker after him. When the son died, his wife continued until she was too old to do so.

Though the cemetery is named Bet Olam, it includes burials from several congregations: Park Synagogue, Beth Am, Zemach Zedek, Oer

Chodesh, Taylor Road, and Liberty Hill Memorial Park. (In some maps it may be listed as Warrensville Cemetery.)

The flat land has row after row of graves.

Courtesy Cleveland Press Collection (CSU)

*Dorothy Fuldheim*

**YOUR VISIT:** Enter from Chagrin Boulevard and turn right. On the right lies Dorothy Fuldheim (1893–1989), one of the first female television news anchors in the country and a Cleveland television icon. Fuldheim was a reporter, commentator, and interviewer. She once stopped an interview with activist Jerry Rubin and told him to leave because of his vulgarity. Fuldheim was still working in her eighties, making her the nation's most senior news commentator. She also wrote a memoir titled *Three and a Half Husbands*.

> **NOTABLE:**
>
> *Bet Olam is typical of most traditional Jewish cemeteries in Cleveland— it has little ornamentation, and little space between markers. Many stones are inscribed in both Hebrew and English, and the most common symbol is the Star of David.*

Proceed to section 5 and look for "Ratner." Leonard Ratner/Ratowezns (1896–1974) came to Cleveland from Poland in 1920. He, his sister Dora, and his brother Max started a creamery. Their brother Charles arrived in 1922, but instead of joining the family business he looked elsewhere for work. He had heard that Cleveland was known as the "forest city," so with his background in carpentry, Charles founded Buckeye Lumber. His siblings soon left the creamery for the lumberyard.

Charles was able to retire, his sister got married, and Leonard and Max changed the name of the business to Forest City Materials and expanded into construction and real estate. The entire family was active in the Jewish community, becoming known for their involvement in fundraising, support for Israel, and educational issues.

OTHER CEMETERIES NEARBY:  Highland Park Cemetery, *p. 96*
                                        Warrensville West Cemetery, *p. 123*
                                        Jackson Burial Plot, *p.102*

# Euclid Cemetery

**ADDRESS:** 20239 Concordia ~ **LOCATION:** Euclid ~ **PHONE:** (216) 289-2726

**ACREAGE:** 5.2 acres ~ **CARETAKER:** City of Euclid; no restrooms on site

**ACCESS:** Grounds open daily dawn–dusk. Records at Euclid City Service Department (216-289-2800), and Euclid Historical Society (216-289-8577)

**NUMBER OF BURIALS:** 4,200+ ~ **OLDEST/FIRST GRAVE:** Unknown

**RELIGIOUS AFFILIATION:** Nondenominational

**ETHNIC AFFILIATION:** German, Irish, Slovenian

**DIRECTIONS:** I-90 to Exit 182A for E. 185th St.; south on E. 185th; left (south) on Dille Rd.; right (west) on Euclid Ave.; left (south) on Grand Blvd.; left (east) on Concordia; on right.

**HISTORY AND SURROUNDINGS:** The Baptist burying ground near Euclid Central Junior High served as the township's first cemetery until 1881. At about that time, the graves were moved to the present Euclid Cemetery. Of course, families also buried individuals on their own property, as in the case of the Peters Farms—an abandoned cemetery near Chardon and Richmond roads.

## "A VOICE WE LOVED IS STILLED"

**YOUR VISIT:** Enter from Concordia Road. About 10 rows down from the entrance on the left are the graves of the Revolutionary War soldiers. John Crosier's is on a pedestal, making it taller than the others. John Crosier (1743 or 1750-1823) was born near Boston and married by the time the

colonists began their fight for independence. He fought as a Minuteman at Lexington, Bunker Hill, Brandywine, Germantown, and Monmouth. Crosier wintered at Valley Forge with General Washington and later told his children stories about the difficulties he endured there. With financial incentives from the Connecticut Land Company, he came to the Western Reserve in the winter of 1816. He had 13 children, 88 grandchildren, and 209 great grandchildren. Eleven generations of Crosiers have lived in Euclid.

*John Crosier is one of five Revolution soldiers buried here*

Very close to Crosier are the other four Revolutionary War soldiers. Jacob Coleman (1762-1838) was a private with the New Jersey Horse Regiment. Nathan Cummins (1759-1838) was with the Massachusetts Regiment, Continental Line. James Jackson (1743-1822 or 1827) was a sergeant in the 2nd Maryland Regiment, Continental Line. David Dille (1753-1835) served as a lieutenant in Crawford1s Virginia Militia. He arrived in Euclid with his wife and five sons in 1798 or 1799. His log cabin on the west bank of Euclid Creek established him as the area's first permanent settler. He and his wife rounded out their family with 14 more children born in Euclid.

**NOTABLE:**

*This is a typical small-town cemetery on a hill overlooking the main street. Familiarity with nearby street names leads to recognition of those same names on many of the gravestones.*

Continue to the flagpole; this is the baby section. Take time to read the stones, reminders of the fragility of life and the difficulties faced by early settlers. Just before the baby section, next to the "Ferrell" stone, is the 8-foot-tall "Wilcox" stone. John Wilcox (1787-1869) was active in the Baptist church, donating land for the church and cemetery. His first wife, Elizabeth, with whom he had three children, died in 1821.He then married Laura, who died in 1850. His third wife, Lucy, lived until 1889 and donated money for the church bell tower. Though the Wilcox stone is here, the family is not; they were removed in the 1930s and reinterred elsewhere.

At the main drive, past the Kassay vault and to the right as you face Euclid Avenue, find the marker for Norman W. Sebek (1919-1941). It has a lovely engraving of a World War II prop plane inside of a cloud. Drive on and turn at the bend near the flag pole, continuing down the hill towards the right. The drive now parallels Euclid Avenue. Stop about thirty feet after the right turn and walk four rows up to find a marker for Gould behind the taller marker for Benson. Raymond Gould (1896-1908) died in the Collinwood School fire, an event that shook the entire Cleveland community, but especially effected Euclid because of its close proximity to the site. Gould's stone has an open book on top of it with this inscription:

> A precious one from us has gone,
> A voice we loved is stilled,
> A place is vacant in our home,
> Which never can be filled

OTHER CEMETERIES NEARBY: East Cleveland Cemetery, p. 35
Lake View Cemetery, p. 105
Nelaview/First Presbyterian Cemetery, p. 51

# Evergreen Cemetery

ADDRESS: 501 E. Main St.  ~  LOCATION: Painesville  ~  PHONE: (440) 639-4891
ACREAGE: 34 acres  ~  CARETAKER: Daniel Mazur
ACCESS: Grounds open daily dawn–dusk; office open Mon–Fri 7:30 a.m.–4 p.m.
Records at cemetery office (including maps and a clippings file); Morley Library in
Painesville has extensive genealogical resources on Lake County (440-352-3383)
NUMBER OF BURIALS: 18,000+  ~  OLDEST/FIRST GRAVE: Unknown
RELIGIOUS AFFILIATION: Nondenominational
ETHNIC AFFILIATION: Finnish, German, Hungarian, Irish, Scottish, Slovenian
DIRECTIONS: SR 2 to SR 283 (Painesville/Fairport Harbor); south on SR 283; left (east)
on US 20 (Mentor Ave./Erie St.); right (north) on Casement Ave.; on right.

**HISTORY AND SURROUNDINGS:** In 1860, the purchase of 24 acres of land
established Evergreen Cemetery. In 1877, lot owners of the Old Burying
Ground on the south side of Washington Street were
notified that a school was to be built there and all
bodies were to be removed. Most of those removed
were reinterred at Evergreen.

"NOT GUILTY"

More land was acquired throughout the years,
with the final two acres purchased in 1938 bringing the total to 34 acres.
The cemetery is on the hilltop of Main Street and Casement Avenue and
offers a nice view of the nearby recreation park. There are many trees
and shrubs throughout, including red Japanese maples. Division 10 has
a grave with a trellis around it.

**YOUR VISIT:** Maps are available at the office. To get there, head south on
Casement Avenue until it dead ends at East Main Street. Turn right onto
Main Street and right again at the bottom of the hill. The office is set
back from the road.

Return to Main Street, drive back towards Casement, and enter the
cemetery from Casement. Stop just before the Gothic-style receiving
vault. On the left, find the tallest obelisk in the section. John Flavel
Morse (1801–1884) moved to Painesville in 1826. A building contractor, he was the architect for the church at Route 306 and Eagle Road in
Kirtland. Morse became a state representative and worked for repeal of
the black codes, discriminatory laws that regulated the lives of African-
Americans. He was speaker of the Ohio House of Representatives and
was later elected to the Ohio Senate.

President Lincoln's treasury secretary, Salmon P. Chase, offered

Morse the position of architect on public buildings. Morse served in that post for 14 years. Much of his work involved repairing buildings damaged in the Civil War. Of the 13 children he and his wife had, only two lived to adulthood. His son Benjamin was responsible for several major projects in Cleveland, including the Superior Street viaduct and Union Station at Terminal Tower. Morse is buried under a Washington monument–style obelisk. (division 1)

Between Main Drive and Morse is a white female figure. Annie E. Gage (1837–1873) received her nickname "Hard Luck Annie" from cemetery workers because of the difficult life she had. Two of her infant children died, and then she herself died at the age of 36. To make matters worse, in 1991 vandals broke the head and one hand off the statue at her grave. A local man, Paul Cordaro, restored "Hard Luck Annie" for free. (division 1)

Turn right and on the right is Storm Rosa's ten-foot-tall obelisk. Rosa was the town doctor. He and his wife were both proponents of homeopathic medicine. He was also active in the abolitionist movement.

Nearby is General Potter's nine-foot-tall gray obelisk, easily seen from the drive. Joseph Adams Potter (1816–1888) is one of two Brevet Brigadier Generals at Evergreen. (Brigadier General is the rank between colonel and major general. The title Brevet promoted the officer to a higher rank, allowing him to assume the duties of a general at times; however, it offered no increase in pay. The rank was given toward the end of the Civil War in recognition of faithful and meritorious service.) Potter's mother was a direct descendant of Samuel Adams. Potter's infatuation with firearms led him to journey to Michigan and then to Chicago, where he joined a party of Indians who took him to Madison, Wisconsin. This five-week excursion cured him of some of his romantic notions of life on the frontier, and he returned home. He declined an appointment to West Point, became a civil engineer, and then moved to Painesville in 1837. There he met and married Catherine Rosa, daughter of Dr. Storm Rosa. Catherine died in 1853.

During the Civil War, Potter was stationed in Chicago where he met and married Hattie Spafford. In 1867, Potter, his wife, and their infant son were sent to Galveston Texas. There they became sick with yellow fever. Within days, the entire household was dying. Potter's wife died and he and his son were unconscious; when Potter recovered, he found his son alive, the house taken over by strangers, and his wife's jewelry and other valuables stolen. Potter is buried in Division 10 next to Catherine, his first wife. His grave can easily be seen from the road, right after you pass the holding vault. It is a gray stone, about two feet tall, in front of the white Storm Rosa monument.

A little farther on is Jennings/Casement. At one time there was a cast-iron statue of a dog at the grave of their son, Charlie, who died when he was four. The statue was removed after repeated damage from vandals. The stone slab where the dog was mounted remains, at the far side of the monument.

John (Jack) Stephens Casement (1829–1909) is the other Brevet Brigadier General buried at Evergreen. Casement moved from New York to Ohio in 1850 to lay track for the railroad. He met his future wife, Frances Jennings, on the job. She did not work for the railroad, but it did run through her father's farm. The workers would go to the Jennings' well for water, and it seems Frances took a keen interest in quenching their thirst.

In the Civil War, Casement fought at the Battle of Cross Lanes and was credited with saving his regiment. He defeated Stonewall Jackson (Jackson's only defeat) at the Battle of Winchester, after which Casement found ten bullet holes in his cape. He was with Sherman on his march to the sea.

After the war, General Dodge contacted Casement to help complete the continental railroad. In 1866 Casement and his brother Daniel contracted to lay 1,044 miles of track from Omaha, Nebraska, to Promontory Point, Utah. One of his challenges was feeding the workers. He used a scout, William F. Cody, to supply him with buffalo meat. That is how Cody (see East Cleveland Cemetery) earned his nickname "Buffalo Bill." By the time he died, Casement had laid more railroad track than any other person in the country. A liberty ship launched during World War II was named the John S. Casement.

Frances Jennings Casement (1840–1928), called "Frankie" by her husband, organized and was the first president of the Ohio Women's Suffrage Association. She, along with friends Elizabeth Cady Stanton and Susan B. Anthony, worked for the adoption of the 19th amendment and the passage of the 18th amendment (Prohibition).

Continue around Division 10. The "Treat" monument is about 20 feet to the left of "Paige," which is about 20 feet high and near "Patterson." Treat's flat bronze Medal of Honor stone is next to his two-foot-tall gray headstone. Howell B. Treat

*Howell B. Treat, the only Medal of Honor recipient buried in Lake County*

(1833–1912), the only Congressional Medal of Honor recipient buried in Lake County, was not acknowledged as such until 1998. Thanks to the research and perseverance of cemetery intern Bonnie Walker, a ceremony held September 13, 1998, gave Treat the recognition he deserved.

In June 1862, Treat enlisted in the Ohio Infantry and fought in numerous Civil War battles. Treat's heroism in rescuing a fellow soldier at Buzzard's Roost, Georgia, May 11, 1864, earned him the Medal of Honor. A wounded soldier had fallen dangerously close to Rebel lines, and the enemy continued to fire bullets into the man, who was still alive. Treat, sickened by the sight of this, asked for volunteers to help save the man. Two privates accompanied Treat on the rescue mission; the privates were both killed and Treat was wounded in the head and body. But Treat managed to reach the soldier, hoisted him onto his shoulders, and carried him to safety. A cheer went up and down the Union lines in acknowledgment of Treat's bravery.

After the war, Treat returned to Painesville, and in 1869 he married Eliza A. Elias. His Medal of Honor was not awarded until 1894. The 30-year delay between the incident and receipt of the medal was not unusual, as Congress had only initiated this medal during the Civil War and there were many nominations to investigate. (division 10)

Next, walk toward division 22, turn right at the paved path and then left at the second path. This is division 24. Stop at the Celtic cross for "Doolittle" and walk three stones back and nine stones in, to where Sophia Kimball (1863–1936) is buried. Sophia's husband, Ambrose Kimball (1839–1915), served in the Civil War as an assistant engineer in the U.S. navy. Sophia Kimball knew her husband's health was deteriorating and wanted to be able to provide for her family. She sold a patent to Barton Reed and Company for a spoon she had invented for feeding invalids and babies. They paid her $1,300, which she used to pay for dental school at Ohio University. She opened her practice in Painesville and was known as a "bread-winning mother." Behind Sophia's grave is that of her only child, Cyrus Carter Kimball (1892–1914), who died in a motorcycle accident. (division 24)

Turn right at next corner and right again, noticing the Nims and Tillotson mausoleums. This road dead-ends into Main; go right until you see a vault and take the first left. Stop at the Windecker mausoleum on the right. Look through the glass doors at the Tiffany window inside.

Clifton Windecker was instrumental in developing Diamond Alkali, which then became Diamond Shamrock Corporation. Robert and Charles Windecker were pioneers in the development of beryllium. The company's work with magnesium kept them very busy making bombs during World War II. (division 2)

Continue and turn left at the first crossroad. On the right is the "Chilson" mausoleum with its Corinthian columns. Baby Austin is buried near the front of it. George B. Austin died of croup before he was two years old—his grave is marked by the statue of a child lying on his side with his head on a pillow. Because both baby boys and girls wore dresses for the first few years of life, many people mistake the Austin statue for that of a baby girl. Local folklore refers to the statue as "the girl who turned to stone." Children who visit often leave small remembrances; one placed a colored ribbon around the statue's neck and tucked a teddy bear into

*Tiffany window seen through the glass doors of the Windecker mausoleum*

its arms. This sculpture was once encased in glass but was vandalized so much that the glass was not replaced. (division 5)

Turn right at the second drive and proceed to the flagpole. As you approach it, on the left look for "Crofoot" and behind it Gibson. Gladys Gibson (1900–1929) lived in Cleveland while working as a switchboard operator at the Cleveland Clinic. She was at work on that fateful day, May 15, 1929, when the disastrous fire broke out in the basement of the Clinic. Although she was told to leave her post and go to safety, Gibson chose to stay, calling for help and assisting others. She died of suffocation from gas fumes.

Gibson was awarded the Theodore N. Vail Medal for Noteworthy Service. Of the seven employees of Ohio Bell who have received this medal, Gladys Gibson is the only woman. Embedded in her gravestone are the medals she was awarded posthumously. Her marker states: "She gave her life to devotion to duty at a time of public disaster in Cleveland May 15, 1929."

Continue left onto the drive that parallels Casement Avenue (the street you entered from). On the right, about halfway between here and the entrance (Main Drive), is the three-foot-tall brownish-red Linhart marker. Joseph Linhart (1867–1921) was certainly not the only person accused of murder who claimed he was not guilty. However, he might be the only one whose grave marker has "NOT GUILTY" written on it. Linhart, from Leroy, Ohio, was accused of throwing his wife down a well. While in county jail he asked for a razor to shave with, was left alone by a guard, and killed himself. Though many people thought his attorney ordered this marker, it was actually bought by Linhart's relatives several years after his death. (division 18)

**NOTABLE:**

In 1877 lot owners of the Old Burying Ground on the south side of Washington Street were notified that a school was to be built there and all bodies were to be removed. Most of those removed were reinterred at Evergreen.

Continue straight, pass Main Drive, and find "Adams," five stones to the left. This stone belongs to Helen Marie Adams (1922–1992), who was called Marie. Her husband placed a memorial for her on the Adams plot, though her ashes are scattered in Kentucky. Adams was a WAVE in the navy during World War II and worked as a telephone operator in Washington D.C. She handled the communication between Washington and the commanders of the Normandy invasion, and had to be guarded 24 hours a day because she had advance notice of the date of the invasion.

Behind Adams's stone is the grave of Marie's young brother-in-law, Robert Adams (1913–1918). The family once believed Robert died from eating a crayon, which at that time was made of arsenic. However, further investigation revealed that Robert had become jaundiced. His other brothers had hepatitis, so it is likely that Robert died of hepatitis as well.

Back up and proceed on Main Drive, again stopping at Division 3 to look for Samuel Huntington. Huntington (1767–1817) became Chief Justice of the Ohio Supreme Court in 1804. In 1808 he was elected Ohio's second governor. Once, while living in Cleveland, Huntington rode two miles down what is now Euclid Avenue followed by a gang of snapping wolves. He used his umbrella to beat them off.

There are several Revolutionary War soldiers buried at Evergreen. Here are some whose graves are most easily found:

Isaac Rosa (1767–1841) served in the New York Militia under Colonel Abraham Culer. He married Agnes Storm and they were the parents of Dr. Storm Rosa. (division 10)

Eleazer Paine, nephew of Edward Paine, was born in East Windsor, Connecticut, and was a drummer boy in 1764 in Captain Britt's company, 2nd Regiment. He came to Painesville in 1800 with his uncle and brought his family back in 1803. (division 4)

Captain Abraham Skinner (1775–1826) answered the Lexington alarm with Captain Amasa Loomis's company and served with the Connecticut Line under Colonel John Durke. In 1798 Skinner came to the Western Reserve, returning again in 1803 with Eleazer Paine. In 1805 he went east to bring his family to his new home. From Buffalo they traveled by sleigh over frozen Lake Erie, and his daughter fell through the ice, but she survived. He later planned and laid out the village of Fairport. (division 4)

**MORE TO KNOW:**  The Jennings Casement House. At 436 Casement, is a large red brick building that was once known as Jennings Place. It was built in 1870 as a belated wedding present for Frances Jennings and John Casement. The basement, dug in 1868, was allowed to settle for two years before construction continued. Five gas wells on the property provided heat and light for the home for 40 years (according to local historians, this served as the first private utility in northeastern Ohio.) The house even had air-conditioning—separate wooden ducts built into the walls brought cool air in from under the porches.

The house has had just four owners in 128 years. The original owners, the Jenningses, gave it to Jack Casement and their daughter Frances Jennings Casement. The Casements left it to their only surviving son, Dan Dillion Casement (not to be confused with the Dan Casement who was Jack Casement's brother). In 1953 Mr. and Mrs. Robert Sidley, the current owners, purchased the home.

It is now home to the executive offices of R. W Sidley Inc., a concrete and building supply company. Behind this building are quarry facilities and an airfield. Across the street is a nine-hole golf course whose clubhouse is a century home also built by Charles Jennings.

~ SUPERSTITIONS ~

If 13 people sit down at a table to eat,
one of them will die before the year is over.

# Highland Park Cemetery

ADDRESS: 21400 Chagrin Blvd.  ~  LOCATION: Shaker Hts.  ~  PHONE: (216) 348-7210

ACREAGE: 140 acres  ~  CARETAKER: On site; restrooms at office

ACCESS: Grounds open daily dawn–dusk; office open Mon–Fri 8 a.m.–4:30 p.m., Sat 8 a.m.–4 p.m. Records at cemetery office, and Western Reserve Historical Society (216-721-5722)

NUMBER OF BURIALS: 130,000+

OLDEST/FIRST GRAVE: First: Caroline Herron, March 31, 1905 (sec 1, lot 516)

RELIGIOUS AFFILIATION: Nondenominational

ETHNIC AFFILIATION: African-American, Hungarian

DIRECTIONS: I-271 to Exit 29 for US 422 (Chagrin Blvd.); west on US 422 (Chagrin) on left at Belvoir Blvd.

**HISTORY AND SURROUNDINGS:** Mayor Tom Johnson's administration deserves credit for having the foresight to establish this then-remote parcel of land as a cemetery in 1904.

The huge doors near the office lead to the first municipal mausoleum in America, built in 1926. (Louise DeWald was Commissioner of Cemeteries at the time, the first woman in America to hold that position.) Inside, the white marble walls make the world seem calm and serene. At the end of the first corridor to the left is a chapel in such disrepair that visitors are not permitted to enter. Highland also includes an urn garden, a crematory, and a plot for the indigent.

## CLEVELAND'S SYMBIOTIC CONNECTION TO PATTY HEARST

The wall above the stairwell near the mausoleum entrance has a hand-painted mural depicting the urn garden. The painting, done in the 1960s by Highland supervisor William Hahn, is signed at the bottom.

There are more than 130,000 people buried here, and Highland's sprawling expanse—141 acres—offers a welcome contrast to the brick and glass of the neighboring business district.

**YOUR VISIT:** As with other very large cemeteries, it is difficult to give complete directions here. It's best to go to the office for section maps, which can more specifically lead you to the sites spotlighted below. The office, which looks like an old castle, is important because of the many cemetery records it maintains—aside from keeping its own records, Highland serves as the repository for records from all other city-owned cemeteries as well: Alger, Brookmere, Denison, Erie, Harvard Grove, Monroe, Scranton, West Park, and Woodland.

Harold Burton (1888–1964) moved to Cleveland in 1911 or 1912 after graduating from Harvard. He was a state representative and law director before becoming the mayor of Cleveland from 1935 to 1940. While mayor, he appointed Eliot Ness as safety director.

Later, Burton was elected to the U. S. Senate (1940–45) and was appointed by President Truman to the United States Supreme Court. Burton wrote the court's opinion outlawing

*Government gravestone with the Medal of Honor insignia for a marine who served in two conflicts*

racial segregation on railroad dining cars. He also participated in the landmark *Brown vs. Board of Education* decision that outlawed school segregation. During World War I, he received a Purple Heart and Belgian Cross. Burton is also the namesake of the Harold H. Burton Memorial Bridge. (section 1, not far from the office, visible from the road)

David Clark (?–1806) was a private in Walbridge's Vermont Militia in the Revolutionary War. He was originally buried at Erie Street Cemetery. His flat marker notes his military service. (section 1, lot 700)

Donald DeFreeze (1943–1974) was known more for his deeds than his name. In 1974, DeFreeze, known as "Cinque," appeared on the front page of hundreds of newspapers (including those owned by the Hearst family) as the leader of the Symbionese Liberation Army, which abducted Patty Hearst. After several months in hiding, DeFreeze and others in his terrorist group were killed in a shoot-out with Los Angeles police. On the day of his funeral at Highland Park, workers in nearby offices were cautioned not to go near the windows—the FBI thought Patty Hearst might attend the funeral and were prepared for trouble. There was none. (section 17, marker #219)

Lucious "Luke" Easter (1915–1979) played for the Cleveland Indians and hit the longest home run in Cleveland Stadium. Easter also played for the Homestead Grays of the Negro National League and the San Diego Padres. With the Padres he hit 25 home runs in 80 games in the Pacific Coast League. During the off season, he played in Hawaii and Puerto Rico.

In 1955 his contract was sold to the Charleston Senators, but in 1969 Easter returned to Cleveland as a coach for the Indians. He was killed near a Cleveland Trust Bank after cashing a $40,000 payroll check. In 1980 the former Woodland Hills park was renamed Luke Easter Park. (section 16, lot 297, tier E ½)

James Kingsbury (1767–1847) was, at age 29, the first settler in the Western Reserve. He and his wife, Eunice Waldo Kingsbury, were the parents of the first child born to white settlers in the Western Reserve.

At the time of the birth, Mr. Kingsbury was out of town, having gone east for supplies. After the baby was born, Mrs. Kingsbury became ill, the cow supplying the baby's milk died, and the infant starved to death. Some historians claim the child was never named. But one claims it was a boy, named Albert, who lived for about two months. The cow was said to have died from eating the browse of oak trees. The couple went on to have twelve children.

The Kingsbury family lived at the corner of Kinsman and Woodhill.

**NOTABLE:**

*Highland Park has a large veterans' section. By 1948 there were more than 1,850 veterans buried here; now there are more than 22,000.*

They built their house, then built a sawmill to provide lumber for others. The part of town the Shaker Rapid travels through on its way to downtown Cleveland was once known as Kingsbury Run, most likely named for this early settler. Kingsbury was originally buried at Erie Street Cemetery but was reinterred here in 1916. His beige granite marker is about 5 feet tall, next to a large urn. (section 1, lot 315)

Joe Vosmik (1910–1962) began his baseball career in the minor leagues and in 1930 was signed by the Cleveland Indians. His best year as a pro was in 1935, when his batting average was .348. With 216 hits, 47 doubles, and 20 triples, Vosmik led the league. In the all-star game in Cleveland's then-new Municipal Stadium, Vosmik struck out, then drove in a run with a single. He was traded in 1936 and spent 18 seasons in the major leagues before becoming a scout for Cleveland. (section 14, lot 1036)

Steve Nagy (1913–1966) was born in Pennsylvania and came to Cleveland as a young boy. Nagy's early exposure to bowling came from his father, who operated a bowling club called the Hungarian Businessman's Club. A cabinet maker by trade, Nagy gave up that career as he became increasingly successful and well known as a bowler. Among his many awards, the Bowling Writers Association named him bowler of the year in 1952 and 1955; he was ABC Tournament Regular Doubles champion in 1953; president of the Professional Bowlers Association in 1964; and a member of the Cleveland Bowling Association Hall of Fame. His highest score was 698. (section 15, lot 379 west)

The East Ohio Gas Memorial is near the center of the park. It was erected in memory of the 61 unidentified or unclaimed people who died in the St. Clair-Norwood-area fire October 20, 1944. A plaque on the memorial lists 40 names and states that 21 bodies remained unidentified. On the other side of the monument is the inscription:

> Social progress attuned to industrial achievements
> for the benefit of the living shall be a memorial
> to these whose lives were unwittingly sacrificed.

Did they purposely neglect to mention that 130 people lost their lives in this disaster? (section 25)

OTHER CEMETERIES NEARBY:   Bet Olam Cemetery, *p. 85*
Warrensville West Cemetery, *p. 123*

~ SUPERSTITIONS ~

# The soul of a dying person can't escape the body and go to heaven if any locks are locked in the house.

# Hillcrest Cemetery

ADDRESS: 26700 Aurora Rd.  ~  LOCATION: Bedford Hts.  ~  PHONE: (440) 232-0035

ACREAGE: 32 acres  ~  CARETAKER: On site; restrooms at office

ACCESS: Grounds open daily dawn–dusk; mausoleum open Mon–Fri 8 a.m.–4:30 p.m., Sat 9 a.m.–3:30 p.m., Sun 11 a.m.–3:30 p.m.; office open Mon–Fri 8 a.m. –4:30 p.m., Sat 9 a.m.–3 p.m., Sun 11 a.m.–3 p.m. Records at cemetery office

NUMBER OF BURIALS: 19,000+

OLDEST/FIRST GRAVE: First: Charles Holliday, 1930 (sec 497)

RELIGIOUS AFFILIATION: Nondenominational, Bahai, Christian, Jewish

ETHNIC AFFILIATION: Hungarian

DIRECTIONS: I-271 to Exit 26 for Rockside Rd.; east on Rockside; right (south) on SR 43 (Aurora Rd.) on right.

**HISTORY AND SURROUNDINGS:** This is actually the newest cemetery in Cuyahoga County, having opened in 1930. Senator Taft dedicated the original chapel. William Gall, the president of Hillcrest, has been working here since it opened in 1930.

Originally, offices were downtown and staff living quarters were located near the entrance gate. During World War II, employees were unable to get gas to drive back and forth to Cleveland, so Gall moved his offices to the cemetery grounds, where they remained until the new offices were built in 1961.

> **RETURN IT "TO THE OLD BASTARD WHO SENT IT"**

It was 57 steps up to the office on the fourth floor, with a chair placed on the third floor for those who needed a rest. The first floor held the furnace, the second floor was a laundry, the third floor was a kitchen, and the fourth floor was converted into an office.

"We never had a complaint," says Gall. He explains that by the time clients reached the fourth floor, they felt sorry for the staff who had to make the climb daily.

The entrance gate is a well-designed architectural point of interest.

**YOUR VISIT:** The mausoleum behind the office has the remains of Shondor Birns. To find Birns, enter through the door surrounded by columns (8 a.m.–4:30 p.m. weekdays; 9 a.m.–3:30 p.m. Saturday; 11 a.m.–3:30 p.m. Sunday), turn left down the first hallway, flipping on the lights as you enter, and then right down the next hallway. There on the left at about eye level are the remains of Alex and Ellie Birns.

Alex "Shondor" Birns (1907–1975) was a mob enforcer who ran the numbers racket in Cleveland (see Lakewood Park Cemetery) and was at odds with Danny Greene over competition in their illegal businesses.

According to an April, 1977 *Cleveland Magazine* article, a bomb meant for Greene did not go off but fell from under his car. He was heard to say he wanted to return it "to the old bastard who sent it"—meaning Birns. One day after that incident, Birns got in his car, turned the ignition and the bomb went off. That was the end of Alex "Shondor" Birns.

While in the mausoleum, walk through and see some of the beautiful stained glass. The next hallway over from Birns has an Old Testament theme. The stained-glass window has a Star of David, the burning bush, Moses in the rushes, and the tablets of the Ten Commandments.

In a nearby hallway, on the crypts of Gertrude and Leroy Robinson, are Bahai symbols affixed on marble. On other crypts there are praying hands, a cross, a dove, Masonic symbols, a picture of the Madonna, and a rose.

The outside of the building is adorned by three angels in relief, with the words *love, hope,* and *faith* under each figure. Trees are planted carefully throughout the grounds, and though most of the markers are at ground level, one section has above-ground monuments.

OTHER CEMETERIES NEARBY: Bedford Cemetery, *p. 177*
Calvary Cemetery, *p. 24*

*This massive gate housed the cemetery office until 1961*

# Jackson Burial Plot

ADDRESS: Landerwood Plaza  ~  LOCATION: Pepper Pike  ~  PHONE: None
ACREAGE: 0.2 acres  ~  CARETAKER: Unknown
ACCESS: Grounds always open. Records at Western Reserve Historical Society
(216-721-5722)
NUMBER OF BURIALS: approx. 4
OLDEST/FIRST GRAVE: Oldest and first: Raw Jackson, 1859
RELIGIOUS AFFILIATION: N/A  ~  ETHNIC AFFILIATION: English
DIRECTIONS: I-271 to Exit 29 for SR 87 (Chagrin Blvd.); east on SR 87 (Chagrin); on left
after Lander Circle.

**HISTORY AND SURROUNDINGS:** Raw Jackson, an English settler, deeded this land as a family cemetery after immigrating here in 1835. Though it is no longer used, the Jackson plot is beautifully maintained by the local merchants' association. Shrubs and flowers are planted around the markers and it is a pleasing sight, particularly in spring and summer.

**SHOP TILL YOU DROP?**

**YOUR VISIT:** There are only a few stones here. A dedication plaque on a large boulder has the names of family members inscribed on it. There are individual stones for Raw Jackson (d. 1859), Jane L. Jackson, his wife (d. 1861), their son, Lansdale (d. 1887), and their daughter, Jane (d. 1906).

In 1965 Harry G. Jackson, a fifth-generation descendant, was operating a wholesale meat outlet on part of the original property (bought in 1835 for $12 an acre). The 94 acres Raw Jackson purchased were valued at $284 with taxes of $1.84. Also, as recently as 1965, a barn built by Raw Jackson in 1845 still stood on the Chagrin Boulevard property.

Until the Regal theaters in Middleburg Heights were built, this was the only cemetery in Ohio located in a shopping center.

OTHER CEMETERIES NEARBY:
Bet Olam Cemetery, *p. 85*
Highland Park Cemetery, *p. 194*
Knollwood Cemetery, *p. 103*

*Jackson family plot near the parking lot of Landerwood Plaza*

# Knollwood Cemetery

**ADDRESS:** 1678 SOM Ctr. Rd.  ~  **LOCATION:** Mayfield Hts.  ~  **PHONE:** (440) 442-2800
**ACREAGE:** 52 acres  ~  **CARETAKER:** On site
**ACCESS:** Grounds open May–Sept daily 7 a.m.–7 p.m., Oct–April daily
7 a.m.–5 p.m.; mausoleum open Mon–Fri 8:30 a.m.–4 p.m., Sat 9 a.m.–4 p.m.,
Sun 10 a.m.–4 p.m.; office open Mon–Fri 9 a.m.–5 p.m., Sat 9 a.m.–noon.
Records at cemetery office
**NUMBER OF BURIALS:** 41,000
**OLDEST/FIRST GRAVE:** First: Georgia Sampson, February 17, 1910 (sec 19 lot 238)
**RELIGIOUS AFFILIATION:** Nondenominational  ~  **ETHNIC AFFILIATION:** N/A
**DIRECTIONS:** I-271 to Exit 34 for US 322 (Mayfield Rd.); east on US 322 (Mayfield);
right (south) on SR 91 (SOM Center Rd.); on right.

**HISTORY AND SURROUNDINGS:** Knollwood opened in 1909 and has
Ohio's largest mausoleum. The imposing gates lead to well-manicured
grounds.

**YOUR VISIT:** Enter the mausoleum through the main entrance. Take an
immediate right, head down the stairs, and follow signs for the women's
restroom. (This route takes you through the mausoleum, which offers
beautiful stained glass throughout.) Outside the
door to the women's restroom are steps leading
back upstairs a different way. Take these. Go right
at the top of the stairs.

CLEVELAND
MURDER CASE
INSPIRES
"THE FUGITIVE"

On the second section of wall, nine names from
the end at about waist level, is the name Marilyn
Reese Sheppard. Dr. Sam's name was not yet on it
when we last visited, though his ashes are there.
Follow "exit" signs out and you will get a chance to
see more beautiful stained glass. The art is both
religious and secular, ornate and understated.

If you don't wish to take the stairs or see other parts of the mausoleum take this route: Enter through the main entrance. Go right down
the second hallway, left at the first hallway, and left again. Now on the
left, on the first full section of wall, is "Sheppard" at waist level.

The Sheppard case has been a topic of much discussion in the Cleveland community for over forty years. In 1998, Sam Reese Sheppard sued
the state of Ohio for the ten years that his father spent in prison.

Marilyn Sheppard (1923–1954) wife of the well-to-do doctor Sam

Sheppard and resident of the upscale suburb of Bay Village, was murdered in her home in 1954. Her husband was tried and convicted of her murder, but always insisted a stranger had entered the house and killed her. It is widely conceded that this was a case of trial by the press, with allegations that authorities withheld certain information because it conflicted with their theory that Sheppard murdered his wife.

**NOTABLE:**

Knollwood probably would like to be known as something other than the location of the Sheppards' crypt. Because of that, staff is sometimes reluctant to give out information on how to find their burial site.

The television show *The Fugitive* was based on this case. Sheppard was acquitted at a retrial in 1966 and died of liver disease just four years later.

Dr. Sam Sheppard (1923–1970) was originally buried in Forest View Cemetery in Columbus. His flat marker had the letters VQP on it—Latin for "endure and conquer." In September 1997, Sheppard's body was exhumed and brought to Cleveland, where blood samples were taken for the purpose of DNA testing. He was then cremated and his ashes placed in a crypt next to the remains of his wife Marilyn, reuniting them for the first time in 43 years.

Sheppard's DNA was compared with blood samples found on his wife's body and at the crime scene. The DNA of Richard Eberling, a prisoner at the Orient Correctional Institution convicted of murdering a Lakewood widow in 1989, was also analyzed. Eberling had been a handyman at the Sheppard home, and his DNA, collected 44 years later, placed him at the crime scene. Eberling, who seemed to enjoy taunting interviewers with his knowledge of the case, died in July 1998. It is interesting that although Eberling had family nearby, no one came forward to claim his body—leaving Eberling, possibly the missing piece of the puzzle, now dead and buried in Columbus.

OTHER CEMETERIES NEARBY:
Jackson Burial Plot, *p. 102*
Bet Olam Cemetery, *p. 85*

*Sheppard's murder sparked controversy that continues*

# Lake View Cemetery

ADDRESS: 12316 Euclid Ave. ~ LOCATION: Cleveland Hts. ~ PHONE: (216) 421-2665
ACREAGE: 285 acres ~ CARETAKER: On site; restrooms at office
ACCESS: Grounds open daily 7:30 a.m.–5:30 p.m.; office open Mon–Fri 8:30 a.m.–
5 p.m., Sat 8:30 a.m.–12:30 p.m. Records at cemetery office, and Western Reserve
Historical Society (216-721-5722)
NUMBER OF BURIALS: 97,000
OLDEST/FIRST GRAVE: First: Captain Louis Germain Deforest (1838–1870)
RELIGIOUS AFFILIATION: Nondenominational
ETHNIC AFFILIATION: African-American, German, Italian
DIRECTIONS: West: I-90 to Exit 173B for Chester Ave.; east on Chester Ave.; left (east)
on US 20 (Euclid Ave.); right (east) on US 322 (Mayfield Rd.); on left at Kenilworth.
East: I-90 to Exit 177 for Martin Luther King Blvd.; south on MLK; left (east) on US
20 (Euclid Ave.); right (east) on US 322 (Mayfield Rd.); on left at Kenilworth.

**HISTORY AND SURROUNDINGS:** Established in 1869 by a group of Cleveland's most prominent residents, Lake View has provided a final resting place for many of the city's best-known citizens. Considering that the city of Cleveland ended at East 55th Street when the cemetery was established, the purchase of this 285-acre tract of land proved prescient. In the 1890s, the number of Sunday visitors was such that admission tickets had to be issued.

**HOW MANY SONGS UNSUNG?**

This garden-style cemetery is located on hilly ground. Many of the trees and shrubs are labeled with both their scientific name and common name. Trees within the grounds include bald cypress, dawn redwood, dogwood, eastern hemlock, ginkgo, and Japanese maple, just to name a few. More than 100,000 daffodils show off their beauty every spring. There are nine miles of roads, more than 90,000 graves, and the largest concrete-poured dam in the U. S. east of the Mississippi (Lake View Cemetery Dam is 114 feet high and 520 feet wide).

The Italian stonemasons employed at Lake View looked for a nearby area to settle in, thus founding the community we now call Little Italy.

**YOUR VISIT:** Lake View offers such a broad historical panorama of Clevelanders who made a difference, it is impossible to see everything in a single trip. If this is your first visit, I suggest going to Wade Chapel, the Garfield Monument, and Rockefeller's grave. For others, following a theme (sculpture, famous women, African-Americans) is the best way to manage your visit. Or you could decide to visit by section. As with other large burial grounds, the office has very helpful maps of each section.

Lake View hosts a variety of tours and events, including an annual

tree-trimming event at Schwan's grave site, and Daffodil Sunday in May. Throughout the year, Lake View organizes walking tours covering Angels of Lake View, Women of Lake View, geology, and horticulture sites.

Charles F. Brush (1849–1929) invented the arc lamp and was responsible for lighting the city in 1879. He also invented the Brush dynamo, predecessor to the generator. (section 10)

Raymond Johnson Chapman (1891–1920) played with the Cleveland Indians when they won their first world championship. As shortstop he was an excellent fielder and also a good hitter. He married Kathleen Daly in 1920, vowing that that would be his last season. The Indians took the news hard, as they were battling for first place and Chapman was central to the team's winning spirit. On August 16, 1920, while playing against the Yankees at the New York

*Impressive memorial to inventor Charles F. Brush*

Polo Grounds, Chapman was hit on the temple by a pitch from Carl Mays. Chapman had surgery, fell into a coma, and died the next morning. Chapman is the only professional baseball player ever killed in a major league game. The Indians dedicated the season to Chapman; that year was the first time the Indians won the American League pennant and world championship. Chapman's wife is buried at Calvary. (section 42, grave 16)

*Collinwood School Memorial.* On March 4, 1908, 175 people (172 students) died in this, the country's worst school fire, at Lakeview Elementary School. School safety precautions across the nation were changed as a result. A memorial garden is located at Memorial School. (section 25)

*Garfield Monument.* James Garfield was the 20th president, shot by an insane man just three

*Visitors often leave baseball items on Chapman's tombstone*

*President Garfield's monument and tomb*          *Tears appear to stream down the face
                                                   of the angel that marks the Haserot grave*

months after taking office. Garfield finally surrendered to his wounds 80 days after the shooting. When Garfield died in 1881, he became the fourth elected president to die while in office, after William Henry Harrison (1841), Zachary Taylor (1850), and Abraham Lincoln (1865). Four more presidents have since died in office: William McKinley (1901), Warren Harding (1923), Franklin D. Roosevelt (1945), and John F. Kennedy (1963). All of these except Taylor were elected at twenty-year intervals.

Before becoming president, Garfield had been a teacher, preacher, state representative, and congressman. He was a major general and hero in the Civil War. He is credited with preventing a riot after President Lincoln's assassination. (section 15)

Gertrude Anna Harrison (1871–1938) invented a golf ball return machine to be used in teaching golf. She was the first women's golf professional in the country, and built the first golf course in Cleveland—a three-hole course in her backyard. (section 24, lot 767A)

Francis Haserot (1860–1954) has a six-foot-tall, 1,500-pound angel on her grave that was sculpted by Herman Matzen in 1924. Made of bronze, the angel stands on a granite base with arms outstretched as it leans on an overturned torch. (section 9)

The monument to John Hay (1838–1905), erected in 1915, depicts the archangel Michael, arms folded above a pillar on which rests a sword and snake. Hay was personal secretary to President Lincoln for four years, and ambassador to Great Britain. As secretary of state for President McKinley, Hay formulated the Open Door Policy for China in 1899. When Hay died, President Theodore Roosevelt, the vice president, and the cabinet members all came to Cleveland for his funeral. (section 10)

*The elaborate marker for John Hay includes sword, snake, and archangel Michael*

John D. Rockefeller (1838–1937) moved to Cleveland when he was fourteen years old and attended Central High School from 1853 to 1855. He then took courses at a business college and worked as an assistant bookkeeper for commission merchants. When he was refused a raise, he and co-worker Maurice Clark started their own commission business.

Rockefeller entered the oil business in 1863 and in 1870 established the Standard Oil Company. By 1865, Rockefeller owned 28 refineries in Cleveland and was a financial success. He soon controlled all aspects of the industry: shipping, refining, and distribution.

The Rockefellers had several homes but for tax purposes could not stay beyond a certain date each year in their vacation homes. But John's wife Laura ("Cettie") became gravely ill in 1914, and he extended his stay in Cleveland. His enemies declared him a permanent resident and presented him with a 1.5-million-dollar tax bill. Legal battles ensued. Rockefeller had to wait four months to bury his wife at Lake View and then only under the cover of secrecy. He did not return to Cleveland until his death.

Many people think Rockefeller would have been more generous to Cleveland if he had been treated with greater sensitivity. Speaking of sensitivity, Rockefeller was very sensitive about a condition he had, known as alopeceia, which caused him to become completely hairless. He always wore a wig and fake eyebrows in public.

In later years, Rockefeller tried to overcome his reputation for sternness and austerity by giving out dimes to children wherever he went. Visitors often leave pennies or dimes at his grave in remembrance of this habit. The monument, an obelisk almost 70 feet high, is the tallest private monument here. It weighs over 400,000 pounds. (section 10)

Wade Chapel is available for funeral services but also hosts weddings.

Classical in design, it is the cemetery's most notable architectural work. The stained glass window depicting the resurrection of Christ won a gold medal at the 1900 Paris World Exposition.

Jeptha Wade's family, who had been searching for a suitable memorial to him, purchased the award-winning window and then hired Louis Tiffany, the window's designer, to build a chapel around it. On either side of the chapel are 32-by-8-foot mosaics of glass depicting "The Voyage of Life"; one side relates to the Old Testament, the other to the New. The lamps were each carved from a single block of alabaster and weigh 700 pounds. The bronze doors weigh four tons. Because Tiffany thought fumes from gas and kerosene might cloud the glass, Wade Chapel uses electricity—probably one of the first public buildings in Cleveland to do so. This is one of the few intact

*Pennies and dimes are often left at the base of the Rockefeller monument*

buildings in the world designed entirely by Louis Tiffany. Be sure to walk around the outside of Wade Chapel to see the reflecting pond. The chapel is on the National Register of Historic Places and is open April through October. (section 5)

Newton D. Baker (1871–1938) was mayor of Cleveland from 1912 to 1916. Under his leadership, Cleveland received the first city charter in Ohio. His appointment of Mildred Chadsey (buried in section 8) as health director made her the first woman cabinet member in city government. Baker's charismatic speech at the Democratic National Convention secured the nomination of Woodrow Wilson for president (possibly also securing Baker's own position as U.S. Secretary of War from 1916 to 1921). After World War I, Baker worked for the establishment of the League of Nations. In 1928, he received the U. S. Distinguished Service Medal—becoming one of the first civilians ever to receive this award. (section 30, lot 198)

Ernest Ball (1878–1927) was a composer and lyricist who wrote "Will You Love Me in December As You Do in May?" and collaborated on "When Irish Eyes Are Smiling." Ball also wrote scores for the musicals *Isle of Dreams* and *Barry of Ballymore*. Flowers sent to his grave from New York arrived with an anonymous note stating: "How many words unwritten? How many songs unsung?" (section 2, lot 109)

Helene Hathaway Robison "Bigsby" Britton (1878–1950) inherited

*The Ball monument*

the St. Louis Cardinals from her uncle, making her the first woman owner of a major baseball club. Her father was Frank Robison. (section 16B)

Albert "Starlight" Boyd (1871– 1921) saved the money he earned as a book-keeper to buy a Canal Road tavern in 1896. His establishment became a place to see and be seen. Boyd, whose nick-name referred to his love of diamonds, was an excellent political player during the era when ward politicians could "turn out votes." He once led a parade of African-Americans in a protest against the film *Birth of a Nation*. (section 18, lot 311)

Charles Chesnutt (1858–1932), a son of slaves, dropped out of Howard School for lack of money. When the principal offered him work, Chesnutt accepted, becoming the youngest teaching assistant at the school. He later became school principal, then studied law and in 1887 passed the bar.

Chesnutt's first book *The Wife of his Youth and Other Stories of the Color Line*, was published in 1889. Next he wrote *The Conjure Woman* and *The House Behind the Cedars*. Although the publisher knew it, he purposely withheld from the public the fact that Chesnutt was African-American, After ten years, he finally went public about it at Chesnutt's insistence. Chesnutt was the first African-American in the country widely recognized as a professional writer and the first to write about race from a black person's perspective. In 1905, he had the distinction of being the only Clevelander invited to Mark Twain's 70th birthday party. (section 5, lot #888)

Henry Chisholm (1822–1881) earned his wealth manufacturing iron and steel. He was responsible for the building of Euclid Avenue Baptist Church in 1877. Employees paid for his monument. (section 1, lot 4)

Genevieve Rose Cline (1877 or '78–1959) became the first woman federal judge to serve on the U.S. Customs Court. She was appointed by Congress in 1928. (section 16)

Laura Mae Corrigan (1888–1948) married a rich playboy and shamelessly flaunted her money and lifestyle. After her husband James died, Corrigan spent more than 5 million dollars in two years on enter-tainment. In Europe, where she was known as the "Dollar Queen," she partied with King Edward VIII and the future Queen Elizabeth II.

It was in Paris, when World War II broke out, that Corrigan did an about-face, helping others and risking her own safety. She founded La Bien Venue, a relief organization for French refugees, and volunteered at a London officers' club. When restrictions prevented her from using personal funds, Corrigan sold her jewels to finance her charitable efforts. She is one of the few women awarded the French Croix de Guerre and Great Britain's King's Medal. (section 11, lot 122)

Dr. George W. Crile (1864–1943) was a military surgeon during the Spanish-American War. He helped arrange for the army's first base hospital in France during World War I. In 1906 he performed the first successful human blood transfusion. Crile was co-founder of the Cleveland Clinic. (section 30, lot 51)

Harvey Cushing (1869–1939) became the first neurosurgeon in the U.S. He received the Pulitzer Prize for his biography of Sir William Osler, his mentor. (section 10, lot 57)

Bishop Edward Demby (1869–1957) wrote five books on race relations. In 1918 he was voted the first and only African–American suffragan bishop of the Episcopal Church in the United States. For many years his grave was unmarked. Although he made plans for his burial and marker, he never completed payment to the monument company. Through the efforts of family and supporters, a marker was bought and placed on the grave in 1992. (section 2, lot 420D)

Perino "Pete" DiGravio (1926–1968) was murdered on the Orchard Hills golf course in Geauga County. He was allegedly involved in loan sharking activities with possible connections to organized crime. DiGravio was known as the "Mayor of Little Italy." His son, William, died in 1974 in a boat explosion in Florida, which family members believe was not an accident. (section 49)

Nathaniel Doan (1762–1815) was one of the original members of Moses Cleaveland's surveying party to the Western Reserve, and the only member to settle in Cleveland. He was given land in return for his services as a blacksmith. (section 1, lot 69)

Frank (Franz) Xavier Frey (1837–1900), a member of the 37th Ohio Volunteer Infantry, received the Congressional Medal of Honor for bravery. (section 24, lot 1011)

Theodatus Garlick (1805–1884) was one of the first plastic surgeons in the country. He was so astute at transferring what he read into practical applications that he built a camera after reading Daguerre's writings and built the first chicken hatchery in the U.S. based on other studies. He was also the first American to breed fish artificially. Garlick was also a noted sculptor and painter: Andrew Jackson and Henry Clay sat for him. (section 2, lot 311)

Zelma Watson George (1903–1994) worked at the YMCA and was a probation officer at juvenile court and director of the Job Corps Center. She was the first African-American to play a leading role in musical theater on Broadway. She also served as a UN ambassador. (section 4, lot 740)

Marcus Hanna (1837–1904), a U.S. senator, made his wealth in coal and iron. In an era that openly combined wealth and politics, he was known as a political kingmaker. Hanna formed the Cleveland Business Man's Marching Club, the country's first political action committee. He was the largest contributor to McKinley's campaign and a close advisor to the president. Teddy Roosevelt called him "the most influential man of politics this nation has ever known." (section 9, lot 8)

Anna M. Harkness (1837–1926) gave away more than $40 million in her lifetime. Her husband, Stephen, was a partner of Rockefeller's. She was one of the few American women to establish a major foundation, the Commonwealth Fund. (section 6, lot 58)

Coburn Haskell (1868–1922) invented the modern golf ball by winding a rubber thread around the core. After patenting his invention in 1899, he sought advice from others on an efficient production method. (section 9, lot 31)

Myron T. Herrick (1854–1929) was governor of Ohio and later ambassador to France. He was the first person to meet and congratulate Charles Lindbergh after his successful transatlantic flight. (section 9, lot 25)

William Hopkins (1869–1961) Cleveland's first city manager, was responsible for the country's first municipal airport, which now bears his name. He also built the country's first control tower. Of all the nation's major airports, Cleveland Hopkins is the closest to a top-20 American city, and it's the only one with no major air disasters. (section 38, lot A)

Jane Edna Hunter (1885–1971) organized the Phyllis Wheatley Association in 1911. Its purpose was to offer housing for homeless black women and girls. (section 4)

William G. Keller (1876–1963) was a private in the Spanish-American War. He received the Congressional Medal of Honor for rescuing wounded soldiers under fire and carrying them more than a mile to safety during the Battle of San Juan Hill. (The cannon on Public Square was captured during that war.) He later was an honor guard at President Franklin Roosevelt's second inauguration. (section 44)

Dayton Miller (1866–1941) was the first person to photograph sound waves. He also produced the first full-body x-ray, of himself. The x-ray is still on file in the CWRU physics department. The exposure time he used was one hour! (section 10 lot 116C)

Lottie Pearl Mitchell (1883–1974), an African-American, was

responsible for a "pool party" at the Garfield Pool—she and others showed up as their way of suggesting the pool be integrated. Officials responded by draining the water from the pool. She and a group of friends made a similar statement by showing up at Euclid Beach Park. Officials there stopped the music and called the police. Mitchell was a singer, musician, and actress and was in the Cleveland Play House's first integrated production. (section 22, lot 736 P-1)

Garrett A. Morgan (1877–1963) was an African-American inventor whose gas mask was first used in the waterworks tunnel explosion of 1916. He and his brother, Frank, were called upon to help, but because they were black only two other men were willing to go in the tunnel with them. Donning Morgan's gas masks, they made four trips into the tunnel. Five of the people they pulled out were alive when rescued, but only one survived. Afterwards, as accolades were handed out to the rescuers, Morgan's name was not mentioned. In 1930 he was at last given the recognition he was due, along with the $2,000 reward. Soldiers in World War II used the gas mask invented by Morgan.

Morgan overcame discrimination again in 1923 when the city of Cleveland refused to allow him to test his traffic light. He took it instead to Willoughby where it gained attention from General Electric to the tune of $40,000. His other inventions include hair straightener. (section 50)

Eliot Ness (1903–1957) earned his reputation as a crime fighter and leader of the "Untouchables" in Chicago. Mayor Burton hired him and brought him to Cleveland in 1935, making Ness the youngest safety director in Cleveland's history. He kept that office for seven years, cleaning up the corrupt police department and starting the first police academy. His ashes were scattered across Wade Lake on September 10, 1997. (section 7)

John Strong Newberry (1822– 1892), a geologist, was one of the first Americans to be awarded the Murchison Medal of the Geological Society of London, in 1888. (section 2, lot 364)

Gloria Pressman (1923–1991), known on the stage as Mildred Jackson, was one of the original Little Rascals. She was in *The Jazz Singer*, the first talking movie, with Al Jolson, and also appeared in *Moby Dick* and *The Virginian*. (section 43, lot 678)

*A stone marker memorializes Eliot Ness, whose ashes were scattered in Wade Lake*

James Salisbury (1822–1905), a doctor and nutritionist, was the creator of Salisbury Steak, which he introduced as healthy diet food. (section 3)

Heinrich Christian Schwan (1818–1905) is considered the father of the American Christmas tree. He was pastor of Zion Evangelical Lutheran Church when he brought a candle-lighted tree into church for a Christmas Eve service. The occasion, in 1851, was the first time a lit Christmas tree was used in a church service in the United States. (section 25, lot 928)

Belle Sherwin (1868–1955) was president of the National League of Women Voters and is credited with originating its policy of nonpartisanship. She was the first president of the Consumer League of Ohio and co-founder of the Women's City Club. (section 1, lot 69)

Carl B. Stokes (1927–1996) was the first African-American mayor of a major U.S. city. He later served as judge and ambassador to the Seychelles. The inscription on the base of his stone reads: "He fought, never gave up may not have won but fought a good fight." This likely refers to his fight for integration. (section 5C, lot 116A)

Jeremiah Sullivan (1844–1922) was named a bank examiner in 1887 by President Cleveland—the first Irish-American to reach such a high position in the financial world. Sullivan founded Central National Bank and was a supporter of the Federal Reserve Act. He was likely responsible for Cleveland being designated as the location for a Federal Reserve Bank. (section 35)

Oris Paxton Van Sweringen (1879–1936) and Mantis James Van Sweringen (1881–1935) share a headstone. The Vans, as they are popularly called, were railroad tycoons who built the Terminal Tower and were responsible for developing Shaker Heights. They felt their Shaker properties might suffer from a lack of public transportation, so they built what we now know as the Rapid Transit. However, they were not always successful businessmen: One of their real-estate deals sent them into default. To get out of the fix, they used their sisters' names (Edith and Carrie) until their own credit was reestablished. (section 10, lot 117)

Jeptha Wade (1811–1890) was a painter and portrait artist who is credited with taking the first daguerreotype (an early photograph) west of New York. As a businessman he developed the first telegraph network in Cleveland and eventually became the first president of Western Union. His invention, the Wade Insulator, allowed him to encase telegraph lines to protect them from the weather. Wade was the first person to route cables underwater (in Mississippi). He was the president and one of the founders of Lake View Cemetery. (section 3)

Hazel Mountain Walker (1889–1980) was one of the first African-

American women admitted to the bar, and the first African–American school principal in Cleveland (1936). She gave the Karamu Theater its name. She was widowed twice by two unrelated men named Walker. (section 52, lot 167)

William White (1850–1923), a store owner, found his fortune when he purchased what he thought was an empty barrel. He found instead that it contained Mexican chicle, a resin used to enhance flavor. He and his wife discovered that it became soft and chewable when boiled. They flavored it with mint and sold it as "Yucatan." Called chewing gum by the public, it soon became the most popular item in his store. White took on two partners and by 1889 was president of American Chicle Company, the world's largest chewing-gum company.

> **NOTABLE:**
>
> *There are nine miles of roads, over 90,000 graves, and the largest concrete-poured dam in the country east of the Mississippi (114 feet high and 520 feet wide).*

White's good fortune took a turn for the worse starting in 1906 when his wife divorced him for being a ladies' man. A day later, he married his 25-year-old girlfriend. Discord with his partners forced him out of the business, leaving him with no money. White made another fortune with a gum company in Niagara Falls but lost it all in a court case.

White fell on some ice on the street in Cleveland and died of an infection related to the accident. His grave was, for some reason, unmarked until 1996, when the Early Settlers Association and Kotecki Monuments remedied the situation. The inscription reads: "Founder of the Chewing Gum Industry." (section 5, lot 615)

Alonzo Wright (1898–1976) was working as a garage attendant in Cleveland when a customer offered him an office job. Wright refused— his dream was to have his own business. But the customer, Standard Oil president Wallace Holliday, was still impressed with Wright and made him a better offer: a franchise.

Wright became the first African-American in the country with a gas-station franchise. Attendants at his station, at East 93rd Street and Cedar Avenue, offered to clean windshields and check air in the tires, earning it the reputation as the best place in town to stop for gas. By the 1930s Wright owned 11 gas stations, and by the '40s he employed more young African-Americans than anyone else in the country. He also devised a plan to help young African-Americans work their way through college.

Jesse Owens was one of many who took advantage of this opportunity. Later, when Owens was in Germany for the 1936 Olympic Games, Wright heard that he was not getting enough money for necessities from the Olympic Committee and sent him $200. With his investments in real estate, Wright became a millionaire, and in 1961 *Ebony* magazine called him Cleveland's richest and most prominent Negro. (section 4, grave 732)

OTHER CEMETERIES NEARBY:  East Cleveland Cemetery, p. 35
Mayfield Cemetery, p. 119

~ SUPERSTITIONS ~

A person who dies at midnight
on Christmas Eve will go
straight to heaven because the gates
of heaven are open at that time.

# Lower Cemetery

ADDRESS: Memorial Drive ~ LOCATION: Burton ~ PHONE: None

ACREAGE: 1.48 acres ~ CARETAKER: Not on site; no restrooms

ACCESS: Grounds open daily dawn–dusk. Records at Burton Library and Geauga County Historical Society (440-834-4012)

NUMBER OF BURIALS: ~ OLDEST/FIRST GRAVE: Unknown

RELIGIOUS AFFILIATION: Nondenominational ~ ETHNIC AFFILIATION: N/A

DIRECTIONS: US 422 to Rapids Rd.(after Auburn Corners); north on Rapids; right (east) on Carlton St. in Burton; right (south) on S. Cheshire St.; right (west) on Memorial Rd.; on left.

**HISTORY AND SURROUNDINGS:** Burton was the first of the 16 townships in Geauga County to be settled. The cemetery is located near a water-treatment plant, but its isolated setting provides a solemn atmosphere.

**YOUR VISIT:** This cemetery does not have clearly defined rows or section markers. Start at the back and work your way to the entrance.

The seven tall, rose-colored stones, some partially broken on top, are for the Fox family.

Mathias Fox (1763–1846) was a private in the Pennsylvania militia.

John Ford Esquire (1763–1842) was a private in the 2nd regiment, Connecticut Line.

Seth Hayes (?–1815) was a private in Mosely's Massachusetts Regiment.

Libbeus Herrick (1749–1821) served as a private in the 57th Connecticut Regiment.

Moses Hutchins (1756–1834) was a private in the Massachusetts militia.

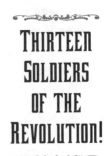

THIRTEEN SOLDIERS OF THE REVOLUTION!

David Dayton (1749–1828) served as a private in the Connecticut troops.

Nathan Parks (1758– 1849) served as a private in Colonel Woolbridge's Massachusetts

*Identical monuments for the Fox family*

Regiment and was discharged in 1777. He enlisted again in June 1778 in Colonel Shephard's regiment and was discharged February 1781. His original stone still stands, and he has a new one in addition.

James Goff (1762–1849) was with Chapman's company in Connecticut as a private.

Amos Beard (1746–1821) was a private with Patterson's Massachusetts Regiment and served seven years in the military. His visits home can be marked by the subsequent births of his children, whom his wife, Hannah Needham, raised on her own. Hannah died when the eldest, Jedidiah, was 14 years old.

**NOTABLE:**

*There are thirteen Revolutionary War soldiers buried here. Many of the older markers have been replaced with new ones, and most of them lie flat on the ground.*

Jedidiah had to work to keep the family together and prevent the children from being placed as indentured servants until their father returned from the war. Upon his return, Amos married Isabella, Hannah's cousin. Jedidiah became a colonel in the War of 1812. He died from poisoning when he accidentally ate an acid mixture meant for polishing brass—he thought it was salts.

Andrew Durand (1758–1834) was a private in the Connecticut militia.

David Brooks (?–1821) was a private in the 2nd Connecticut Regiment.

Caleb Fowler (1755–?) enlisted and fought in the 6th Connecticut Regiment. One Sunday during the Battle of Monmouth, while the British were eating breakfast, Fowler stole a musket belonging to one of the British soldiers. The musket is in his family to this day. Fowler moved to Burton with his second wife Olive in 1812.

Benjamin Johnson (1761–1828) was a sergeant in the 2nd Connecticut Regiment.

Easther Ford (1805–1822) the daughter of John and Easther Ford has this inscription on her marker:

> Alas not youth with all its rose a'bloom
> can save from death or rescue from the tomb
> yet this fair flower untimely snatched away
> we trust will flourish in immortal day

# Mayfield Cemetery

ADDRESS: 2749 Mayfield Rd.  ~  LOCATION: Cleveland Hts.  ~  PHONE: (216) 321-1733

ACREAGE: 25 acres  ~  CARETAKER: On site

ACCESS: Grounds open daily 8:30 a.m.–5 p.m.; office open Mon–Sat 8:30 a.m.–5 p.m. Records at cemetery office, Cleveland Jewish Genealogical Society (440-449-2326), and Western Reserve Historical Society (216-721-5722)

NUMBER OF BURIALS: 10,500

OLDEST/FIRST GRAVE: Oldest: Simpson Thorman (1812–1881)

RELIGIOUS AFFILIATION: Jewish  ~  ETHNIC AFFILIATION: German, Hungarian, Lithuanian

DIRECTIONS: West: I-90 to Exit 173B for Chester Ave.; east on Chester Ave.; left (east) on US 20 (Euclid Ave.); right (east) on US 322 (Mayfield Rd.); on left.

East: I-90 to Exit 177 for Martin Luther King Jr. Blvd.; south on MLK; left (east) on US 20 (Euclid Ave.); right (east) on US 322 (Mayfield Rd.); on left.

**HISTORY AND SURROUNDINGS:** Mayfield Cemetery opened in 1890 and is the only garden-style Jewish cemetery in greater Cleveland. If this is your first visit to a Jewish cemetery, you maybe surprised by some of the customs. Many Jewish burial grounds have little, if any, ornamentation on the gravestones, and what does exist is usually in keeping with a religious theme—a Star of David or a menorah.

### CLEVELAND RABBI SPEAKS AT UNITED NATIONS

**YOUR VISIT:** In section 8 is Alfred Benesch (1879–1973), safety director under Mayor Baker and a member of the Cleveland Board of Education. Benesch served on the Board continuously for 37 years until 1962. A prominent lawyer, he obtained better police protection for Jewish peddlers.

In section 4 is Aaron Marx (1834–1901), who enlisted in the Civil War in Erie, Pennsylvania. He settled in Cleveland afterward and was Cleveland's first Jewish policeman.

Also in section 4 is Morris Ullman (?–1908 ), a Confederate soldier in the Civil War. In 1869 he and his brother founded a wholesale liquor business. The brothers merged with Leopold and Herman Einstein and their firm survived until prohibition. They made their own liquor under the label Black Cat and published a recipe book containing a recipe for Ohio grape brandy.

Across from section 4 is section 3. Here is the grave of Sigmund Shlesinger (1848–1928), who emigrated from Hungary with his parents in 1864. He made his way to Kansas, and was sutler (vender of supplies to soldiers) in the camp of the 10th U.S. Calvary. Shlesinger joined Colonel George Forsythe's frontier scouts in 1868 and participated in the Battle of Beecher Island in Colorado, where they defeated Cheyenne Chief Roman Nose. Shlesinger was cited for bravery. He came to Cleveland in 1870.

Simpson Thorman (1811–1881), a fur trapper, was the first Jewish settler in Cleveland. He was originally buried at Willet Street but, was reinterred here in 1916. Thorman's marriage to Regina Klein in 1840 was the first Jewish wedding in Cleveland. In 1865 he was elected to Cleveland city council.

**NOTABLE:**

*One custom, seen in the film* Schindler's List, *is to place stones on the grave as a way for family members to communicate with each other about who has been there to visit. The stones are sometimes removed before the High Holy Days, and the cycle of visiting and marking the grave starts over.*

Continue to the back of the cemetery and go in the mausoleum. Sam Gerber (1898–1987) was a cruise ship physician after his medical internship. He then graduated law school and passed the bar. As Cuyahoga County coroner from 1937 to 1986, Gerber was involved in everything from the Torso murders to the Sam Sheppard case. His remains are in the mausoleum on the first floor (down steps as you walk in).

Turn around and come back toward the entrance, with section 8 on your left. Max Kalish is buried here. Kalish (1891–1945), born in Lithuania, was sculptor for the Pan Pacific Exhibition in San Francisco in 1914. He was a scholarship student at the Cleveland Institute of Art, where he won first prize for life modeling. His piece *Rebecca and Judas Maccabeus* was judged best student sculpture ever exhibited. Kalish's bronze statue of Lincoln, dedicated in 1932, is in front of the Cleveland Board of Education.

There are several family mausoleums here including those for the Joseph, Fishel, Sampliner, and Hays families. The Glauber mausoleum has a domed top, and others offer stained-glass patterns which can be seen through the doorways.

Turn the corner with section 4 on the left and look for the large boulder marking the grave of Rabbi Abba Hillel Silver (1893–1963). Rabbi Silver's oratory brought standing-room-only crowds to The Temple

*Rabbi Abba Hillel Silver with his son Daniel*

Courtesy Cleveland Press Collection (CSU)

at East 105th Street and Euclid Avenue. The Temple (now Temple Tifereth Israel) became the largest Reform congregation in the country. Silver spoke at the United Nations in 1947 about the issue of partitioning Palestine. He was considered to be highly influential in getting President Truman to recognize the state of Israel in 1948.

Look toward the right for a bench. This is the burial site of Barnett Brickner (1892–1958), spiritual leader of Fairmount Temple for 33 years. Brickner's debate with Clarence Darrow in 1928 on the subject "Is Man a Machine?" drew nationwide attention. Rabbi Brickner received the Medal of Merit for his service as a chaplain in World War II.

Close by is the granite marker for Rabbi Arthur J. Lelyveld (1913–1996), a leader in the civil rights movement. He participated in several demonstrations in the southern states and marched with Dr. Martin Luther King Jr. His epitaph alludes to his belief in the equality of all.

Section 1 is now on the left. David Berger (1944–1972) was an athlete representing Israel in the 1972 Olympic Games in Munich, Germany. Palestinian terrorists broke into the Olympic Village, murdered two of the team's coaches, and took 9 of the 18 team members hostage. All 9 of the hostages, including Berger, were killed in a bungled rescue attempt.

**MORE TO KNOW:** Outside the Mayfield Jewish Community Center at 3505 Mayfield Road stands the David Berger National Memorial. The sculpture, by David E. Davis, is of the Olympic rings, broken yet placed close together, giving the impression of movement and offering hope that they might come together again.

OTHER CEMETERIES NEARBY: Lake View Cemetery, p. 105
East Cleveland Cemetery, p. 35

~ SUPERSTITIONS ~

# If the left eye twitches there will soon be a death in the family.

# Shaker Burial Ground

ADDRESS: 16740 South Park Blvd.  ~  LOCATION: Shaker Heights  ~  PHONE: None

ACREAGE: 0.1 acre  ~  CARETAKER: Unknown

ACCESS: Grounds always open. Records at Shaker Historical Society (216-921-1201), and Western Reserve Historical Society (216-721-5722)

NUMBER OF BURIALS: 1  ~  OLDEST/FIRST GRAVE: Oldest: Jacob Russell

RELIGIOUS AFFILIATION: N/A  ~  ETHNIC AFFILIATION: N/A

DIRECTIONS: West: I-480 to Exit 23 for Broadway Rd.; left (south) on Broadway Rd.; left (east) on McCracken Rd.; left (north) on Lee Rd.; right (east) on South Park (after Shaker Blvd.); on left

East: I-480 to Exit 24 for Lee Rd.; north on Lee; right (east) on South Park (after Shaker Blvd.); on left

**HISTORY/SURROUNDINGS:** Shakers were originally English Quakers who, in 1747, formed a separate sect. Ralph Russell founded the North Union Shakers, who lived in the area now called Shaker Heights. Ralph donated this land for use as a cemetery in 1859, by which time he had moved to Bentleyville because of disagreements with his neighbors. Ralph and others who were committed to a Shaker cemetery drew lot numbers from a hat. Lot number five was Ralph's. In it is buried his mother, his wife, his six-year-old daughter Laura, and his two sons, Ralph Ellsworth and Gershom Sheldon. Lot 28 was for strangers. Records report 137 burials at this original site. In about 1905, expansion and development of this area necessitated the removal of all remains but those of Jacob Russell. The rest are buried in a common grave at Warrensville West Cemetery.

## LOT 28 WAS FOR STRANGERS

**YOUR VISIT:** The only grave remaining is that of Revolutionary War veteran Jacob Russell, Ralph Russell's father, who died in 1821. It is under a large maple tree, marked by a boulder and surrounded by an iron fence.

*The only remaining grave belongs to Jacob Russell*

OTHER CEMETERIES NEARBY:
Warrensville West Cemetery, *p. 123*
Highland Park Cemetery, *p. 96*

# Warrensville West Cemetery

ADDRESS: 2110 Lee Rd. ~ LOCATION: Shaker Heights ~ PHONE: None
ACREAGE: 1.3 acres ~ CARETAKER: City of Shaker Heights
ACCESS: Grounds always open. Records at Shaker Historical Museum (216-921-1201), and Western Reserve Historical Society (216-721-5722)
NUMBER OF BURIALS: 200 ~ OLDEST/FIRST GRAVE: First: Lovisa Warren, 1811
RELIGIOUS AFFILIATION: Nondenominational, also North Union Shakers
ETHNIC AFFILIATION: Manx
DIRECTIONS: West: I-480 to Exit 23 for Broadway Rd.; left (south) on Broadway Rd.; left (east) on McCracken Rd.; left (north) on Lee Rd.; on right.
East: I-480 to Exit 24 for Lee Rd.; north on Lee; on right.

**HISTORY AND SURROUNDINGS:** Many people from the Isle of Man in the Irish Sea emigrated to America and found their way to the Western Reserve. Known as Manx, these settlers played an important role in early Warrensville Township and later in Cleveland. With over half the burials here of Manxmen, this is often called Old Manx Cemetery.

WHAT HAPPENED TO THE OTHER 47?

Warrensville Township is named for Moses Warren, but it was Daniel and Margaret Warren who built the first log cabin near Lee and Chagrin in 1809. The death of their two-year-old daughter Lovisa led to the need for the cemetery.

**YOUR VISIT:** There is no real gate or entrance to the cemetery, but you can enter by taking a large step up the retaining wall that was built in 1932. Walk to the boulder at the southeast portion of the cemetery. In 1949 the Shaker Historical Society placed it here with a plaque in memory of the North Union Shakers reinterred from their own cemetery. This boulder, marking the common grave of the Shakers, was taken from a Shaker farm.

The original Shaker burial ground was located where South Park Boulevard and Lee Road now intersect. As Cleveland grew, development plans caused the Shaker Burial Ground to be moved. In about 1905, the remains of all but Jacob Russell were gathered, placed in boxes, and buried in this common grave. Records show 137 burials at the original Shaker burial ground and 89 reinterred here at Warrensville West.

Jacob Russell's grave is still on South Park, but what happened to the other 47? We can only guess that there were multiple burials in the original plots and that during the reinterment the body count was less than precise.

There are supposed to be 200 graves here. Almost half the legible markers have the names of persons under age 21—attesting to the high rates of infant mortality and death from communicable diseases.

**NOTABLE:**

*This is the oldest landmark in Shaker Heights and one of the oldest cemeteries in Cuyahoga County. It is now in front of a supermarket.*

Though the following graves could be found several years ago, they are now impossible to locate:

James Prentiss (1755–1817) fought in the Revolutionary War.

Moses Warren (1760–1851) was the original settler who bought this land from the Connecticut Land Company. Warren was a private in Captain Seth Newton's company, Colonel Abijah Stear's Massachusetts Regiment. The name Warrensville Township was chosen at a housewarming party when Moses' wife was asked to propose a name for the town her husband had founded.

Robert Carran (1812–1914) came to Cleveland in 1845 and began farming in Warrensville Township. He was a school director for 58 years, justice of the peace for 24 years, and the official flag raiser for Cleveland. He is buried here with his wife Ann and six of their children.

OTHER CEMETERIES NEARBY: Shaker Burial Ground, *p. 122*
Highland Park Cemetery, *p. 96*

Tablet marks the mass grave
of those removed from Shaker
Burial Ground

The gravestone of Lydia Russell,
who died in 1839

# Willoughby Cemetery

ADDRESS: Sharpe Rd.  ~  LOCATION: Willoughby  ~  PHONE: (440) 953-4360

ACREAGE: 17 acres  ~  CARETAKER: Alan Lemieux

ACCESS: Grounds open daily dawn–dusk. Records at the cemetery office; Morley Library in Painesville has Lake County genealogy resources

NUMBER OF BURIALS: 10,200  ~  OLDEST/FIRST GRAVE: First: 1823

RELIGIOUS AFFILIATION: Nondenominational  ~  ETHNIC AFFILIATION: N/A

DIRECTIONS: I-90 to Exit 189 for SR 91 (SOM Center Rd.); north on SR 91 (SOM Cetner); right (east) on US 20 (Euclid Ave.); left (west) on Sharpe Ave.

**HISTORY AND SURROUNDINGS:** Little is known about the early history of this cemetery. The memorial gates at the main entrance were built in 1931, and the lots are laid out so precisely, it's as if there were a tape measure underneath the grass.

**YOUR VISIT:** As you enter the main gates, go immediately to the left. Four rows down and toward the fence is a white military sandstone marker for John F. Broderick, who was awarded the Silver Star for gallantry in 1938.

Proceed along Hickory and look for the "Girl in Blue." Her stone is in the center section by a mulberry tree. (From Hickory and Evergreen, walk diagonally toward the mulberry tree and you will notice the stone near the tree.)

## THE GIRL IN BLUE

The "Girl in Blue" is this cemetery's claim to fame. On December 22, 1933, an attractive young girl was put off a streetcar in Kirtland because she could not pay the fare. Someone noticed her wandering around and took her to a boardinghouse in Willoughby. The next day, the girl asked directions to church but got lost on the way and ended up at the railroad tracks. She was found dead on Christmas Eve, killed by a train. She had no identification; only ninety cents and a train ticket to Corry, Pennsylvania, were found in her purse. Wearing a blue dress and blue shoes, she was dubbed "the girl in blue."

More than 3,000 local residents went to the funeral home to say good-bye to a girl they never knew. Donations from the community paid for her headstone, and the few dollars left over were put in a fund for flowers. Newspapers carried the unusual story. Families with missing daughters wrote seeking more information, but the mystery continued.

*Top: Josephine Klimczak will forever be the "Girl in Blue"*

*Bottom: A sundial contributes to the uniqueness of the Rogers family plot*

In 1938, a visitor to the cemetery identified his sister in a picture shown to him by the sexton. The man explained that he and his sister, Sophie, had left their parents' home during the Depression to look for work. They both had trouble finding work, so he gave Sophie money for a train ticket home.

According to the sexton, the man (who donated two dollars for flowers for the grave) looked very much like the girl.

As time passed, clues developed and police records indicated her last name was Kincau or Kingcoe. The funeral director thought it was Kincov.

Finally, a story in the *News Herald* on the 60th anniversary of the accident led to the resolution of the mystery. After reading the story, a local realtor contacted a title agency, which researched records from the sale of a property in Warren County, Pennsylvania. In settling the estate of his parents, Leo Klimczak had to prove the whereabouts of his sister Josephine, or "Sophie," another possible heir. Pennsylvania authorities declared Josephine Klimczak the person killed in an accident in Willoughby, Ohio, on December 24, 1933.

Lake County records, however, have not changed. The death certificate still lists her as "The Girl in Blue."

Continue along Cherry. Six rows past Evergreen, toward the office, is a sundial on the Rogers family plot—the first sundial I've seen in a cemetery. The inscription on the sundial, originally written by Mark Twain after the death of his wife and two daughters, reads:

> warm summer sun, shine kindly here,
> warm southern wind blow softly here,
> green sod above lie light, lie light
> good night dear heart, good night good night.

OTHER CEMETERIES NEARBY: Single Marker for Edward Paine, p. 127

# Single Marker

**NAME:** Edward Paine

**LOCATION:** Mentor Ave. and Washington St. (across from Lake Erie College)

**DETAILS:** Edward Paine was the founder of Painesville. In 1900 his statue was unveiled during a July 4th centennial observance, and on July 21, 1900, his remains were removed from Washington Street and placed in the monument's masonry base. The point where the statue stands is known as Charter Oak Point.

*Statue of Edward Paine*

OTHER CEMETERIES NEARBY: Evergreen Cemetery, *p. 89*
Willoughby Cemetery, *p. 125*

# WEST

## Adams Street Cemetery

ADDRESS: 94 Adams St. ~ LOCATION: Berea ~ PHONE: None

ACREAGE: 2 acres ~ CARETAKER: City of Berea; no office or restrooms on site

ACCESS: Grounds open daily dawn–dusk. Records at Western Reserve Historical Society (216-721-5722); related documents at Berea Historical Society (440-234-2541)

NUMBER OF BURIALS: Unknown

OLDEST/FIRST GRAVE: Oldest: Susan Briden,1843, age 20

RELIGIOUS AFFILIATION: Nondenominational ~ ETHNIC AFFILIATION: German

DIRECTIONS: I-71 to Exit 235 for Bagley Rd.; west on Bagley; left (south) on Eastland Rd.; right (west) on Bridge St.; left (south) on Adams St.; on right.

**HISTORY AND SURROUNDINGS:** Officially started by a cemetery association on September 17, 1861 (there had already been some burials on the property), Adams Street became a village cemetery for Berea. Across the street from the cemetery, John Baldwin built the log hut which was the first residence in Berea; and the cemetery is on land that was originally part of the Baldwin estate. In 1913, the Cleveland Stone Company purchased the unused portion of the lot, but their quarrying began to cause landslides, and public protest stopped the company from further activity. Today, Adams Street Cemetery sits next to an American Legion post in a residential neighborhood.

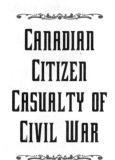

CANADIAN CITIZEN CASUALTY OF CIVIL WAR

Jennie Wade Wright was buried in 1931. Because of a city ordinance, burials here had been stopped at the time of her death, but an exception was made so that she could be buried with her husband and family. The ordinance was either changed or not followed because there are also markers dated 1955 and 1977.

There are 14 Civil War veterans buried here. Sadly, several of their markers are no longer visible. Only a few that can be found are readable.

**YOUR VISIT:** Park on one of the side streets and enter through the gate. The rectangular section on your left is dedicated to veterans. Cross to the right side of the gate and find Turanchik.

The stone for Robert W. Turanchik (1946–1977) has messages on both sides. The side facing the entrance reads:

> But through a sudden gate there stole
> the universe and spread in my soul;
> Quick went my breath and quick my heart;
> And I looked at God with lips apart.

On the other side is:

> Evening night darkens the green earth,
> The wheel turns, death follows birth;
> Strive as you sleep with even breath;
> That you may wake past day, past death.

Behind Turanchik and to the right is Nachtrieb's white marker showing a hand with its forefinger extended. John Gottleb Nachtrieb (?–1875), a student at German Wallace College, was the son of a man who worked at the German Methodist Orphans Asylum. Nachtrieb died from drowning.

Walk toward the back of the plot and to the left side. Directly across from the fifth parking space of the American Legion post is a white, two-foot-tall marker for Simpson. It stands behind a tall pine tree with unusual nodules protruding along the length of the trunk. William S. Simpson, a jeweler, was the last soldier to be buried here.

After finding Simpson, walk toward the front of the cemetery and look for the Crockett stone by the edge of the American Legion building. Robert Crockett died November 8, 1955; other than that date, only "friend" is written on his gravestone.

*The gate at Adams Street Cemetery*

*Dedicatory plaque to those known and unknown buried here*

Continue toward the gate and notice the large granite stone about six feet tall with a plaque dedicating this section as a garden. It reads:

To the memory of all souls who laid to rest within these humble boundaries. Our grandmothers and grandfathers, our aunts and uncles, our neighbors and our friends. They quarried the stone that helped build nations and turned Berea O into the sandstone capital of the world. For those whose names can no longer be read or whose stones have been lost to time, though their names are lost they are loved and will not be forgotten.
(Boy Scout Eagle Project BF 1996)

**STORY BUT NO STONE FOUND:** George Huckins (?–1862) graduated from Baldwin University in 1859, joined the Methodist ministry, and worked in the Berea Schools as a teacher and later principal at Wooden School. Although a Canadian citizen, Huckins volunteered with the Berea contingent in the Civil War. He died from disease in a hospital in Tennessee, becoming Berea's first casualty in the war. Before he enlisted, Huckins had been engaged to marry Hannah Foster, a teacher. She never married. His marker cannot be found.

**NOTABLE:**

*Near the back of the cemetery, there is supposed to be a small marker with no writing on it and a flag flying overhead. It was a tribute to Berea's Unknown Soldier. No one knows for sure if there is anyone in the grave. The marker can no longer be found.*

OTHER CEMETERIES NEARBY: Woodvale Cemetery, p. 171
Hepburn Cemetery, p. 140

~ SUPERSTITIONS ~

# Pregnant women should not attend funerals.

# Brainard / Broadview Cemetery

ADDRESS: Next to 2044 Broadview Rd.  ~  LOCATION: Brooklyn  ~  PHONE: None
ACREAGE: 6 acres  ~  CARETAKER: Unknown
ACCESS: Grounds open daily dawn–dusk; Records at Western Reserve Historical Society (216-721-5722)
NUMBER OF BURIALS: approx. 50  ~  OLDEST/FIRST GRAVE: First: Simon Chester, 1821
RELIGIOUS AFFILIATION: Nondenominational  ~  ETHNIC AFFILIATION: Irish, Scottish
DIRECTIONS: I-480 to Exit 16 for SR 94 (State Rd.); north on SR 94 (State); right (north) on US 42 (Pearl Rd.); right on Broadview Rd.; on left.

**HISTORY AND SURROUNDINGS:** This land originally belonged to the Brainard family; Seth and Delilah Brainard established it as a cemetery in 1852. The property was to be returned to their heirs if it ever stopped being used as a cemetery. In 1913, the city acquired it from the state, which had taken possession of it due to nonpayment of taxes. In the book *Ohio Cemeteries*, published by the Ohio Genealogical Association, this cemetery is listed as "abandoned."

## THIRTY-SIX BURIED IN A SINGLE GRAVE

Portions of the land were sold and resold in the 1930s and '40s, leading to questions about ownership rights and disputes with area residents who had proof they owned burial plots here. In 1941, a corner of the original plot was sold, once again because of delinquent taxes. In 1962, the owners wanted to develop the site for commercial purposes. The matter was taken to court, where it was decided that the portion in dispute had not been used as a burial ground. There were, and probably still are, area residents who would argue the truth in that statement.

In recent times, neighborhood children played baseball here and used the grounds as a school shortcut. It is now cared for, with flowers planted around the few remaining gravestones and the grass trimmed. On Memorial Day flags are placed alongside some of the stones.

**YOUR VISIT:** Park on one of the side streets, Spring or Treadway, and walk to the parking lot of the restaurant. As you look beyond the fence you will notice the gravestones barely visible from the street. One of these is for H. Carl Kohlman (1826–1899), a nurse in the Civil War.

Walk onto Broadview and enter the cemetery. Look for a cluster of three small stones. One is for Allen S. McDiarmid who was released from an insane asylum where he had been treated for four years. Records indicate he was "let out unimproved." When he died in 1897 he was 18 years old.

Although this is public land, visitors should be aware of the private property adjacent to it.

**NOTABLE:**
*Sometime in the 1890s there was a flood in the Cuyahoga Valley, and a boat with 36 people aboard capsized. All of the victims are buried in a single grave.*

**STORY BUT NO STONE FOUND:** Although you won't be able to find his grave, Daniel Fish, son of the first settler of South Brooklyn, is buried here.

OTHER CEMETERIES NEARBY: Brookmere Cemetery, p. 134
Riverside Cemetery, p. 54
Denison Cemetery, p. 32

*H. Carl Kohlman served as a nurse in the Civil War*

~ SUPERSTITIONS ~

**If a mirror in the house falls and breaks by itself, someone in the house will die soon.**

# Brookmere Cemetery

ADDRESS: Broadview  ~  LOCATION: Brooklyn  ~  PHONE: (216) 348-7216
ACREAGE: 3.5 acres  ~  CARETAKER: City of Cleveland
ACCESS: Grounds open Mon–Sat 9 a.m.–3 p.m.; Records at Highland Park Cemetery
(216 348-7210)
NUMBER OF BURIALS: 3,300  ~  OLDEST/FIRST GRAVE: Oldest and first: Bertha Albers, date
unknown, but prior to 1832
RELIGIOUS AFFILIATION: Nondenominational  ~  ETHNIC AFFILIATION: German
DIRECTIONS: I-480 to Exit 16 for SR 94 (State Rd.); north on SR 94 (State Rd.); right
(north) on US 42 (Pearl Rd.); left (west) on Broadview Rd. to cemetery entrance.
OR I-71 to Exit 246 for US 42 (Pearl Rd.); south on US 42 (Pearl); right (west) on
Broadview Rd. to cemetery entrance.

**HISTORY AND SURROUNDINGS:** Brookmere Cemetery was founded when ten farmers donated part of their land for the first cemetery in the community, then known as Brighton Village, population 267. Cleveland acquired it in 1906. There have been more than 2,700 burials in this modest refuge of trees and greenery in an otherwise commercial area of the city. As in many cemeteries, names on several of the monuments, such as Biddulph and Schaaf, match local street names.

## BELLS, BELLS: NO EVIL SPIRITS HERE

**YOUR VISIT:** As you enter, one of the first few rows on the right has a seven-foot-tall pedestal for Johnson. In front of it are stones for Angenette, "grandma," and John L. Johnson (1824–1911), "grandpa." Johnson took money he made in the gold rush and built a hotel called Johnson House at the corner of Broadview and Pearl.

About seven rows farther down on the same side is the Ohnacker monument with a poem inscribed on it in German. The five sons, Rudolph, Jacob, Ludwig, George, and Philipp, all died in a fire September 18, 1851. The poem attests to the family's grief and their continued faith in God:

> Rest therefore in this quiet vault till the Savior
> calls you. Meanwhile we praise Him quietly and
> suffer as His will requires it.

Continue toward the back, looking on the left for a group of stones

*Above: Enclosure of chain surrounds the Selover family plot*

*Right: Detail of ornamental bell*

inside a wrought-iron fence belonging to the Selovers. Notice the hanging bells, which were often used in cemeteries to ward off evil spirits. Asher (1796–1896) and Ruth (1805–1872) Selover came to Cleveland from New York. He owned a hotel on Public Square along with a barn and livery stable. His Cleveland House Hotel later became the Cleveland Hotel, which no longer exists.

Toward the back of the cemetery, on the left but before the road turns, is the gray Brainard pedestal marker with several names on it. Amos Brainard (1758–1832) fought in the Revolutionary War and served with General Washington at Valley Forge.

In the oval at the back of the cemetery is the Gates family plot. This striking monument features an angel holding a palm leaf. The angel stands over the figure of a mourning woman holding flowers. On the other side of the monument are in bas-relief pictures—likely those of Jeremiah (1795–1870) and Phebe (1795–1881) Gates.

Their son, Charles, and his wife, Mary, are buried here, together with their three children: Lafayette, Mary Gates Bratten, and Howard. Jeremiah and Charles (father and son) worked together operating gristmills. Howard and Lafayette (brothers) manufactured mineral paint. Howard continued on his own to manufacture fertilizer and then began buying land, including property along Big Creek that had belonged to

Asahel Brainard and later became Brookside Park, now the home of the Cleveland Metroparks Zoo.

**NOTABLE:** Mathilda Meny (1902–1956) has an epitaph I call the "as you pass by" epitaph:

> Dear friend take notice as you pass by
> As you are now, so was I
> Where I am now you will be
> Prepare for death and follow me

OTHER CEMETERIES NEARBY: Brainard/Broadview Cemetery, *p. 132*
Denison Cemetery, *p. 32*
Riverside Cemetery, *p. 54*
Memorial for Wolf and Foote, *p. 83*

*Grief and angel appear on stately Gates family monument*

# Butternut Ridge Cemetery

ADDRESS: SR 252 and Butternut Ridge Rd.  ~  LOCATION: North Olmsted

PHONE: None  ~  ACREAGE: 5.2 acres  ~  CARETAKER: City of North Olmsted; no restrooms on site

ACCESS: Grounds open daily dawn–dusk. Records at Olmsted Historical Society (440-777-0059), and Western Reserve Historical Society (216-721-5722); maps at North Olmsted City Hall, Engineering Department (440-777-8000)

NUMBER OF BURIALS: approx. 2,500

OLDEST/FIRST GRAVE: Oldest: Isaac Scales, July 15, 1821

RELIGIOUS AFFILIATION: Nondenominational  ~  ETHNIC AFFILIATION: English, Scottish

DIRECTIONS: I-480 to Exit 6 for SR 252 (Columbia Rd.); south on SR 252 (Columbia); right (west) on Butternut Ridge Rd.; on right.

**HISTORY AND SURROUNDINGS:** Charles Hyde Olmsted, who at one time owned about one third of what is now North Olmsted, donated this land for use as a cemetery in 1835. While it obviously was used as a cemetery prior to that, it is not known if there were burials earlier than 1821. A gravel drive through openings in a split-rail fence provides access to this small plot of land.

**FAMILY BUSINESS**

**YOUR VISIT:** Enter on the gravel road closest to Route 252/Columbia Road and look to the left for the broken-tree-trunk monument for Rice close to Butternut Road. On it are listed the dates of death of their five children. The inscription:

> Deaths doings
> recorded here
> heartaches elsewhere

The Rices had five children, all of whom died before their seventh birthdays. Rev. Jonas F. Rice (1825–1905) came to Olmsted when he was 17 years old. He was a minister in the Universalist Church and one of the carpenters who, in 1847, helped build the sanctuary of the First Universalist Church in North Olmsted.

Walk north and look for Briggs's aging, white, seven-foot-tall obelisk. Arthur Briggs (1857–1861) at age three years, five months died of accidental hanging. His father put him up in an apple tree to look at something. The boy, who was wearing a cape around his neck, accidentally stepped off the tree branch—the cape pulled tight around his neck, strangling him to death.

On the other side of the gravel road, find what looks like a book on a table. This is a fine example of a book monument with nice attention to detail. The stone is carved to look like cloth drapes over the pedestal that holds the book, and the tassel hanging down marks the page. This book reveals that L. J. Jennings died Jan 31, 1870, age 33 years, 7 months, 12 days.

**NOTABLE:**
*Like many early burial grounds, this one was used as a cemetery before being officially so designated. In fact, the first person buried here, Isaac Scales, was actually buried in his front yard.*

Continue up the gravel road and turn left. On the right before the vault is Samuel Porter's two-foot-tall headstone. It is near the road and has a slight arch on top. Samuel Porter (1747–1840) fought in the Revolutionary War. He was in Captain Whipple's company of the Massachusetts Guards.

Proceed toward the vault, stopping just before it. On the left side of the gravel road you'll find Southworth, four stones over and behind the new gray speckled stone that reads: "Molly wife of Jonathan Spencer". Esther Spencer Southworth (1836–1872) poisoned three of her children with strychnine on July 7, 1872. They were: Arthur, age 9; George, age 7; and Silas, age 3. Her fourth child, Henry, had died just six months earlier on Jan 5, 1872, at less than two months of age. She may have been so distraught over Henry's death that she killed the others. The three children are buried in separate coffins, all in the same grave. Esther died exactly two months later on September 7, 1872.

Past the vault on the right is "Powell." The marker has a Masonic symbol on the top and three small stones beside it for Elroy King (1868–1926), father; Emily Helen (1914), baby; and Sabra Stearns (1877–1956), mother. Elroy King Powell married Sabra Stearns after the death of his first wife, who was the mother of Dawn Powell, a noted author. (Powell's works, including *Angels on Toast* and *The*

*A broken portion of the Southworth monument lies on the ground*

*Locusts Have No King*, have been receiving wide interest lately.) On January 17, 1914, Sabra gave birth to a baby girl, Emily Helen, who was born four months premature. The infant died five days later. Several months afterward, Sabra arrived at the elementary school her stepdaughter Phyllis attended (Dawn, Phyllis's sister, had already run away from home) to take her home on "family business." At home the youngster was told to get the white dress of her one and only doll. Sabra took the dress and, with husband and stepdaughter in tow, came to Butternut Ridge, dug up the infant's body, and reburied it in the doll's dress.

OTHER CEMETERIES NEARBY: Sunset Cemetery, *p. 163*
Immanuel Evangelical Cemetery, *p. 46*

~ SUPERSTITIONS ~

## If a clock that has not been working suddenly chimes, there will be a death in the family.

# Hepburn Cemetery

ADDRESS: Hepburn Rd.  ~  LOCATION: Middleburg Heights  ~  PHONE: None

ACREAGE: 0.2 acres  ~  CARETAKER: Unknown

ACCESS: Grounds always open. Records at Western Reserve Historical Society (216-721-5722); related documents at Berea Historical Society (440-243-2541); plaques on site provided by the SWAMP CO. (Sons, Wives, Ancestors for Middleburg's Preservation Coalition) offer detailed historical information

NUMBER OF BURIALS: 18  ~  OLDEST/FIRST GRAVE: Unknown

RELIGIOUS AFFILIATION: Nondenominational  ~  ETHNIC AFFILIATION: N/A

DIRECTIONS: I-71 to Exit 235 for Bagley Rd.; west on Bagley; right (north) on Hepburn Rd. (after Middleburg Towne Square Plaza); on right.

**HISTORY AND SURROUNDINGS:** The land for Hepburn Cemetery was disbursed by lottery agents who worked for the Connecticut Land Company, which surveyed the Western Reserve. Gideon Granger (postmaster under Thomas Jefferson) drew the lot for range 14, township 6, later known as Middleburg Township. With no inhabitants on this land, Granger offered 50 acres to the first settler; Jared and Rachel Hickox arrived in 1809 and received the 50 acres.

## PLAYING AT A THEATER NEAR YOU

Much later, in 1827, Morris Hepburn arrived in Cleveland from New York; in 1832, he married Hilda Ann Pease. Morris was skilled at real estate dealings and was responsible for 30 property transactions in Cuyahoga County from 1835 to 1855. In 1854 he bought the claim to the 50-acre Bagley farm (originally the Hickox property) for five dollars from a tavern keeper named Abijah Bagley. This is the land that became Hepburn Cemetery.

The burial ground is located in an unlikely spot at the rear of a theater parking lot.

*Jared Hickox's tombstone*
*with Regal theater in background*

**YOUR VISIT:** The Hickoxes' grandsons, Asor and Nathaniel, are buried here. Asor died September 12, 1809, of typhoid fever and Nathaniel died of the same illness two months later.

Morris and Ann Hepburn and their son, Willis, are also buried here. Willis's stone is original but records indicate that no stone ever existed for Morris or Ann. Official records cannot be found, but descendants of the family agree that this is, indeed, the final resting place of Morris and Ann Hepburn.

**NOTABLE:**

*A small gate surrounds the cemetery and has detailed history written on plaques at the site, which provide visitors enough information for a self-guided tour. It's truly amazing that this area was preserved— thanks to the Historical Society and others.*

OTHER CEMETERIES NEARBY:

Woodvale Cemetery, *p. 171*
Adams Street Cemetery, *p. 129*

~ SUPERSTITIONS ~

# If you dream of death. it's a sign of a birth: if you dream of birth. it's a sign of death.

# Johnson's Island
# Confederate Cemetery

ADDRESS: Confederate Rd.  ~  LOCATION: Marblehead Peninsula  ~  PHONE: None
ACREAGE: 1 acre  ~  CARETAKER: Under federal control; no restrooms available
ACCESS: Grounds open daily dawn–dusk. Records at Port Clinton Public Library
(419-732-3211)
NUMBER OF BURIALS: 206  ~  OLDEST/FIRST GRAVE: Oldest: Elijah Gibson, May 29, 1862
RELIGIOUS AFFILIATION: Nondenominational  ~  ETHNIC AFFILIATION: Native-American
DIRECTIONS: SR 2 to SR 269; east on SR 269; right (south) on Danbury North Rd.;
left (east) on Bay Shore Rd.; right (south) on Gaydos Dr. (after Skyline Rd.) to toll
causeway (becomes Confederate Rd.).

**HISTORY AND SURROUNDINGS:** This island was known as Bull Island until L. B. Johnson purchased and renamed it.

CONFEDERATES GET NEW OUTLOOK ON LIFE

Prior to the opening of Johnson's Island, the Union sent prisoners, both officers and enlisted men, to Camp Chase in Columbus, Ohio. As Camp Chase became overcrowded, the government searched for a separate, isolated spot for Confederate officers. Kelleys Island and Put-in-Bay were both considered, but their commercial wineries and growing populations made them unsatisfactory. Situated in Sandusky Bay, Johnson's Island has a great view of Sandusky and Lake Erie.

When the prison opened in April, 1862, it could hold 1,336 prisoners and 168 guards. Eventually there were as many as 3,200 prisoners at one time, and when it closed in September 1865, Johnson's Island had housed a total of 8,700 prisoners, including 27 Confederate generals and five slaves accompanying their masters.

Because the prisoners were officers, they could not be forced to work. As a result the barracks were often filthy—probably adding to the sickness already common among the troops.

The prisoners amused themselves by learning baseball from their Northern captors. Entrepreneurial types set up a tailor shop, an ice-cream shop, and a lemonade stand. The theatrically inclined organized the Rebelthespians, writing and putting on plays such as *The Battle of Gettysburg* which enjoyed a long run. Others played chess or designed jewelry, and some even bought a washing machine to set up a laundry business.

After the prison closed, a workman tearing down the barracks found this poem on a wall. The unknown prisoner wrote:

> Hoarse sounding billows of the white-capped lake,
> That 'gainst the barriers of our hated prison break
> Farewell! Farewell thou giant inland sea;
> Thou, too, subservest the modes of tyranny,
> Girding this isle, washing its lonely shore
> With moaning echoes of thy melancholy roar,
> Farewell, thou lake! Farewell, thou inhospitable land!
> Thou has the curses of this patriot band—
> All save the spot, the holy sacred bed,
> Where rest in peace our Southern warriors dead!

Thirteen buildings comprised the prison complex; the last one burned down in the 1940s. This is the only dedicated military Masonic cemetery in the U.S. United Daughters of the Confederacy purchased the land for $1 in 1905 and turned over control to the federal government in 1932. A national radio broadcast announced the event—the cemetery was declared a federal national cemetery.

In 1991 developers announced plans for 340 condominiums and town houses as well as a boat marina on the island. Despite numerous town meetings, and protests from environmentalists, historians, and

Courtesy Cleveland Press Collection (CSU)

*Statue honoring Confederate dead outlined by iron fence*

*Typical government markers at Johnson's Island Confederate Cemetery*

property owners, the project was approved. Until this project began, the island had only 30 to 35 year-round residents and about 300 in the summer.

Many consider this the most important Civil War site in Ohio.

**NOTABLE:**
*The earliest graves are in the middle of the cemetery. Most of the deaths were due to illness—such as pneumonia, dysentery, or typhoid fever—related to unsanitary conditions.*

While at Marblehead, look for the battle marker for the War of 1812 on the south side of Bayshore Road (0.5 miles west of Gaydos Drive). This is the site of the first land battle in northern Ohio. In September of 1812, three months after the War of 1812 began, militiamen from Camp Avery near Milan, Ohio, went to Marblehead in response to reports that two men had been killed by Indians. Joshua Giddings, who later was an Ohio congressman and also served as President Lincoln's ambassador to Canada, was a 16-year-old participant in the battle. The monument commemorates the six who lost their lives at the Battle of Marblehead.

**YOUR VISIT:** At the cemetery entrance, a marker offers historical information about the site. Notice that all the stones are the same government-issued markers. Because of poor record-keeping and the fact that the original stones were made of wood, there are 54 unknowns buried here; by the time government markers were ordered, the names on many of the wooden markers were illegible. The grave of one of the unknowns is in the fifth row from the gray building, about 11 graves from the road. It is next to E. M. Orr.

Ruben Stout is the only Union soldier buried here. Stout went home on furlough and stayed with his father-in-law. His host, a "Copperhead" (a Northerner who sympathized with the South), convinced him to take a secret oath and fight no more. Several months later, Stout went to visit his father in Delphi, Indiana, and was caught by bounty hunters at the top of the stairs in his father's home. He shot and killed one of the bounty hunters on the spot. After signing a long confession with an "X," Stout was executed on Johnson's Island as a deserter on October 23, 1863. Stout's is grave #70, 11th Arkansas.

The one Native American buried here is S. V. Hamilton, Captain 2nd Choctaw Cavalry, who died from diphtheria on February 4, 1864. He was a Mason and was cared for by other Masons in his final days. He is in grave 154.

Although there is a tombstone for John Dow, according to Roger Long, local librarian and Johnson's Island expert, no one named Dow died at Johnson's Island. Instead, Robert W. Crow, 2nd lieutenant, company I of the 11th Arkansas, is buried in grave 68. He was captured in Mississippi on April 8, 1862, arrived at Johnson's Island on April 26, and died from typhoid fever on July 21, 1862. Wear on the original markers along with poor record-keeping may account for the discrepancy.

Long knows of other mistakes as well. For example, John J. Nickell (the stone reads Nichols), of the 2nd Kentucky Mounted Rifles, in grave 170 (near the clubhouse fence), was listed as a "surgeon" but was actually a sergeant. Pro-Union sympathizers had killed Nickell's uncle. While

*Sir Moses Ezekial's monument to the Confederate soldiers silhouetted against the sky*

Courtesy Cleveland Press Collection (CSU)

home on leave, Nickell retaliated by killing two of his uncle's assailants (one of whom was Logan Wilson). He was sent to Johnson's Island, the nearest federal facility, where he was hanged.

There are many graves marked "Jon"—this probably stood for John or Jonathan.

At the end of the compound near the lake is "Outlook," a monument to all the Confederate soldiers. It was designed by Sir Moses Ezekiel (a graduate of Virginia Military Institute whose statue of Stonewall Jackson is on the VMI campus), and was dedicated in 1910. The monument is of a soldier looking out over Lake Erie. Some like to think the soldier is looking longingly toward the South. Basic knowledge of geography disproves that theory.

**STORY BUT NO STONE FOUND:** Lieutenant Elijah Gibson was returning to his barracks past curfew after visiting a friend. He was asked to halt, and did so, but as he tried to explain his actions he was shot and killed by a guard. This bold display of power almost caused a riot.

**MORE TO KNOW:** A ghost story. After the war, a group of Sicilian workers were employed at a nearby quarry. A storm hit the island, and they left their flimsy shelters to run for protection behind the "Outlook" sculpture.

One of the workers, Nicolai Rocci, was crouched behind the monument and told his friends that during the height of the storm he was suddenly aware of something. He looked up toward the graves and saw 206 soldiers rise up, form ranks, and march southward across the lake.

The Sicilians left the island, never to return.

~ SUPERSTITIONS ~

# You will have bad luck if you do not stop the clock in the room where someone dies.

# Lake Side Cemetery

ADDRESS: West of 29014 Lake Rd.  ~  LOCATION: Bay Village  ~  PHONE: None
ACREAGE: 0.5 acres  ~  CARETAKER: City of Bay Village
ACCESS: Records at Bay Village Historical Society (440-871-7338) and Western Reserve Historical Society (216-721-5722)
NUMBER OF BURIALS: approx. 271
OLDEST/FIRST GRAVE: First: Rebecca Smith (Mrs. Abner), 1811
RELIGIOUS AFFILIATION: Nondenominational
ETHNIC AFFILIATION: English, German, Norwegian
DIRECTIONS: I-90 to Exit 156 for Crocker Rd.; north on Crocker (becomes Bassett Rd.); right (east) on Lake Rd.; on left.

**HISTORY AND SURROUNDINGS:** This small, almost austere cemetery, one of the oldest in Cuyahoga County, offers beautiful vistas of Lake Erie.

**YOUR VISIT:** Drive in at the eastern entrance. On the left about one-third of the way back is the Wischmeyer plot.

Henry and Matilda Wischmeyer operated a private wine orchard, with two acres of grapes and a wine cellar with a capacity of 10,000 gallons. Though the country was in a major depression, Wischmeyer took a chance and opened a resort hotel in 1874. Located at 26556 Lake Road, with a clubhouse near the beach, the hotel could accommodate 70 guests. It became a popular spot for businessmen traveling between Sandusky and Cleveland as well as for well-to-do Clevelanders. With the introduction of the interurban railway, the hotel was even more accessible. The business was forced to close in 1927 when local laws changed and would not permit businesses on Lake Road. In 1962 the building was razed.

> "SLEEP ON
> SWEET ONE,
> NOT DREAM
> ALONE"

Continue as the drive curves left. The Cahoons have the tallest and most impressive monument here. Joseph Cahoon was the first settler in this northwest section of Cuyahoga county. He and his wife had seven children—all are buried around them. The Cahoons gave a lot of land to the city as well as a park, which, according to their bequest, is not to be used on Sundays. The Cahoons also started the local library in their home.

Now walk into the center section of the cemetery. Winsor's marker is lying flat. It is closer to Lake Road than to Lake Erie. Nancy Maria Winsor (1839–1849), daughter of H. and M.Winsor, died at the age of 10; she has an interesting inscription, particularly for someone buried near the shore of Lake Erie:

> sleep on sweet one not dream alone
> is the path of light while our thoughts hath gone
> for we know in the land where our loved one dwells
> there are no partings and no farewells,
> and when the dream of life is o'er
> may we meet again on that far distant shore

In the center section you'll also find the Foot grave, with an SAR marker. David Foot (1760–1851) is one of two Revolutionary War soldiers buried here. He was a Minuteman and served with the Massachusetts Troops from 1777 to 1780.

Near Foot is the other Revolutionary War soldier, Saddler.

After viewing the stones in the center section, go toward the back of the cemetery and look for Selden Osborn, one of the sons of Reuben and Sarah. An herb doctor who received his training in a doctor's office, Selden grew his own herbs and his wife brewed them. He traveled by horse with one saddlebag for his own use, the other for his medications. On July 20, 1853, Governor Robert Lucas made him a captain of the 7th

*Inscription depicts loss of beloved child*

*Grave of David Foot commemorated by a Sons of the American Revolution plaque*

company's first rifle regiment, 2nd brigade, 9th division in the Ohio Militia.

As the road curves left again toward the exit road, find "Aslaksens" on your right. Olaf Aslaksens (1869–1957) and Louisa Malvena Aslaksens (1877–1948) arrived in the United States from Norway. Louisa Malvena met Olaf, a ship's captain, when his ship sailed to the Falklands, where she was living with her parents. They married and lived in Chile, Argentina, and Norway before coming to the U.S. in about 1903. John Aslaksens (1901–1921), their son, was killed in a car accident.

**NOTABLE:**
In the center of Lake Side Cemetery is a flagpole and near it is a grave for an Unknown Soldier.

OTHER CEMETERIES NEARBY:
Alger Cemetery, p. 21
Lakewood Historical Society, p. 150

~ SUPERSTITIONS ~

**Dropping an umbrella on the floor means that there will be a murder in the house.**

# Lakewood Historical Society

ADDRESS: 14710 Lake Ave.  ~  LOCATION: Lakewood  ~  PHONE: (216) 221-7343

ACREAGE: 0.2 acres  ~  CARETAKER: The Lakewood Historical Society/Museum

ACCESS: Grounds open daily dawn–dusk. Records at Lakewood Historical Society (216-221-7343), and Western Reserve Historical Society (216-721-5722)

NUMBER OF BURIALS: 11  ~  OLDEST/FIRST GRAVE: Oldest: Peter Hall, 1847

RELIGIOUS AFFILIATION: Nondenominational  ~  ETHNIC AFFILIATION: English

DIRECTIONS: I-90 to Exit 165 for W. 140th/Bunts Rd.; north on Bunts; left (west) on Clifton Rd.; right (north) on Belle Ave.; left (west) on Lake Ave.; on right.

**HISTORY AND SURROUNDINGS:** When Wagar Cemetery closed, most of the bodies were reinterred at Lakewood Park Cemetery, and some stones ended up behind the Lakewood Service Department. Those stones were brought here and placed in an herb garden behind the house, which is now home to the Lakewood Historical Society museum.

Built by Scottish weaver John Honam in 1838, the building served as a residence, post office, shoe-repair shop, grocery store, doctor's office, and barbershop before being moved here in 1952. It was then restored and opened as a museum. The museum and garden are maintained in keeping with the period of the 1850s. The stones are part of the herb garden.

## HERB GARDEN SERVES DUAL FUNCTION

**YOUR VISIT:** There are only six stones here, and on some the writing is so worn it is unreadable. The one closest to the house mentions Hannah, wife of Jonathan Bates, born June 19, 1828, died December 22, 1884. To one side is the stone for Jonathan Bates, born December 22, 1825, died July 1880, with the inscription: "Though I walk through the valley of death I will fear no evil." Above that inscription is written, "how desolate our home bereft of thee."

OTHER CEMETERIES NEARBY:
Alger Cemetery, p. 21
Lake Side Cemetery, p. 147

*Herbs and gravestones share space adjacent to the Historical Society building*

# Lakewood Park Cemetery

**ADDRESS:** 22025 Detroit Rd.  ~  **LOCATION:** Rocky River  ~  **PHONE:** (440) 333-1922

**ACREAGE:** 55 acres  ~  **CARETAKER:** Available Mon–Fri 8:30 a.m.–12:00 p.m. and 1:00 p.m.–4:30 p.m.; Sat 8:30 a.m.–12:00 p.m.

**ACCESS:** Grounds open daily dawn–dusk; office open Mon–Fri 8:30 a.m.–4:30 p.m. (closed noon–1 p.m.), Sat 8:30 a.m.–noon. Records at cemetery office, and Western Reserve Historical Society (216-721-5722)

**NUMBER OF BURIALS:** 26,200+  ~  **OLDEST/FIRST GRAVE:** Unknown

**RELIGIOUS AFFILIATION:** Nondenominational  ~  **ETHNIC AFFILIATION:** German, Irish

**DIRECTIONS:** West: I-90 to Exit 161 for Detroit Rd.; west on Detroit; on right.

East: I-90 to Exit 162 for Hilliard Rd.; right (west) on Westway Dr.; left (west) on Detroit Rd.; on right.

**HISTORY AND SURROUNDINGS:** In 1914 farmland was purchased on this part of Detroit Road, then considered "way out of town." The mausoleum, made of granite and marble, was built in 1921, and the office, including a fireproof record room, was built in 1957. The remains from the old Wagar Cemetery at Detroit Road and St. Charles Street, 84 in number, were placed in section 1. In 1957 the unknown remains from Kidney Cemetery were placed here in section 2.

**FOREVER CAMELOT**

As its name suggests, this cemetery is meant to create a park-like setting. The 55 acres are bordered on the west and south by wooded ravines. The grave markers are all flat, so it looks like you're driving through a park.

**YOUR VISIT:** Because this is a memorial park, all markers are flat and therefore somewhat difficult to locate. For additional help, stop by the office for maps of the individual sections. Lot numbers are on the bottom right of the markers, but not on every one. Using the map, park by the corner of section 4 closest to the office.

Sammy Kaye (1910–1987) graduated from Rocky River High School in 1928 as Samuel Zarnocay, Jr. Kaye formed a band with himself on clarinet to help pay college expenses. In 1938 his band opened in New York, at the Commodore Hotel. He changed his name to Kaye and called his act "Swing and Sway with Sammy Kaye." The band had several hit songs during the big-band era: "Daddy," "There Will Never Be Another You," and "Harbor Lights." On December 7, 1941, Kaye's radio show was interrupted by news of the attack on Pearl Harbor. "Remember Pearl Harbor" was written that night. There is some dispute as to the authorship of the song, with some books saying Don Reid wrote it with Kaye. The song, released eight days later, was the first American war song of World War II. Kaye's band played at the inaugurations of presidents Richard Nixon and Ronald Reagan. (lot 352)

Proceed to the part of section 9 close to sections 8 and 7. Walk in six rows to lot 312. The Seltzer plot is about 50 feet from a bench in section 7, lot 312. Louis B. Seltzer (1895–1980) was editor of the *Cleveland Press* from 1928 to 1966. His newspaper career began when he was 12 years old, working as an office boy at the *Cleveland Leader*. Two years later he had his own column, and by the time he was 18 he was a city editor.

Drive to section 14 in the back. Park and walk down the steps by the retaining wall. As you descend the stairs, "Sansom" is six rows to the left in lot 89. Art Sansom (1922–1991) was the creator of the cartoon strip *Born Loser,* which has been syndicated in more than 1,200 newspapers in 26 countries and has appeared in nine languages. *Born Loser* received the Reuben Award, the highest honor given by the National Cartoonists Society, in 1987 and again in 1991, six weeks before Sansom died. Chip Sansom worked with his father on the strip beginning in 1978 and took it over after his death. Art Sansom's stone has an etching of *Born Loser* and Sansom's signature as creator of the cartoon. The inscription reads "Forever Camelot."

Drive back toward the mausoleum but stop at the middle of section 1. About nine rows in, there are two trees with a large patch of ivy between them. "Stouffer" is lot 463 just behind the trees. Vernon Stouffer (1901–1974) graduated from the Wharton School of Business and then worked at a lunch counter owned by his father. Along with his brother

*From Cleveland to this Chicago site and beyond, Stouffer's food prospered*

Gordon, he helped the modest quick-lunch business grow into a large food-service company. Their frozen foods became available in 1951, and dinner in American has never been the same.

The family expanded its business interests into real estate and hotels in the 1960s. Stouffer even bought the Cleveland Indians in 1966, hoping to cure the financial weakness of the team. After five years and little success, he sold it to Nick Mileti's investment group.

Walk into Lakewood Abbey, the mausoleum. Neville Chandler, Jr. (1946–1994) was a beloved Cleveland sportscaster who, after Gib Shanley retired, was known as the voice of the Cleveland Browns. Chandler's cremains are in a glass niche, #159, on the south wall

Proceed toward the office, parking in a visitor space. In section 12, between the office and the entrance road and about nine rows in, is Carney in lot 210. John Carney (1911–1994) and his brother James were active real-estate developers in Cleveland. The brothers worked for their

**NOTABLE:**
*As its name denotes, Lakewood Park Cemetery is meant to create a park-like setting. The 55 acres are bordered on the west and south by wooded ravines. The grave markers are all flat, so it looks like you're driving through a park.*

father's West Park Excavating Company by driving teams of horses and later trucks for the business. Carney was appointed deputy treasurer of the county in 1933 and was elected to the Ohio House of Representatives in 1936. He held numerous other state positions culminating in the post of common pleas judge from 1975 to 1981.

On the other side of the office, still in section 12, about five rows from Detroit Road is Butler in lot 370. John Patrick Butler (1905–1996) was part of the renowned "Four Horsemen" football team at the University of Notre Dame. Butler's operatic voice helped him work his way through college. Unfortunately, in 1938, he lost his ability to sing after being beaten and robbed. He became a lawyer, with such a phenomenal command of the English language that people flocked to the courtroom to hear him expound. He worked for Cleveland mayors Ray Miller and Thomas Burke, as well as racketeers Alex "Shondor" Birns (see Hillcrest entry) and Danny Greene, adhering to the philosophy that everyone deserves good legal representation.

Now drive back to section 15, walk in ten rows, and on the left find Jacobs in lot 160. David Jacobs (1921–1992), with his brother, Richard, was a major player in developing Cleveland's modern skyline, with such notable successes as the Galleria at Erieview and the Society Center project. The two brothers worked together for 37 years (with Richard as the dealmaker, David the on-site supervisor) on 41 regional shopping centers and numerous office buildings and hotels; they bought the

Cleveland Indians in 1986. A little-known fact: David piloted blimps during World War II.

**STORY BUT NO STONE FOUND:** Janet Blood (?–1930) was the victim of an unsolved murder. Two years before Janet's death, her mother died and her father lost his job at Taylor's department store after suffering a nervous breakdown. Janet dropped out of school in her senior year to nurse her father back to health.

On January 3, 1930, Janet left her West 108th Street home to visit her friend, Edward Decker, who lived at 10220 Clifton Boulevard. At West 106th and Clifton, she was approached by a stranger who demanded money. When he found out she had none, he took her coat and shot her in the heart.

Janet languished in the hospital for two weeks. After a neighbor donated a pint of blood, the entire basketball team at West High offered to do the same. But by that time, Janet was too far gone and she died. Her murder remains unsolved. She was buried beside her mother, but with no stone because her father could not afford one. In April 1998 someone bought a marker for her grave.

A detailed account is found in *The Maniac in the Bushes*, by John Stark Bellamy II.

OTHER CEMETERIES NEARBY:  Alger Cemetery, *p. 21*
Lake Side Cemetery, *p. 147*

~ SUPERSTITIONS ~

# If a dead person's eyes are left open, he'll find someone to take with him.

# North Royalton Cemetery

ADDRESS: 6170 Royalton Rd. (No sign)  ~  LOCATION: North Royalton
PHONE: (440) 237-4866 (city offices)  ~  ACREAGE: approx. 11 acres
CARETAKER: City of North Royalton; no restrooms on site
ACCESS: Records at cemetery office (440-237-4866) and North Royalton Historical Society (440-582-3231)
NUMBER OF BURIALS: Unknown  ~  OLDEST/FIRST GRAVE: Unknown
RELIGIOUS AFFILIATION: Nondenominational
ETHNIC AFFILIATION: English, French, German
DIRECTIONS: I-71 to Exit 231 for SR 82 (Royalton Rd.); east on SR 82 (Royalton); on left after SR 3 (Ridge Rd.).

**HISTORY AND SURROUNDINGS:** The township's original cemetery was on the village green in the center of town near the town hall. In the 1860s, the area was being neglected and most graves were moved to the new cemetery. It is believed that those who had died of smallpox were not reinterred.

The current site, established in 1866, was cared for by a group of women who formed a Cemetery Association for that purpose. As families needed to bury loved ones, they would be asked to pay dues of one dollar a year and thus became part of the association. Until 1927, the Cemetery Association held a fundraising dinner every Memorial Day in the hall above J. N. Veber's store.

**UNION SPY OUTWITS CONFEDERATES**

The building on the west side of the lot was built in 1879 to hold bodies during the winter months when the frozen ground made manual grave digging impossible. In the 1880s the charge to store a body in the vault was twenty five cents a week. The price for a lot with eight graves was $8.

Even though there are stores nearby, the informal aspect of the grounds—there isn't even a sign—gives a rural feeling to North Royalton Cemetery.

Five soldiers of the American Revolution are buried here.

**YOUR VISIT:** Enter on the westernmost entry road and look to the left for the Keyes grave about two-thirds of the way before the road curves. The rose-colored stone, about one by four feet, is easily seen from the road.

efort55

Elias Keyes (1763–1849) was born in New Marlborough, Massachusetts. He enlisted in the Revolutionary War in June of 1779 under Captain Collar, and enlisted again in April of 1780 under Captain Samuel Warner's Company in Colonel Brown's Regiment. He served for six months and fought in the Battle of Stone Arabia. On November 6, 1832, he applied for a pension.

At the curve in the road, park your car and walk in a few rows. You should easily find Miner's narrow white marker. John Miner/Minor (1762–1847) was born in Lyme, Connecticut. He enlisted May 8, 1775, and was discharged November 9, 1775. He later served in the 9th company of Knowlton's Rangers and the 7th Connecticut Regiment. Private Miner was commanded by Colonel Heman Swift and served for four months in Captain Judson's Company.

**NOTABLE:**

*Township records from 1927 list rules for the cemetery, including "no vehicle may drive in the cemetery faster than a walk, no horse left without a driver, and no person shall catch, wound, kill or attempt to injure any birds or remove or disturb bird nests." (History of North Royalton 1811-1991)*

A few rows farther toward the center of the cemetery and toward Royalton Road is the monument for Hall. John Hall (1763–1836) was an apprentice on the *Dean*, a frigate that was commanded by Captain Samuel Nickolson. His white stone is difficult to read.

Two stones farther toward Royalton Road in the same row is Shephard. John Shephard (1729–1847), born near Philadelphia, was a member of Colonel Washington's command at the time of Braddock's defeat. He served three years and nine months in the Revolutionary War and also fought in the French and Indian War. He did not arrive in Ohio until 1816, at the age of 88. He was the driver of the first team of horses to enter this township.

Accounts by his grandchildren reveal Shephard's personality and pioneer work ethic. He is described as standing about five feet, nine inches tall, with light brown hair that never turned gray. He spoke often about being in the battles of Brandywine and Germantown and never complained about how anyone treated him. He didn't start losing his health until age 112, and died on January 3, 1846, at the age of 117 years, 9 months, and 17 days.

One grandchild tells of his grandfather going into a cornfield with a chair and a long butcher knife. After coming in for dinner and resting for half an hour, the 112-year-old Revolutionary War veteran went back to the cornfield to continue his work. The next day, Shephard's family measured how much corn had been cut. By himself, Shephard had cut two acres of corn in one day.

Now walk toward the vault to find the marker for Irwin Edgerton (1844–1921) near the mausoleum's northwest corner. It is an arched

stone made of granite, about one foot wide by two feet high. Edgerton was a spy for the Union army. As evidence of one of his close calls, he kept a coat with a tear from a Confederate bullet in the left shoulder. Once, in a narrow escape on horseback, Edgerton jumped over a river while being chased by the Confederates. The Confederates' horses refused to jump, thus insuring his getaway.

Proceed up the gravel road near the vault to the back of the cemetery. Turn right. About one third of the way between the gravel road and the next road (near Route 94) is Stewart's three-foot-tall stone, between the Coates cast-iron marker and the Johnson monument, which portrays a seated lady. From the road, Stewart is the first in its row.

*Revolutionary War veteran John Shepard died at the age of 117 years, 9 months, and 17 days*

Samuel Stewart (1749–1827) was born in Londonderry, New Hampshire. He served in Captain Hugh McClellen's company of Minutemen, then reenlisted May 1, 1775, in Captain Robert Oliver's company. He also served eight months with Colonel Ephraim Doolittle's regiment. Stewart served as a sergeant in Captain L. Kemp's company at Ticonderoga and was also at the Battle of Bennington. His wife Elizabeth died February 4, 1836, aged 76.

Now walk in toward the Masonic Temple building to find the graves of Worthy and Welthy Green, about two-thirds of the way toward the Temple. Worthy S. Green (1842–1936) and his wife, Welthy A. Green (1848–1905), remind us that names were once used to refer to characteristics. What does that say about their son, Harry Green (1881–1901)?

OTHER CEMETERIES NEARBY:

Pritchard Cemetery, *p. 158*
Strongsville Cemetery, *p. 210*

*Quick thinking and an able horse helped Edgerton outwit the Confederates*

# Pritchard Cemetery

ADDRESS: 9354 Edgerton Rd. ~ LOCATION: North Royalton ~ PHONE: None

ACREAGE: 0.2 acres ~ CARETAKER: Unknown; cemetery is abandoned

ACCESS: Grounds open daily dawn–dusk. Records at North Royalton Historical Society (440 582-3231)

NUMBER OF BURIALS: Unknown ~ OLDEST/FIRST GRAVE: Oldest and first: 1818

RELIGIOUS AFFILIATION: Nondenominational

ETHNIC AFFILIATION: English, German

DIRECTIONS: I-71 to Exit 231 for SR 82 (Royalton Rd.); east on SR 82 (Royalton); right (south) on Valley Pkwy.; right (south) on Edgerton Rd.; on left.

**HISTORY AND SURROUNDINGS:** It's hard to imagine a quiet abandoned burial site just five miles from the bustling South Park Mall. Yet here is the oldest existing cemetery in North Royalton.

In 1839, for the price of one dollar, Jonathan and Betsey Sarles gave North Royalton Township some land on Slate Road by the Hinckley border for use as a cemetery. That cemetery is no longer in existence.

Pritchard Cemetery began as a family plot which later was also used by neighbors. The deed for the cemetery, dated January 21, 1841, states that Knight Sprague sold Thomas Pritchard this one-acre section of land to be used as a burying ground. The only requirement was that the trustees erect a fence around the lot.

## WHAT A RELIEF TO FIND THIS

**YOUR VISIT:** Park at the commercial property on the corner and walk up onto the knoll. You'll easily find the headstones of Parley and Relief Austin. The dates are somewhat obscured, but Parley's date of death appears to be 1862. The Austin house, located at 17325 Bennett Road, overlooked a branch of the Rocky River. The house, most likely built in 1839, was the only saltbox-design house left in the township as of 1991. Township records list the various branding marks used by early settlers; Parley Austin's was "swallows fork in right ear." Near Parley and Relief is the marker for Hannah E. Austin, their daughter, who died January 16, 1861, age 21 years.

Walk around to find the headstone for John Smith, who died in 1823 at age 32. By the tree you'll see the marker for Maria, wife of John Smith, late of Devonshire, England, who died July 24, 1865, aged 65 years and 11 months.

Thomas Redrup's grave shows he died April 29, 1853 at 13 years of age; and Maria, daughter of Robert and Emma Pritchard, was born December 20, 1836, and died January 7, 1859.

The last person buried here was Thomas Sanders, who died in 1887.

OTHER CEMETERIES NEARBY: North Royalton Cemetery, *p. 155*
Strongsville Cemetery, *p. 210*

*Brush half hides the gravestone of Electa*

*Left and right: Parley and Relief Austin lie side by side*

# Riverside Golf Club Cemetery

ADDRESS: Columbia and Sprague Rds.  ~  LOCATION: Olmsted Falls
PHONE: (440) 235-8006  ~  ACREAGE: Unknown  ~  CARETAKER: Riverside Golf Club
ACCESS: Grounds open daily dawn–dusk. Some of the staff at the Golf Club have tid-bits of information
NUMBER OF BURIALS: Unknown  ~  OLDEST/FIRST GRAVE: Unknown
RELIGIOUS AFFILIATION: Nondenominational  ~  ETHNIC AFFILIATION: N/A
DIRECTIONS: I-480 to Exit 6 for SR 252 (Columbia Rd.); south on SR 252 (Columbia); left (east) on Sprague Rd.; right (south) on East River Rd.; on left.

**HISTORY AND SURROUNDINGS:** This typical pioneer graveyard was located on family property. It is now in the wooded area of a golf course—a nice view, but few come to see the cemetery.

**In THE ROUGH**

Early settlers in this area had something other than golf in mind when they established their farms on this land. Those who settled here were part of the Waterbury Land Company. In April of 1807, for the sum of $21,600, they bought land in this area from the Connecticut Land Company. The trip from Connecticut to Ohio was strenuous. The group arrived in Buffalo in December and had to suffer cold winter winds as they continued toward Cleveland.

**YOUR VISIT:** To find the cemetery, head toward the pro shop; directly across the green is a wooded area. As you get close to the woods, you will see the stones.

This is certainly an unusual place to find a graveyard. Most of the stones are difficult to read. One for Calvin and Miriam's son, Marshal, who died when he was 17 years old, is still legible. Also found here in one grave are Sophia J. Porter, Samuel Hoadley's granddaughter, and her one-day-old son. The date of death is

*Eternal rest and modern recreation meet at cemetery's edge*

*Markers give evidence to age and neglect*        *View of stones in wooded area*

1863. Because they are buried together, we assume she died in child-birth. For many years, her son, Orlando Porter, made regular trips from Michigan to repair the cemetery fence. The fence no longer exists.

Other names visible on the markers are "Baker" and "Hickox."

The last burial was that of Bethia Baker in 1912.

**STORY BUT NO STONE FOUND:** Calvin Hoadley (1769–1846) arrived in 1807 with his five children, ages 2 to 17 years, and his wife Miriam. Miri-am died in 1811. Hoadley's brother, Lemuel Jr., came later, bringing his own family and their father, Lemuel Sr.

Calvin Hoadley attained the rank of captain when commissioned by Governor Huntington to command a military company in the area. During the War of 1812, Hoadley's company was ordered to defend Cleveland, but Captain Hoadley refused to leave the local people defenseless should the British or Indians attack from the west first. After Hull's surrender at Detroit, Hoadley was listened to more carefully.

Following orders, Hoadley established military headquarters and a blockhouse on the eastern shore of the Rocky River. Soon after, there was a report that the British had landed at Huron, and area residents gathered at the blockhouse for safety. To everyone's relief, resident Levi Bronson arrived from a visit to Cleveland with the news that the men who had landed were American prisoners of war released by the British after Hull's surrender.

Colonel Samuel Hoadley and his wife, Constant Barnes, are also buried here. Samuel was another brother, who arrived in 1825 at the age of 50. By that time, brothers Luther and Lemuel, and brother-in-law, Riley Whiting, had a thriving business going. They'd started making wooden clocks in 1808. Two years later they were using a secret process to cast church bells. So closely guarded was their secret that the work was done in a detached building and no outsiders were permitted. Soon a wire factory was added to the clock factory.

**NOTABLE:**

*This typical pioneer graveyard was located on family property. It is now in the wooded area of a golf course—a nice view, but few come to see the cemetery.*

We don't often read about women traveling alone to the Western Reserve, but Molly Parker came in Captain Hoadley's original party from Connecticut. She was a widow whose husband had been a shoemaker, and she knew people would need shoes wherever they lived, so she brought and used her husband's shoemaking equipment. James Geer, a hat maker, was also in the original party. Hats were not in demand on the frontier, and when Geer fell in love with Molly Parker he learned how to make shoes. Their son, Calvin, was the first male born to settlers west of the Cuyahoga River.

At one time, the grave of Revolutionary War soldier John Reynolds could be located here. He died March 3, 1810. His inscription read:

> Here in the tomb beneath the soil,
> lies all that's mortal of the man,
> Who's soul surrendered up to God,
> To finish what he had begun.

OTHER CEMETERIES NEARBY:  Sunset Memorial Park, *p. 163*
Butternut Ridge Cemetery, *p. 137*

~ SUPERSTITIONS ~

# Nothing new should be worn to a funeral, especially new shoes.

# Sunset Memorial Park

ADDRESS: 6265 Columbia Rd.  ~  LOCATION: North Olmsted

PHONE: (440) 777-0450  ~  ACREAGE: 165 acres  ~  CARETAKER: On site; restrooms at office

ACCESS: Grounds open May–Sept Mon–Fri 8 a.m.–8 p.m., Sat & Sun 8 a.m.–6 p.m., Oct–April daily 8 a.m.–5 p.m.; office open Mon–Fri 8:30 a.m.–5 p.m., Sat 9 a.m.– 4 p.m., Sun 10 a.m.–4 p.m. Records at cemetery office

NUMBER OF BURIALS: 37,000  ~  OLDEST/FIRST GRAVE: First: John C. Riegler, 1935

RELIGIOUS AFFILIATION: Nondenominational

ETHNIC AFFILIATION: Hungarian, Latvian, Russian

DIRECTIONS: I-480 to Exit 6 for Sr 252 (Columbia Rd.); south on SR 252 (Columbia); on left after Butternut Ridge.

**HISTORY AND SURROUNDINGS:** This 165-acre privately run cemetery was started in 1935. Because it's a memorial park, all of the markers are at ground level. There have been more than 37,000 burials on this expansive, well-planned, manicured land. When it first opened, concerts were held here on a regular basis.

**OUTDOOR PAINTINGS A REAL STEEL**

Although there is a Latvian section, not all members of the Latvian community choose that site for burial. The cultural expectation is that fresh flowers will be placed every week at the grave, and few people wish to be talked about in church on Sunday for failing to supply the weekly floral arrangement.

**YOUR VISIT:** I suggest driving through for a few minutes just to get a sense of size and design. Stop by the office (from the entrance, it is straight back) and get a map.

Then drive to the Garden of Religion (section F) and walk through it. This is a sunken garden with pictures designed by former Clevelander Daniel Boza. The pictures, reproductions of famous European masterpieces, are painted in porcelain enamel on steel. This is certainly one of the most unusual art galleries in the state—consider how well these paintings have withstood the forces of nature for more than 40 years.

Now drive to section 43 to see the National Hungarian Memorial, erected to honor those who gave their lives in World War II. It was dedicated in 1986 and has the Hungarian crest in its center with a bronze eagle on top.

Next drive to Westwood Abbey, the mausoleum near the office. There are a number of beautiful memorials to view.

The Prells, Charles M. (1887–1960) and Mary (1887–1967), have two sarcophagi (stone coffins above the ground) with mosaics above them. These can be found downstairs by the back doors.

The Brown family, whose son Kevin Charles (1952–1989) died in a boating accident, has a scene painted on the ceiling. It depicts a helicopter through the clouds. The inscription reads: "Only one life that soon is past/ Only what's done with love will last." The family has a private room located on the chapel floor; enter from the front door and take the first corridor on the right.

OTHER CEMETERIES NEARBY: Butternut Ridge Cemetery, p. 137

*Detail from "Creation of Man" by Michelangelo*

Courtesy Sunset Memorial Park

# Westwood Cemetery

ADDRESS: 429 Morgan St.  ~  LOCATION: Oberlin  ~  PHONE: (440) 775-7252
ACREAGE: approx. 24 acres  ~  CARETAKER: On site; no restrooms on site
ACCESS: Grounds open daily dawn–dusk; office open Mon–Fri 8 a.m.–4 p.m.
Records at cemetery office, the Oberlin College Archivist, and the Oberlin Historical
and Improvement Organization (440-774-1700)
NUMBER OF BURIALS: 8,000
OLDEST/FIRST GRAVE: First: Samuel Montgomery, August 1863 (section V)
RELIGIOUS AFFILIATION: Nondenominational
ETHNIC AFFILIATION: African-American, Slovak
DIRECTIONS: I-480 to Exit 1 for SR 10; west on SR 10 (becomes US 20) to SR 58;
north on SR 58; left (west) on Morgan St.; on left.

**HISTORY AND SURROUNDINGS:**  Oberlin's original cemetery was on
Morgan and Professor Streets, on land leased from the college in the
1830s. At that corner is a statue marking the site of
the original cemetery. The statue is of Giles Waldo
Shurtleff (1831–904). The inscription at the base
states:

> believing in the ability of the Negro to aid in
> the fight for his freedom he organized the first
> regiment of colored troops raised in Ohio.
> Inspired by his leadership they offered their
> lives for the freedom of their race.

## A YOUNG FUGITIVE SLAVE IS REMEMBERED

When the needs of the community outgrew the
original space, the Oberlin Cemetery Association was formed, and two
years later, in 1863, 28 acres on the present site were bought for $1,470.

There are more than 30 varieties of trees, including shagbark hickory,
white spruce, Kentucky coffee, sweet gum, ash, eastern hemlock, cot-
tonwood tulip, and yellowwood. Rabbits, raccoons, blue heron, frogs,
turtles, and muskrats have been seen in the cemetery and nearby pond.

In 1944, Westwood became the cemetery for the city of Oberlin.

**YOUR VISIT:** Enter from Morgan Street after passing the golf course. At
the first structure, a receiving vault, turn left, wind around, and take the
first right. You are directly in front of the stone memorializing Lee
Howard Dobbins and other fugitive slaves. It reads: "In memory of the

fugitive slaves whose journey to freedom brought them to Oberlin," followed by this epitaph:

> shielded by an almighty arm
> thy griefs and sufferings now are o'er
> beyond the reach of tyrant's harm,
> freed spirit rest forever more;
> lone little wanderer now no more
> mid stranger hearts to seek for love;
> thou'st gained thy home, thy native shore
> and boundless love thy bliss will prove.
> thy father called thee suffering one
> he knew and felt thy untold grief
> to him complexions all are one
> He died alike for their relief

At the bottom is written: "Lee Howard Dobbins aged 4 years died in Oberlin a fugitive slave orphan March 26, 1853."

This is a large cemetery. I suggest using the map and looking for sites on the outer edges first—sections C, D, H, K, R; and then go to MR, N, M, I, E, and A. The sections are well marked.

Charles Finney (1797–1875), a charismatic minister and founding member of the Oberlin colony, gave up law for the ministry. He subscribed to the views known as "Oberlin Perfectionism"—the belief that people have an endless capacity to repent. Finney agreed to establish the theological department at Oberlin on condition that the school admit blacks. He was the second president of Oberlin, serving from 1851 to 1865. His is the most visited grave here. (section C, five-foot-tall marker, six rows from the path by section D)

James Monroe (1821–1898) was teaching school by the age of 14. His antislavery oratory won the attention and encouragement of William Lloyd Garrison. An Oberlin graduate, Monroe served in the Ohio General Assembly and the state senate. He was influential in passing a bill voiding the effects of the Fugitive Slave Law, and advocated property rights for married women. He unsuccessfully tried to recover the body of John Copeland, a

*Deaths of young and old slaves memorialized on an Underground Railroad marker*

participant in John Brown's raid. President Lincoln appointed Monroe ambassador to Brazil. (section C, four-foot-tall marker behind Finney)

Wilson Bruce Evans (1824–1898), a free black, came to Oberlin in 1854. He was active in the Underground Railroad and jailed for his part in the Oberlin-Wellington Rescue. Evans fought for the Union for one year in the Civil War. He has a government marker, "Civil War Co D 178th OVI." (Sec C in front of tall "Vance" and across from huge tree across from the pond)

Albert Allen Wright (1846–1905) was the first Oberlin College faculty member born in Oberlin. After serving in the Civil War, Wright worked on Ohio's second geological survey. He was instrumental in developing laboratory projects for science students. Wright is credited with initiating Ohio's first topographical survey. (section C—a glacial rock across from the Rawson-Hinde vault)

Lewis Clarke (1815–1897) was a slave on a Kentucky plantation, and his family published the story of their lives as slaves in 1842. An outspoken abolitionist, he met Harriet Beecher Stowe later and claimed the George Harris character in her famous novel was modeled after him. The inscription reads: "original George Harris of Harriet Beecher Stowe's book Uncle Tom's Cabin." When he died, the governor of Kentucky arranged for his body to lie in state (a public viewing of the casket as an honor to the deceased). (section D, a flat gray marker near "Strong")

Harriet Keeler (1846–1921), an 1870 graduate of Oberlin, was one of only five women permitted to study the more difficult men's course at the college. She was president of the Cuyahoga County Suffrage Association and assistant principal of Central High in Cleveland. In 1912 Keeler became the first woman superintendent of the Cleveland Public Schools. She wrote 11 books, mostly on wildflowers and shrubs, and in her honor a 300-acre preserve at Brecksville Reservation bears her name. (section D, her marker is easily missed—it is only about two feet high, in the back, near stock pile.)

Francis Jewett (1844–1926) was a popular chemistry professor at Oberlin who dared his students to find a way to make aluminum on a commercial basis. One of his students, Charles Hall (see below), did just that. (section E, gray, four feet tall, and about three feet wide; with section A on left and E on right, visible from road.)

Charles Hall (1863–1914), took up Professor Jewett's dare and discovered the process for extracting aluminum from ore. He opened the Pittsburgh Reduction Company in 1888; it became Aluminum Company of America (ALCOA) in 1907. Hall is in the Inventors Hall of Fame in Akron. (section E, light gray, six feet tall)

Henry Churchill King (1858–1934), a graduate of Oberlin, taught mathematics and philosophy at the college. King worked in many religious and missionary associations and was president of Oberlin from 1902 to 1927. His work on the Inter-Allied Commission on Mandates in Turkey led to his being made a Chevalier de la Legion d'Honneur by France in 1920. His stone does not mention the award. (section E, old white marker, near bench, about five rows from road by sections F & I)

Alonzo Pease (1820–1881), a self-educated artist, exhibited at the Academy of Design in New York. He painted portraits of several Oberlin College presidents at a price of $50 each. Pease used his artistic talent to help runaway slaves escape by painting their skin to make them appear Caucasian. A captain in the Civil War, he resigned when he learned that his colonel was returning escaped slaves to their masters. (section I, a square vase on top; can be seen if M is on left and I on right. Also visible from the road if I is on right and M is on left, behind obelisk of "Jarvis.")

Courtesy O.H.I.O.

*Funeral urn in stone marks grave of artist Alonzo Pease*

Charles Mosher (1906–1984) was a state senator from 1951 to 1961, then served in the U. S. House of Representatives from 1961 to 1977. He was the only Republican in Congress to vote against funding for U. S. involvement in Vietnam in 1967. Mosher was the first congressman to claim membership in the American Civil Liberties Union. (section I, rose-colored, two feet tall, in center by grove of trees, in front of double marker for "Bosworth")

Helen Shafer (1839–1894) graduated Oberlin in 1863 and taught math there for 20 years. She received her M. A. from Oberlin in 1878 and in 1893 was the first woman to earn an L.L.D. from Oberlin. Shafer was president of Wellesley College from 1888 to 1894. (section I, across from Lee, 30 feet from the road, about four to five feet high. Shafer's grayish-brown monument reads, "Helen"; to the right is "Mosher.")

Petar Pease (1795–1861) is known as Oberlin's first citizen. He moved from Brownhelm in Lorain County to a site now on Oberlin's campus. Pease built his cabin in three days and moved his wife and children into it in April 1833. (section K, seven feet high, old white obelisk near oak tree and to right of footpath behind "Penfield")

Thomas Henderson (1849–1934) was vice president of the Winton Motor Company. He sold the first two automobiles in the world. He also was the first to order auto tires from Goodrich, which was making bicycle tires at the time. (section M, almost white, five-foot-tall, rather wide marker; visible from road when M is at left and P on right)

Henry Lee (1836–1899) was a slave who fled to Syracuse in 1858 via the Underground Railroad. A year later he arrived in Oberlin, where he attended public school and then college. In 1865 while on a train in West Virginia, Lee refused to move to the black section. As the conductor tried to move Lee, Oberlin College president Asa Mahan, who was in the same car, came to his aid. When a similar incident occurred four years later, Lee sued the railroad and won his case.

Lee was also known for some unsavory actions. He was arrested for maltreatment of his wife, and while raising funds for teachers in the South managed to keep most of the money for himself. (section N, tall white marble base with newer rose-colored column on top)

Reverend John Keep (1781–1870) was on the board of trustees of Oberlin College and cast the deciding vote allowing blacks to enter the school. Thanks to him the Lane Rebels (a group of students from Lane Seminary in Cincinnati who wanted immediate emancipation of the slaves) were allowed to register at Oberlin College. (section N, near family plot of "Siddall." Keep has a gray obelisk nine feet tall, one of the tallest in the section. In front of it are stones with dates on them.)

> **NOTABLE:**
> The section 3OAP2 on the map was originally a potter's field used for those who could not afford a burial plot. In keeping with Oberlin's egalitarian reputation, this was stopped—it created a needless class division. Those burials now occur throughout the cemetery.

Simeon Bushnell (ca.1829–1861) was a clerk who took part in the Oberlin-Wellington Rescue and was jailed for it. (An escaped slave was discovered living in Oberlin, and abducted to Wellington. Oberlin residents flocked to his rescue and he was hidden in the home of James Fairchild. Thirty-seven people from Oberlin and Wellington were indicted for violating the Fugitive Slave Law of 1850.) (section R, aging white marker between "Mary Fairchild" and "James Fitch")

Mary Kellogg Fairchild (1819–1890) went to Oberlin College in 1837 to study for a B.A. She was one of the first four women to do so. She did not finish her degree but did marry Oberlin College president James Fairchild. (section R, five to six feet tall, gray)

James Fitch (1816–1867) was jailed for activity in conjunction with the Oberlin-Wellington slave rescue. It was he who drove John Price to the secret hiding place. Fitch's home also had secret rooms for hiding fleeing slaves. (section R, aging, white, six feet high, close to mausoleum)

John Steele (1835–1905) fought in many Civil War battles. He was awarded the Congressional Medal of Honor for saving an ammunition train from the enemy at Spring Hill, Tennessee. He was appointed to administer a trust set up by Andrew Carnegie to repay people who had been duped by Cassie Chadwick. Chadwick cheated people by using Carnegie's name, causing the fall of the Citizens Bank of Oberlin. (section R, a government marker, near "Fairchild," no mention is made of the Medal of Honor but it does say "Aide de camp.")

The marker of Andrew Hudacky (1888–1922) is bronze (green with age) with an eagle, lion, and YMCA symbol. Hudacky was born in Kladzan, Slovakia, on May 15, 1888, and died in Oberlin on February

*Epitaph in raised bronze
includes YMCA symbol*

10, 1922. He served as YMCA secretary to the Slovak legionnaires in Siberia during World War I. He was the last student of the Slavic Department of Oberlin Theological Seminary. His inscription reads: "I have fought the good fight, I have finished the course, I have kept the faith. (Timothy)." (section MR)

Richard Lee's (1964–1986) stone has an excellent example of the process of etching on granite markers. It has an etching of a car on it. (section D, right behind the sign for the section)

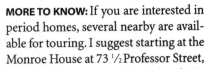

**MORE TO KNOW:** If you are interested in period homes, several nearby are available for touring. I suggest starting at the Monroe House at 73 ½ Professor Street, the site of the Oberlin Historical and Improvement Organization (440-774-1700). There you can go on a guided tour of the building and get information about other historic sites.

# Woodvale Cemetery

ADDRESS: 7535 Engle Rd. ~ LOCATION: Middleburg Heights

PHONE: (440) 826-3455 ~ ACREAGE: 50 acres ~ CARETAKER: On site; restrooms at office

ACCESS: Grounds open daily dawn–dusk; office open Mon–Fri 8 a.m.–4:30 p.m., Sat 8 a.m.–noon. Records at cemetery office, and the Western Reserve Historical Society (216-721-5722)

NUMBER OF BURIALS: 10,000 ~ OLDEST/FIRST GRAVE: Unknown

RELIGIOUS AFFILIATION: Nondenominational ~ ETHNIC AFFILIATION: English

DIRECTIONS: I-71 to Exit 235 for Bagley Rd.; west on Bagley; left (south) on Engle Rd.; on left.

**HISTORY AND SURROUNDINGS:** Early records are rather confusing. One account states that in the 1850s the Klink family gave a half acre of land to the township for a cemetery. Another states that Middleburg Township purchased the cemetery in 1870 and it remained nameless until 1876 when "Woodvale" was suggested. The cemetery's own records were destroyed by a fire in 1890.

## GOLF BALLS IN THE GRAVE

When quarrying activities at the Cleveland Stone Company began intruding on the land at Adams Street Cemetery, many bodies were reinterred here at Woodvale.

The Fowleses were among the first settlers of Middleburg Township, and the road bordering Woodvale is named for them. You will find several graves of Fowles family members as you walk through Woodvale's older sections. Woodvale's 50-acre newer section lacks architectural interest.

**YOUR VISIT:** Enter the cemetery and bear left, heading toward the office, where you can park and get a map. Nearby, in section 3, is the log cabin marker of the Kirk family. This noteworthy marker was carved from a solid block of sandstone. The names and dates reveal early deaths of many of the family members. James died of pneumonia on October 23, 1895, at the age of 22; William died November 27, 1893, at age 27; Collins was 21 when he died of consumption on November 5, 1917; Helen died of measles when she was two years old. Other family members fared better: James Sr. died of a brain fever at the age of 82, and Georgiana was 96 and senile when she died on July 1, 1938.

*This log cabin marker attracts attention*

Walk over to section 10 on the hill beside the office and look for John Baldwin's large white stone to the left of the receiving vault. Baldwin (1799–1884) founded Baldwin College in Berea. The college celebrates his birthday every year with a ceremony at his grave. Though his actual birthday is October 13, the college's observance of Founders Day may vary by a day or two, depending on scheduling considerations.

Baldwin is credited with discovering the value of the stone found in the local quarries. He invented a machine that used water power to make grindstones; he opened the first quarry and shipped the first grindstone in 1833. In 1913, Baldwin College merged with German Wallace College to become what is now Baldwin-Wallace College. Baldwin also founded a Baldwin College in Baldwin, Kansas, and a mission school in Bangalore, India. His old red house was the first Underground Railroad stop in Middleburg. Baldwin was a very religious man who dressed in rags.

The black granite marker near Baldwin is for Bonds. Dr. Alfred Bryan Bonds (1913–1981) was president of Baldwin-Wallace College from 1955 to 1981. He was also assistant executive secretary of President Truman's Commission on Higher Education and was later named special educational consultant for the United Nations Educational Scientific and Cultural Organization (UNESCO). From 1953 to 1956 Dr. Bonds was chief of the U.S. educational mission in Egypt, which helped establish the country's public school system.

Walk over to section A and look for the name Humiston on a slanted stone behind a grove of cypress trees. Drusilla Humiston (1824–1836) married Patrick Humiston. Her early death is attributed to childbirth, and Patrick died 2 years later when he was only 17. Their marker is just barely readable.

Also buried in this section is a Confederate soldier from Mississippi who was a tobacco salesman in Berea after the Civil War. His grave is said to be behind the white pumphouse and across the road from the tall "Robinson" monument.

Drive or walk to the part of section 13 across from section 7. The flat government marker for Marks is five rows from the road and behind "Baker." Thomas Marks (1875–1957) served in the Spanish-American War and World War I, but never fought in any battles. During the Spanish-American War, Marks was in Florida waiting to take a troop ship to Cuba. The vessel was damaged, and the war ended before a replacement arrived. During World War I, because he was 45 years old, Marks remained stateside as a machine gun instructor at Camp McArthur, Texas. He eventually became known as Berea's oldest living veteran of the two wars. He was proud of his record of attending every Memorial Day ceremony from the time he was 14 years old until he was 81, except for the years of his war service.

Proceed to section 7 near East Drive and section 6. There is a three-foot-tall gray monument and a flat Medal of Honor marker at the grave of Alfred Baesel (1892–1918), one of only three World War I soldiers from Ohio to receive the Congressional Medal of Honor. The stone reads: "He sought not glory but his country's good."

Baesel, the son of Henry and Caroline Baesel, married Lydia Cole. He enlisted in World War I and was a second lieutenant in the 148th infantry regiment, 37th division. Near Ivry, France, Lieutenant Baesel gave his life crossing enemy fire to rescue Corporal Sterling Ryan; both he and the corporal died.

Baesel's body, found five years later, was brought back to Ohio. The funeral was held at Baldwin-Wallace on April 11, 1926, with a flag-draped casket transported by a horse-drawn caisson accompanied by military reserve units, the Cleveland Grays, and other guests.

**NOTABLE:**
*Look for the log cabin marker for the Kirk family. This noteworthy marker was carved from a solid block of sandstone.*

In the corner of this section are the Walter children. Jacob Walter (1917–1930) and his sister Juanita (1920–1930) were killed in a tragic accident as passengers on a school bus that was hit by a train. The bus driver and 9 of the 10 passengers were killed. One account recalls the trainman waving the bus driver on, not realizing a train was coming from the other direction. A conflicting account states that the bus pulled directly in front of the train, which had no way of avoiding the accident.

Dorothy McKelvey (1902–1993), a well-known historian and much-beloved community member, is also buried in section 7. She was an authority on the history of Baldwin-Wallace College and was appointed college historian in 1950. She also founded the Berea Historical Society. McKelvey was interested in history outside Berea as well, and served as a trustee of the New England Society of the Western Reserve and a member of the Early Settlers Association.

Proceed to section 15, lot 357 and look for the flat marker of Tom Armstrong (1918–1985), a popular radio personality who loved golf. At his burial, Armstrong's friends tossed $200 worth of golf balls in the ground before the grave was covered by dirt.

OTHER CEMETERIES NEARBY: Hepburn Cemetery, *p. 140*
Adams Street Cemetery, *p. 129*

~ SUPERSTITIONS ~

# If you touch a loved one who has died, you won't have dreams about them.

# Single Marker

**NAME:** Amy Mihaljevic

**LOCATION:** Bay Village Police Department (Cahoon Park)

**DETAILS:** Ten-year-old Amy Mihaljevic was the subject of a statewide search as a missing child. She died February 8, 1990. Though she is not buried here, there is a memorial marker by a tree in the grassy area behind the Police Department.

*Memorial to murdered child and grieving community*

# SOUTH

## Bedford Cemetery

ADDRESS: 66 E. Taylor St. ~ LOCATION: Bedford ~ PHONE: (440) 232-4462

ACREAGE: 15 acres ~ CARETAKER: On-site weekdays 8 a.m.–4 p.m.; restrooms at office

ACCESS: Grounds open Mon–Fri dawn–dusk. Records at cemetery office (440-232-4462), and Western Reserve Historical Society (216-721-5722); related documents and other source material available at Bedford Historical Society (440-232-0796)

NUMBER OF BURIALS: 15,000 ~ OLDEST/FIRST GRAVE: Oldest: Mary Bartlett, 1808

RELIGIOUS AFFILIATION: Nondenominational

ETHNIC AFFILIATION: African-American, English, Hungarian, Romani

DIRECTIONS: I-271 to Exit 23 for SR 14 (Broadway Ave.); west on SR 14 (Broadway); on right.

**HISTORY AND SURROUNDINGS:** The land for the first Bedford city cemetery was bought in 1857 from J. P. Robinson and his wife, and Bedford acquired additional, adjoining land when the Wheeling & Lake Erie Railroad was routed through the original tract. Enclosed by an iron fence, the land slopes gently towards Tinker's Creek and is bordered on three sides by an old farmhouse.

TITANIC SURVIVOR SKIRTS THE ISSUE

**YOUR VISIT:** There are three entrances from Broadway Avenue. For the purposes of this guide book, the most easterly entrance is called "A Road," the next one is "B Road," and the one furthest west is "C Road."

Enter the cemetery on A Road, the most eastern entrance on Broadway—the first entrance you come to. Proceed past sections 2, 4, and 10 and take a left. The building that appears to be built at an angle is actually the cemetery's old receiving vault. It was used to hold caskets during the winter months when frozen ground prevented hand digging of graves. This is the only underground storage vault I've seen and is no longer in use. If you were to continue down A Road you would see two small buildings also no longer in use—these were outhouses.

Section 9 is on the left past the intersection. Mary Godwin is buried behind the rose-colored "Wilhelm" stone, which you'll see near the road. Although her one-foot-high rose-colored stone does not mention it, Mary Davison Godwin (1878–1939) was a survivor of the *Titanic*. Her husband, Thomas Henry "Harry" Davison, was not so lucky. Mary was born in England and came to America with Thomas in 1907. They lived in Bedford but returned to England because Mary missed her family, especially her sister Alice. In 1912 the Godwins made plans to return to America. Thomas originally purchased tickets on another ship, but Mary, like so many others, wanted to be on the *Titanic*'s maiden voyage. Her husband exchanged the tickets to please his wife.

On the night of April 14th, the couple was jarred awake. After getting dressed (Mary put on the skirt made for her by her sister Alice), they reached the top deck and saw how few lifeboats were available. Thomas urged Mary to get in one of the lifeboats telling her "I'll be right behind you." Once in the boat, Mary saw her husband giving his life jacket to someone else. According to Marion Hankey, a relative in Maple Heights, Mary could hear her husband's voice as he sang "Nearer My God to Thee" with the others on board.

Although Mary survived the disaster, she always blamed herself for asking her husband to exchange the tickets.

Return to the intersection just passed and turn on B Road toward Broadway Road. At the next intersection, turn right, and stop where sections 6 and 3 meet. Find "Matthews" 13 rows from the road, to the left of four cypress trees. Thomas E. Matthews was the oldest Civil War veteran in Bedford when he died on March 15, 1928. He has two markers: a typical white government stone for military personnel and another marked "T. E. Matthews."

Continue until this road ends. Nine rows up the footpath, on the left between "Anna Robinson" and "Phyllis Smith," is an area with no markers. This is where Julius Tibbs is buried, but he has no stone. Julius Caesar Tibbs (1812–1903) was a runaway slave who took refuge in a wooded area on what was Joseph Burns's farm in Bedford. According to family legend, Burns discovered the escaped slave in a large hollow tree and took him in. The exact date of Tibbs's arrival at the farm is unknown, but detailed financial records maintained by farmer Burns indicate that on November 14, 1853, Burns supplied Tibbs with 25 pounds of flour for $.85 and one peck of potatoes for another $.65. How long Mr. Tibbs and his family stayed on the farm is unclear, but he remained a resident of the town for another 50 years.

*The Skirt* Titanic *survivor Mary Godwin wore on that fateful night*

Tibbs was well known in Bedford as an orator, philosopher, and humorist. Born in Tuckerahoe, Virginia, he married Clarissa Bongher in 1842. Of the five children who survived him, one son was also named Julius. Another, Isaiah, became known locally for his skills as a baseball player. Julius Tibbs died at the age of 91. He is buried in section 6, lot 65.

*Escaped slave Julius Tibbs became a well known Bedford resident*

Courtesy Richard Squire

Turn left onto C Road and stop about halfway down. Not far from the Taylor mausoleum you'll find a rose-colored marker that resembles a boulder with lumps. It reads "Gates" and "Handyside." The stone for Holsey Gates is just behind it. Holsey Gates (1855–1914) was the grandson of the founder of Gates Mills. In 1876 he bought a gristmill on nearby Tinker's Creek and sold various flours under the name "Gates' Best." He continued to improve and expand the original building to double its size. The mill closed in 1908. By then Gates was involved in other ventures, including the country's first hydroelectric plants, which were constructed in 1891. His house, known as "Handyside House," was completed in 1894, and was the first home in Bedford wired for electricity.

As C Road ends, turn left and stop as section 1 begins. About 8 rows up, there is a five-foot-tall gray stone with "Bartlett" written on the base—Mary Bartlett's was the first burial here. The date on the marker is 1858, but cemetery officials think a daughter of Mary's is buried here. Mary is supposedly buried between the two nearby stones, one of which has the initials SAB on it.

Proceed left on B Road and look on your right for "Duber" on the end near the road. One row closer to Broadway and about 12 stones in from B Road is a four-foot-tall aging white marker labeled "Parsons." The murder of Tamzen Parsons (1796–1865) rocked the village of Bedford in the summer of 1865. Dr. John W. Hughes married Parsons a year before, but failed to tell her he already had a wife. Upon learning of his deceit, Parsons gave her husband his walking papers. Hughes, in turn, shot her on the doorstep of a house on Columbus Street. Though several persons witnessed the crime, none immediately confronted the armed and dangerous Hughes, but he was followed and apprehended as he fled toward Cleveland. Hughes was tried and convicted in February 1866. Parsons lies in section 2.

Toward the end of this section is Richard Sedlon's granite stone with etching on it. Sedlon (1900–1991) was a local artist who made his living as a lithographer. Privately he produced pencil sketches, watercolors, oil paintings, and sculpture. He was particular about doing portraits—he refused to paint people he didn't like.

Turn right at the first intersection past "Sedlon," right onto Road A, and then right again (you are on a road close to and parallel with Broadway). In section two, look for the graves of Rose and Leary

Mitchell, who belonged to a clan of Gypsies. Notice that their graves have pictures on them. At times, such as the anniversary of the death, trinkets are left at these graves.

Gypsy tradition, according to a previous sexton here, includes carrying the casket down the center of the cemetery followed by a brass band. The open casket is lowered into a cement vault, and friends and family toss in jewelry and money. (One Gypsy king was known to love bacon so much that an admirer threw fried bacon on his casket during the funeral.) Wine is passed around and even sprinkled into the casket before the lid is closed. Apparently Gypsies believed they had to buy their way into heaven, thus the need for keeping valuables close at hand. According to

*Photograph and crosses
mark Gypsy grave*

staff at Bedford Cemetery, Gypsies look upon birth and marriage as sad occasions that may bring a future filled with troubles. A funeral, however, is considered the end of trouble and a happy event worthy of enjoyment. This explains a Gypsy funeral some ten years ago which was scheduled to begin at 12:30 p.m. The staff was surprised when at 9:30 a.m. large numbers of people arrived with food, drink, and much merriment.

**MORE TO KNOW:** At 762 Broadway is the ornate home of Holsey Gates, currently owned by a Handyside relative, which will eventually be donated to the Western Reserve Historical Society.

The Bedford Historical Society and Museum is on Park Street behind the Bedford Baptist Church. They have a collection of art by Richard Sedlon (buried at Bedford Cemetery), many artifacts from early pioneer life, and an interesting assortment of radios from the 1920s through the 1940s.

**OF NOTE:**

*Supposedly four Gypsy queens and at least one king are buried at Bedford.*

OTHER CEMETERIES NEARBY:
Harvard Grove Cemetery, p. 191

# Chapel Street / Olde Hudson Township Burying Ground

**ADDRESS:** 50 Chapel St.  ~  **LOCATION:** Hudson

**PHONE:** (330) 342-1759 (city offices)  ~  **ACREAGE:** Not available

**CARETAKER:** City of Hudson/Hudson Cemetery Board; no restrooms on site

**ACCESS:** Grounds open daily dawn–dusk. Records at Hudson Historical Society and Library (330-653-6658), and Superintendent of Hudson Cemeteries (330-342-1759)

**NUMBER OF BURIALS:** 188

**OLDEST/FIRST GRAVE:** First: Ruth Mills Brown, born 1772, died December 9, 1808

**RELIGIOUS AFFILIATION:** Nondenominational  ~  **ETHNIC AFFILIATION:** N/A

**DIRECTIONS:** I-480 to Exit 37 for SR 91 (Darrow St.); south on SR 91 (Darrow); left (east) on Chapel St. (after I-80); on right.

**HISTORY AND SURROUNDINGS:** Although this cemetery was started in 1808, its deed, given to the township by Benjamin Whedon and David Hudson, is dated 1814. This was the township's only cemetery until Markillie Cemetery was founded in 1868. Mrs. Anner Baldwin, daughter of David Hudson and the first child born to settlers in Hudson, was buried here in 1882. The last burial to take place here was in 1900.

This burying ground looks and feels much like a small New England cemetery. This may be due to

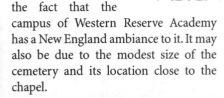

BURIED WITH
HER BABY
IN HER ARMS

the fact that the campus of Western Reserve Academy has a New England ambiance to it. It may also be due to the modest size of the cemetery and its location close to the chapel.

**YOUR VISIT:** Inside the cemetery, about two-thirds of the way back on the left side near the fence, are the graves of a father and his son. Both served in the Revolutionary War. Stephen Thompson

*New dedication marker with stylized weeping willow*

*Wrought iron fences typically enclose family plots*

Sr. (1734–1823) enlisted in June 1776 and fought in battles at Long Island, White Plains, Germantown, Stony Point, and Yorktown. He was at Valley Forge with George Washington. (Look for Sons of the American Revolution markers.) Stephen Thompson Jr. (1762–1841) was only 14 when he enlisted in the First Regiment, Connecticut Line. He served as a drummer boy in the war.

In front of the Thompson graves is the Brown family plot. Owen Brown is buried here next to his first wife, Ruth Mills Brown. (Their son, John Brown, the famous abolitionist, is buried in Elba, New York.) Owen Brown's second wife, Sally Root Brown, is buried here as well. There is a story that she is buried with a baby in her arms (the stillbirth of that baby was thought to have caused her death) however, it's probably just that—a story. Owen's third wife, whom he married when in his 70s, is buried next to her first husband at Markillie Cemetery. Walk to the other side of the cemetery. In the back section are three markers for the Draper family. Look for the SAR marker. John Draper (1750–1845) enlisted on April 17, 1775, and then again on August 27, 1776. He was 95 years old when he died.

Toward the center is another SAR marker and white stone for Joel Gaylord (1753–1827), who enlisted August 15, 1777. Gaylord, a musician and drum major under Colonel Herman Smith, was with Washington at the Battle of Monmouth and served with the main army on the Hudson.

*Grave of David Hudson marked anew with bronze plaque*

Also in the center section is the grave of David Hudson. His original stone is preserved in fragments with a bronze plaque on top. David Hudson (1761–1842) founded the town of Hudson in 1799 when he arrived with two other people from Goshen and Litchfield, Connecticut. Anna Hudson, his first wife, has a new stone near her old one.

**MORE TO KNOW:** David Hudson's house at 318 North Main Street is on SR 91, across the street and to the right as you exit Chapel Street. It is the oldest house on its original foundation in Summit County, and is owned by Western Reserve Academy. It is white, identifiable by a fence that angles inward, marking the spot where the horses were brought in. It is not open to the public.

**NOTABLE:**
*There are four Revolutionary War soldiers buried here.*

If you'd like to see the Hudson home that abolitionist John Brown lived in, it is at 1842 Hines Hill Road. Turn right as you exit Chapel Street and left onto Hines Hill. This, too, is a private home, not open to the public.

OTHER CEMETERIES NEARBY: Markillie Cemetery, *p. 199*

~ SUPERSTITIONS ~

# All windows should be opened at the moment of death so that the soul can leave.

# Crossview Cemetery

ADDRESS: Between 3091 and 3001 Rockside Rd.  ~  LOCATION: Seven Hills
PHONE: None  ~  ACREAGE: 0.2 acres  ~  CARETAKER: City of Seven Hills; no restrooms on site
ACCESS: Grounds open daily dawn–dusk
NUMBER OF BURIALS: 6  ~  OLDEST/FIRST GRAVE: First: Katherina Alber, 1852
RELIGIOUS AFFILIATION: Nondenominational  ~  ETHNIC AFFILIATION: German, Dutch
DIRECTIONS: I-77 to Exit 155 for Rockside Rd.; west on Rockside; right (north) on N. Crossview Dr. and park.

**HISTORY AND SURROUNDINGS:** In 1992 there were visible remains of only four tombstones here; there were as many as 65 markers here in the 1930s. You may feel like you're walking on private property, but this slice of land is a cemetery belonging to the city of Seven Hills. There are only three markers visible, all toward the back half of the lot. None of these stones are standing, all lie flat, although that was not always so.

## DON'T BLINK, CROSSVIEW IS IN SIGHT

**YOUR VISIT:** Approach from North Crossview and notice Katherina Alber's gravestone. Next to it is a stone broken in half, inscribed in German or Dutch.

Across from these is the white stone for Chris Link (1843–1866), who joined the Union Army August 15, 1862, at the age of 19. Link was in the 107th Regiment, Company E, of the Ohio Volunteer Infantry. His unit fought at Gettysburg, but Link himself did not. He had been shot in 1863 and was sent home. His unit was given reinforcements in Cincinnati and went on to defend Washington, D.C. Link was married to Dorothea and they had several children. He was discharged March 19, 1863, in Virginia for a disability.

OTHER CEMETERIES NEARBY:
Darrow Cemetery, p. 185
West Family Cemetery, p. 217
Tinker's Creek/Pilgerruh Cemetery, p. 215

*Grave of Christian Link is one of three visible at Crossview*

# Darrow Cemetery

ADDRESS: Old Rockside Rd.  ~  LOCATION: Independence  ~  PHONE: None
ACREAGE: 0.1 acres  ~  CARETAKER: None
ACCESS: Grounds always open
NUMBER OF BURIALS: approx. 3  ~  OLDEST/FIRST GRAVE: Unknown
RELIGIOUS AFFILIATION: Nondenominational  ~  ETHNIC AFFILIATION: N/A
DIRECTIONS: I-77 to Exit 155 for Rockside Rd.; west on Rockside; right (north) on Pinnacle Pk.; left (west) on Old Rockside Rd.

**HISTORY AND SURROUNDINGS:** Darrow Cemetery appears suddenly—a wooded area in the midst of civilization, not far from the hotels and restaurants of suburban America. It is another example of the custom of burying family members on the family farm.

It only takes a few minutes to find and read the markers, and if you've visited any of the other small family plots, by now you realize it's not that unusual in Cleveland to live near an "abandoned" cemetery.

## DARROW YOU LEARN ABOUT THE OTHERS?

**YOUR VISIT:** The large stone marked "Darrow" is the only one in this burial plot for three members of the family bearing that name. Nearby are the three markers that tell us the relationship of the people whose stones are

found here. Lavina Darrow, Alvah Darrow's wife, died May 4, 1860. Her husband died 21 years later on January 8, 1881. Their daughter, Elizabeth, died February 26, 1895. According to the 1850 census, Lavina Darrow was insane.

OTHER CEMETERIES NEARBY:

Crossview Cemetery, p. 184
West Family Cemetery, p. 217
Tinker's Creek/Pilgerruh Cemetery, p. 215

*Care of gravesite continues at abandoned cemetery*

# Glendale Cemetery

ADDRESS: 150 Glendale Ave.  ~  LOCATION: Akron  ~  PHONE: (330) 253-2317
ACREAGE: 85 acres  ~  CARETAKER: On site
ACCESS: Grounds open daily 8:30 a.m.–5 p.m.; office open Mon–Fri 9 a.m.–
4:30 p.m. Records at cemetery office; related materials at Summit County offices
NUMBER OF BURIALS: Unknown
OLDEST/FIRST GRAVE: Oldest: Gurdon Geer, 1828
RELIGIOUS AFFILIATION: Nondenominational
ETHNIC AFFILIATION: African-American, German, Native American
DIRECTIONS: I-271 to Exit 18 for SR 8; south on SR 8 to Perkins St.; west on Perkins;
left (south) on Union St.; right (west) on E. Market St.; left (south) on Glendale Rd.;
on left.

**HISTORY AND SURROUNDINGS:** Glendale is a rural-design cemetery established in 1839. The hilly grounds are covered with an abundance of trees and shrubs. Many of the bodies here were reinterred from Spicer Cemetery when it closed in the 1870s.

**YOUR VISIT:** As you enter, the cemetery the office is to the left and the historic superintendent's lodge is on the right. I suggest stopping at the office for a map. This is a large cemetery with flat stones that may be difficult to locate.

**THERE'S ONLY ONE ODD THING HERE—FIND IT**

Past the office is the ornate Gothic chapel built in 1876. Stained-glass windows let in natural light, and the original pews remain. A plaque on the door states that the building was designated as a historic landmark in 1980.

The superintendent's lodge was built in 1869 and the bell tower (seen in the woods behind the office) was built 1883. The first floor of the lodge is used by Let's Grow Akron and the upstairs is rented to an employee.

Using the map, follow the cemetery road to section 15. Bettie King's marker, toward the edge of the hill, is only about a foot high. Find the wide "ISBELL" stone; you'll see "King" a few rows behind it. Bettie Washington Steele King (1826–1909), the grandniece of George Washington, married lawyer David L. King on May 1, 1849. They had five children, moved to Cleveland in 1851, and back to Akron in 1855.

Not far from here in section 16 on the left is Shumacher. Ferdinand Shumacher (1822–1908) founded German Mills American Oatmeal

Company in 1856 in Akron. Prior to that, all oatmeal used in the United States was imported. By the time the Civil War began, rolled oats was an accepted breakfast food, and the Union army was Shumacher's customer. In 1886 the business suffered huge losses from a fire. In 1901 Shumacher joined with two other pioneers in oat milling to form Quaker Oats. He was an ardent prohibitionist, contributing heavily to the cause. Shumacher later went into debt over business dealings and died a pauper, but his debts were paid off. A costly monument adorning the grave site led to unfounded rumors of buried treasure.

*The Gothic chapel, built in 1876, is a historic landmark*

Head to section 19 to see the monument for Frank A. Seiberling (1889–1955), co-founder of the Goodyear Tire and Rubber Company. Seiberling and his wife, Gertrude, were in England in 1912 researching castles in preparation for the building of their home in West Akron, Stan Hywet Hall, which is open to visitors. For the return trip, they were booked on the *Titanic* but a change in travel plans saved them from the ill-fated voyage.

You are near section 22; the Buchtel plot is at the corner. There are two huge bushes next to the markers, and a large "B" is visible at the base of the monument, a statue of a rather commanding gentleman. John Buchtel (1820–1892) founded Buchtel University, which later became the University of Akron.

In this same section is "Miller," more than 10 feet tall with several flat, oval stones around it. Each of these individual stones has a green wreath with a cross through a crown. The wreaths match the wreath on the monument. It is interesting to note that Lewis Miller's oval stone is the only one missing a wreath.

*One of several individual stones*

*Angel bestows crown on Miller family graves*

Lewis Miller (1829–1899) was an inventor who applied for several patents—one of them with renowned inventor Cyrus McCormick. His patents include the Buckeye Mower and Reaper, the Buckeye Table Rake, and a self binder. Along with Bishop J. H. Vincent, Lewis founded a religious and educational association, the Chautauqua Association. His daughter, Mina, was Thomas Edison's second wife. They married in the Millers' Akron home.

From here, go to section 28 and the Oddfellows memorial. The International Order of Oddfellows has a large monument displaying their symbol, three "O"s intertwined. The Oddfellows is a fraternal organiza-

*Interlocking "O"s denote Oddfellows monument*

tion dedicated to performing charitable acts. Their name goes back to 17th-century England, where it was "odd" to find a group of people focused on helping others.

With the Oddfellows monument on your left, head back toward section 27 (pass section 28, on the left). You'll see the Chief Big Buffalo monument just inside section 27. Chief Big Buffalo (1861–1956) was an Oglala Sioux left behind in Akron by a carnival. One day he showed up at Glendale Cemetery and just started raking leaves. It is unclear if he was actually a chief, but that didn't matter to the cemetery superintendent who gave him a job and befriended him. When Chief Big Buffalo died at Glendale Cemetery, the superintendent gave him a plot because he couldn't afford one.

Continue to 27ADD for "Wilkes," a flat marker about a third of the way in from the road. Ellen Wilkes (1864–1955) was a third-class passenger who survived the sinking of the *Titanic*. Her stone reads "Titanic survivor."

The stone of another *Titanic* survivor, Elizabeth Hocking (1860–1914), faces backwards in section E, up the hill from the crossroad after Wilkes. Hocking was hit by an automobile as she exited a streetcar. She died on the second anniversary of her rescue from the *Titanic*.

Hocking, Wilkes's sister, was a second-class passenger on the ship. In a newspaper account of the infamous tragedy, she described how a man gave up his seat in a lifeboat for her. Of the family members on the ship with Elizabeth, only her son George did not survive the disaster. Her grave is up the hill by two large trees; the flat stone is dark gray with the name "Hocking."

In section J, look for the "Lane" rock. Samuel A. Lane (1815–1905) was a sheriff, newspaper editor, and sign painter who went west during the California gold rush. There is some debate as to the origin of the boulder that marks his grave. One story suggests that Lane visited

Cleveland, where he saw ore boats unload a huge boulder and leave it on the shore. He somehow brought it to Akron, displayed it in front of his store, and requested that it be used as his gravestone. Another story claims that this stone was a meteor that fell from the sky. Cemetery workers recall astronomers scraping samples of the rock to test it.

Return to section 28 for "Kullberg," a difficult-to-find, flat marker in the middle of the section near a tree. Harold Kullberg (1896–1924) was a World War I flying ace who

*Top: Chief Big Buffalo was abandoned in Akron by a carnival*

*Middle: Third class passenger Ellen Wilkes survived the sinking of the* Titanic

*Bottom: The boulder at Samuel Lane's grave may be part of a meteor*

downed 14 German planes and two observation balloons. His military career ended in 1918 after he was wounded. Afterwards, he worked in commercial aviation in the Akron area.

Kullberg died during a lesson with a student pilot. During the lesson, he collapsed and fell over in his seat, covering the control stick and making the plane unmanageable for the student.

**STORY BUT NO STONE FOUND:** Dr. Jedidiah Commins is rumored to have kept his dead son in a vat of spirits for one year before burying him. Commins was Akron's first pharmacist.

The staff tells an interesting story of a lady who called to buy a marker for a woman buried here. The buyer, a woman in her eighties, had recently been reunited with the son she gave up for adoption some 70 years before; the beneficiary was the adoptive mother. The birth mother was so pleased at being reunited with her son that she wanted to honor the woman who had raised him.

**NOTABLE:**
Revolutionary War soldier Gurdon Geer (1756-1828) served for three years as a private under Colonel Samuel Webb, in Captain Thomas Wooster's company. He fought in the Battle of Rhode Island and was a sergeant in Colonel McClellan's regiment. His upright sandstone marker is in section 1 near Maple Street.

**MORE TO KNOW:** Stan Hywet Hall, the Seiberling mansion located at 714 North Portage Path, is open to visitors. The 65-room estate with 23 fireplaces and 21,000 panes of glass boasts the first use of telephones in Ohio. Surrounding the house are the rose garden, Japanese garden, English garden, and a lagoon. There are tours of both the house and gardens (a fee is charged). Call (330) 836-5533 for schedule and directions.

OTHER CEMETERIES NEARBY:
Mt. Peace Cemetery, *p. 206*

~ SUPERSTITIONS ~

# It's bad luck to count the cars in a funeral cortege.

# Harvard Grove Cemetery

ADDRESS: 6100 Lansing Ave.  ~  LOCATION: Cleveland

PHONE: (216) 348-7216  ~  ACREAGE: 20.82 acres  ~  CARETAKER: City of Cleveland

ACCESS: Grounds open Mon–Sat 9 a.m.–3 p.m. Records at Highland Park Cemetery (216 348-7210), and Western Reserve Historical Society (216-721-5722); related materials at Slavic Village Historical Society (216-341-8199)

NUMBER OF BURIALS: 30,000+  ~  OLDEST/FIRST GRAVE: Unknown

RELIGIOUS AFFILIATION: Mormon  ~  ETHNIC AFFILIATION: Welsh

DIRECTIONS: I-77 to Exit 159A for Harvard Ave.; east on Harvard; left (north) on E. 55th St.; right (east) on Orey St.; left (north) on E 57th. St.; right (east) on Lansing Ave.; on right.

**HISTORY AND SURROUNDINGS:** This property was originally a farm belonging to Isaac Reed. He dammed a local creek known as Burk's Run and dug a pond for his livestock; two manholes in the middle of the cemetery are left as reminders. Graves were transferred here when Axtel Cemetery was abandoned in 1881. Harvard Grove is situated in an old Polish neighborhood, on flat land with rolling hills at the back of the property.

DEATH AND TAKES BOTH FOUND HERE

**YOUR VISIT:** From the entrance make an immediate right and stand in front of the grave for Williams and family. William Wheeler Williams (1760–1831) was born in Norwich, Connecticut. He served in the Revolutionary War as a private with Captain Peter Robertson's Company and with Colonel Heman Swift's 2nd Regiment, Connecticut Line. He had four brothers who also served in the war. In 1799 the Connecticut Land Company contacted Williams to build a flour mill and sawmill in Newburgh Township (an early name for this part of Cleveland) using the waterfall for power. In return for his efforts, he was given materials, 100 acres, and $150.

Williams married Ruth Granger, who came to Newburgh in 1800 at the age of 35. She later became blind but was so adept at using her hearing to compensate that when someone would enter her room she could tell who it was.

*Painting of
Frederick Williams*

Frederick Williams, their eldest son, donated the land for the Kirtland Temple, which was founded by Joseph Smith. (Smith went on to found the Church of Jesus Christ of Latter-day Saints, with Frederick as his counselor.)

Nearby are seven white, government-issue markers. Five are for Revolutionary War soldiers and two are for Civil War soldiers. "USCI" on the marker stands for United States Colored Infantry.

Counting Williams, there are six Revolutionary War veterans buried here—more than at any other location in the city of Cleveland. Their headstones can be found near the entrance:

Nathan Boughton, private; Rossiter's Massachusetts Regiment, died in 1820.

Abner Cochran, private; Shepherd's Massachusetts Regiment, died December 17, 1819.

Charles Miles, captain; Seventh Connecticut Regiment, died 1813.

Joshua Palmiter, private; Rhode Island State Troops, died 1839.

Joseph Upson, Skinner's Connecticut Militia, died December 21, 1855.

Go left up the main drive to section 9. The stone for Morgan is a square turned up and resting on its point. One side reads "Howells" and the other reads "Morgan." Beneath it are footstones reading "mother" and "father."

Jeanette Morgan (1869–1944) was a founder of the Women's Welsh Club. At Harvard School she helped organize a "mothers' club," the precursor to the current Parent Teacher Association. Morgan was also the first woman assessor in Ohio. She was so well known that her death was announced on local radio.

Once, at a political convention in Cleveland, Morgan's daughter, Elizabeth, presented a bouquet of flowers to President Harding's wife.

Morgan's husband David, a foreman in the local steel mill, worked for passage of a law that required parental permission in order for school children to be vaccinated. He is also buried here.

None of the surveyors from Moses Cleaveland's original surveying party settled in Cleveland. The surveyors and their assistants signed a contract with Cleaveland allocating 500 acres to each man in the surveying party on condition he settle on the land and pay the Connecticut Land Company $1 per acre. However, Nathaniel Doan, a blacksmith and member of both the first and second surveying groups, did become a resident of the county, earning the distinction of being the only member of either of the first two surveying parties to reside in Cleveland (he is buried at Lake View Cemetery).

On the way out, and on the other side of the gate, look for "Carter," a rose-colored obelisk with a Masonic symbol. Alonzo Carter (1790–1872), one of Lorenzo Carter's sons, is buried here with his wife Julia (1795–1882). Lorenzo Carter is credited with being the only early settler who stayed in Cleveland. Others fled to avoid the fevers associated with being near the Cuyahoga River (see Erie Street Cemetery).

In this same section but farther into the cemetery is the newer, almost flat stone for Holly. Ezekial Holly (1765–1822) married Lorenzo Carter's sister Lucy (1770–1827). Little recognition has gone to Holly, who came to Cleveland with Carter on October 19, 1799. He was one of only three people who held the office of "fence viewer" (responsible for supervising the erection and maintenance of boundary and highway fences). His stone also lists him as "first constable."

**NOTABLE:**
*You'll find seven white, government-issue markers here. Five are for Revolutionary War soldiers and two are for Civil War soldiers. "USCI" on the marker stands for United States Colored Infantry.*

**STORY BUT NO STONE FOUND:** John Leonard Whitfield (1879–1928) died in the Columbus Penitentiary from gunshot wounds. He was a criminal from Cleveland with several wives, who impregnated a 14-year-old girl and fled, causing police to conduct a five-state manhunt. After killing a Cleveland policeman by the name of Dennis Griffin, Whitfield, an African-American, used a mixture of chemicals to lighten his skin so he would not be recognized. He was followed through 12 states before being caught, convicted of murder, and sent to prison. With the aid of prison guard Oren Hill, Whitfield escaped, but he was discovered in Hill's house and shot. His marker can not be found, but he is buried in section 19, tier 11, grave 2.

Sons of the American Revolution (SAR) records indicate that Edmund Rathburn Sr. (d. January 30, 1849), a private in the Massachusetts Troops, is also buried here. But it is impossible to verify because cemetery records fail to show evidence of this, and his grave could not be found.

OTHER CEMETERIES NEARBY: Calvary Cemetery, *p. 24*
Bedford Cemetery, *p. 177*

# Highland Drive Cemetery

ADDRESS: 9012 Highland Dr. ~ LOCATION: Brecksville ~ PHONE: (440) 526-4351
ACREAGE: 4.25 acres ~ CARETAKER: City of Brecksville
ACCESS: Grounds open daily dawn–dusk. Records at Western Reserve Historical Society (216-721-5722)
NUMBER OF BURIALS: 4,500 ~ OLDEST/FIRST GRAVE: Unknown
RELIGIOUS AFFILIATION: Nondenominational ~ ETHNIC AFFILIATION: N/A
DIRECTIONS: I-77 to Exit 149 for SR 82 (Royalton Rd.); east on SR 82 (Royalton); right (south) on Highland Dr.; on right.

**HISTORY AND SURROUNDINGS:** The early history of Highland Drive Cemetery is unclear. In 1941 the city of Brecksville took over ownership of the land, which lies on the outskirts of the county and includes a water tower. In the early days, most families could not afford the high prices—$25 for seven graves—so they would trade farm produce or labor in exchange for a grave lot.

## YOU COULD GET SNOWED HERE

**YOUR VISIT:** Down the cemetery road toward SR 82 and up the first small steps on the left, you'll find the Snow family's monuments. The Snow family has lived in the area for generations, and Charles Snow's barn served as the first school in Brecksville. Surely nearby Snow Road is named for this family. Dorcas Snow (1902–1994) was a much-beloved music and piano teacher known nationwide. She was also a composer, writer, and expert on local history.

Close by is the Wilcox family. Their stone reveals that the Snow and Wilcox families intermarried. Frank Wilcox (1887–1964) was a painter, printmaker, and leading artist of the Cleveland School. He garnered many awards in the May Show at the Cleveland Museum of Art and also received the 1920 Pelton Medal for sustained excellence. Reproductions of Wilcox's drawings can be seen on the historic markers on the towpath trail in the Cuyahoga Valley National Recreation Area.

Next, walk toward the water tower, staying on the grass. Before reaching the vault, look for the 15-foot-tall obelisk of the Breck family.

Robert and John Breck were brothers from Northampton, Massachusetts; though they never lived here, the city bears their name. The land was actually purchased by John and Robert's father, Robert Breck Sr., who was a colonel in the Revolutionary War and died in 1802. Both brothers inherited the land, but Robert died soon thereafter. Three of John's six children came to Brecksville. Of those, Dr. Theodore Breck (1867–1934) was the last to reside in Brecksville.

Notice the heart-shaped marker for Chauncey and its simple inscription: "at rest." Walk downhill, past Chauncey, to the left. Here are four low rose-colored stones of the Weise family. The demise of three children in rapid succession (1896, 1898, and 1899) reminds us of the hard life and high rates of infant mortality in the 19th century.

Return up the hill and proceed right, toward the other side of the vault. This is the oldest part of the cemetery.

A few rows past the vault is Jonah Stoner's grave. The headstone for this three-year-old (1833–1836) states "died with rosey cheeks." The inscription is:

> His little spirit is gone to God, God gave it and took it. Be ye also ready to meet your God in peace.

The next row has a newer stone with praying hands for the McCreary family.

Two rows farther down and near a tree lies Colonel Quartus Stebbins, who "died of the prevailing fevers" on September 14, 1827. It was common at the time to list the cause of death on tombstones.

About three rows down is the flat bronze marker of Thaddeus Newell (1746–1830). He served with the Continental Line in the Revolutionary War.

Another row back is "Bourne," a small headstone with a design on top. Lemuel Bourne's stone was probably made by an amateur or a family member. Notice the *o* inserted above the line—mistakes like this, if left uncorrected, could lead future genealogists to think the family name was Burne.

Bourne walked the 600 miles from Savoy, Massachusetts, to Brecksville in four weeks. He returned to Massachusetts to marry Delia Waite and came back to Brecksville with her in 1812. The day after her arrival, a rattlesnake surprised Mrs. Bourne near her cabin. She found a weapon and killed the snake.

In the next row lies Sophia Oakes (1794–1830), from another family whose name graces a local street. Oakes died in

*As marker indicates, three-year-old Jonah Stoner died "with rosey cheeks"*

childbirth. Her stone is inscribed:

> The resurrection day will come and
> Christ's strong rein will hurl the lamb,
> the sleeping dead we trust will rise,
> with joy and pleasure in her eyes,
> and ever shine among the wise.

Four rows back is an aging white stone curved on top. No other markers are next to it. This is the grave of Maria W. Hollis, whose simple epitaph is etched about a third of the way down the back of the marker. Look carefully to find "Mother we miss thee."

**NOTABLE:**
*Look for a stone bench, a unique memorial for the Brooks family.*

Look for a stone bench, a memorial for the Brooks family. Notice that the rest of this row has only Allen family members. Look carefully for Joseph Allen who served in the War of 1812.

A few rows farther find the Van Noate family, which had two women with rather unusual names—Ardalise and Mehitable.

OTHER CEMETERIES NEARBY: North Royalton Cemetery, *p. 155*
The single marker for Benjamin Waite, *p. 218*

*A stone bench marks the Brooks family grave*

# Lutheran Cemetery

ADDRESS: 4566 Pearl Rd.  ~  LOCATION: Cleveland  ~  PHONE: (216) 351-1308

ACREAGE: Approx. 28 acres  ~  CARETAKER: On site; restrooms at office

ACCESS: Grounds open May–Sept daily 8 a.m.–6 p.m., Oct–April daily 8 a.m.–
4:30 p.m.; office open Mon–Fri 9 a.m.–4 p.m., Sat 9 a.m.–noon. Records at
cemetery office, and Western Reserve Historical Society (216-721-5722)

NUMBER OF BURIALS: 18,000  ~  OLDEST/FIRST GRAVE: First: Martin Voightschmidt,
November 1894, and Ludwig Kaufmann, November 1894

RELIGIOUS AFFILIATION: Lutheran  ~  ETHNIC AFFILIATION: German, Slovak

DIRECTIONS: I-480 to Exit 16 for SR 94 (State Rd.); north on SR 94 (State); left (west)
on Biddulph Ave.; right (north) on US 42 (Pearl Rd.); on left.

**HISTORY AND SURROUNDINGS:** In 1894 Lutheran congregations on
Cleveland's West Side organized for the purpose of acquiring land for a
cemetery. Four congregations—Christ Lutheran,
Immanuel, St. Matthew, and Trinity Lutheran—joined
and formed the Evangelical Lutheran Cemetery Association. Thirty acres were purchased and ten of those
were made available for burials. St. Luke's, St. Mark's,
and Redeemer Lutheran Church joined in 1903.

**PASTOR
AND GOLFER
SHOW
PASSIONS
IN STONE**

This cemetery has the most uniform feel to it. The
majority of the monuments have religious symbols,
and they are a testimonial to the work of skilled stone-
cutters.

This flat land is home to 16 different kinds of bushes and trees including birch, catalpa, and elm.

**YOUR VISIT:** Enter from Pearl Road and take the first right turn. Go left of
the flagpole so that Section B is to the right and D is to the left. Continue, with H on the right and G on the left. Go around G and park so that
G is on the left and section I on the right. The tall Leopold stone should
be visible. Walk toward it and then right to the podium marker.

Friedrich Conrad Dietrich Wynekan (1810–1876) served as pastor of
Trinity Evangelical Lutheran Church from 1850 to 1864. During that
time he was also president of the Missouri Synod of the Lutheran
Church. His monument has his picture on it.

Keeping section G on the left as you go straight, turn left so M is on
the right and G on the left. From here you can see Wulfman-Frantz. The
Wulfman and Frantz families have a joint monument showing an angel

*One of many angels marking graves at Lutheran*

with her hands filled with roses. It is at least 10 feet tall, with a cross that has a carved rose in the center.

Across from Wulfman-Frantz in section M is the huge Meyer-Kluever monument. Gustav Meyer (1859–1939) and other family members are buried near this monument that displays an angel standing in front of a very large cross.

Toward the end of section G, by a sewer grate, you'll see "Brenner." The stone has a seated angel with the sun rising behind it. There are no dates on the monument itself, but there are headstones behind it with individual names and dates on them (George 1863–1952 and Anna 1861–1914).

The "Pohl" marker, farther toward Pearl Road, stands about seven feet tall. It is six stones from the end of section G, across from D. This family memorial is much smaller than some of the others and has an angel on top, but the angel's head is missing.

Proceed toward the main gate and circle back to section O. This is the section devoted to children and infants. Baby Mikulich is four rows from the fence by Biddulph Road and about 10 rows before the red brick building. Baby Mikulich's headstone has a relief of a cherub, which is the symbol of hope and the promise of heaven. Another popular symbol in this section is the lamb, signifying the innocence of children and of Christ.

Pass the building and go to section P. Two rows from the fence and about 25 stones from the school is the stone for Armin Kunde (1921–1980). It features illustrations of his favorite things—trees near a lake, an airplane flying by, clouds with the sun shining through, and the 11th hole of a golf course.

**OTHER CEMETERIES NEARBY:**
St. Theodosius Cemetery, *p. 71*
Brainard/Broadview Cemetery, *p. 132*

*Favorite pastimes are now commonly etched on stones*

# Markillie Cemetery

ADDRESS: 410 North Main St.  ~  LOCATION: Hudson  ~  PHONE: (330) 342-1759
ACREAGE: 16 acres  ~  CARETAKER: City of Hudson
ACCESS: Grounds open daily dawn–dusk. Records at Hudson Historical Society and Library (330-653-6658), and Superintendent of Hudson Cemeteries (330-342-1759)
NUMBER OF BURIALS: 3,700
OLDEST/FIRST GRAVE: First: Lucy Hurn Markillie, July 30, 1850
RELIGIOUS AFFILIATION: Nondenominational  ~  ETHNIC AFFILIATION: English
DIRECTIONS: I-480 to Exit 37 for SR 91 (Darrow Rd.); south on SR 91 (Darrow); becomes N. Main St. in Hudson; on right.

**HISTORY AND SURROUNDINGS:** This is the largest of Hudson's five cemeteries, encompassing more than a mile of roads. John Markillie was the original owner of this land, and after burying his mother, he portioned out 2.5 acres into burial lots that he willed to the city. After Markillie's death in 1868, the village council elected trustees to run the cemetery. Over the years more land was purchased, and Markillie Cemetery now spans more than 16 acres.

> TALK ABOUT GOING SOUTH FOR THE WINTER

There once was a 30-foot easement road to the south to provide access for the Catholics of St. Mary's in case the Protestants tried to keep them out. About 10 years ago, this easement was sold to developers, resulting in new homes along the back of the cemetery, permitted in spite of a state law preventing houses from being too close to a cemetery.

A provision in James Ellsworth's will provided a trust fund for a Cleveland bank to maintain the family plot, but it ran out of money a few years ago. Now the entire cemetery is operated through the Hudson Cemetery Board.

**YOUR VISIT:** Drive through the entrance, turn right at Front Street and left onto Maple. On the right is the black granite Ellsworth monument, wider than it is tall. Imagine what it must have been like to place this monument here. It was imported from Italy in 1926, before the availability of flatbed trucks, so it was moved in on rollers pulled by oxen.

This cemetery is best known as the burial place of Lincoln Ellsworth. He received the Congressional Medal of Honor from President Hoover in 1931 for his part in the Amundsen-Ellsworth polar and transpolar flights of 1925 and 1926.

*James Ellsworth,*
*October 1897*

Lincoln's father, James Ellsworth, was a very important civic leader, and many amenities currently enjoyed by Hudsonites can be traced directly back to him. James Ellsworth was a banker who also made money in the coal industry. His family was already involved in the oil business when he married Eva Butler, a wealthy woman from Chicago, where he moved after the wedding. After she died, Ellsworth and his two children, Lincoln and Clare, returned to Hudson.

Ellsworth left the children to be raised by their grandparents and returned to Chicago. At the Chicago World's Fair, James purchased a gift for Hudson's Western Reserve Academy—a cross from Christopher Columbus's hometown of Genoa. Ellsworth moved back to Hudson upon his retirement.

During Hudson's financial difficulties in the early 1900s, and after a fire devastated most of Main Street, Western Reserve Academy went bankrupt, closing its doors from 1903 to 1916. Ellsworth came to the rescue, using his personal funds to reestablish the academy and his expertise to help rebuild the city. Two of his suggestions were to put all utilities underground and to build a power plant which would be owned by the town.

Ellsworth was proving to be a great friend to the city of Hudson. But the friendship fell on hard times when local politicians did not support Ellsworth's candidate for mayor. He lessened his generosity with the city, and the townspeople took over the operations of the power plant.

And it was not until the boilers burst from their first load of bituminous coal that the townspeople realized Ellsworth's ingenious trick of building a power plant that could only be fueled by anthracite coal, which his coal company mined.

Meanwhile, the Ellsworth children were reaching adulthood. Clare married Bernon S. Prentiss, while Lincoln got thrown out of both Dartmouth and Yale. Lincoln was interested in exploring and began to communicate with Roald Amundsen, a Norwegian explorer. Amundsen, who obviously had his own agenda, agreed to Lincoln's participation in an expedition on condition that Lincoln's father finance it.

The expedition took off in the airship *Norge*, on May 11, 1926. Because no one had heard from the expedition for some time, it was assumed Lincoln and the others died. James was notified of this by telegram. James Ellsworth died before learning that the trip had been, in fact, a success, and that Lincoln had survived.

When James died, his land in Hudson was given to Western Reserve Academy. Other gifts from Ellsworth include Hudson's landmark clock tower and an important piece from his art collection, Rembrandt's *Portrait of a Man*. The painting—purchased in France and the first Rembrandt to be brought into the United States—was given to the Metropolitan Museum of Art in New York when Lincoln's widow, Mary Louise Ulmer, died in 1993.

Lincoln Ellsworth returned to a hero's welcome. His interest in exploration continued, and he went on to explore the South Pole and more than 100,000 miles of Antarctica.

Clare Ellsworth Prentiss, who aided and encouraged Lincoln in preparation for his expeditions, was dead by the time her brother received the Congressional Medal of Honor that made him famous.

> **NOTABLE:**
> *It is difficult to tell where Markillie Cemetery ends and St. Mary's Cemetery begins. This shared boundary came in handy. Catholic cemeteries did not permit non-Catholics to be buried on their hallowed ground, so spouses in mixed marriages could have one member buried at St. Mary's and the other at Markillie.*

Several feet behind the Ellsworth monument is a white sandstone monument for Eliza Post (1825–1856), wife of Bradford Post. On it is a version of an epitaph that was common in the middle of the 19th century. It aptly conveys the realistic yet spiritual attitude toward death held by many early settlers. It reads:

> Remember well as you pass by,
> All you that here pass long must die,
> your cheeks will lose their youthful bloom,
> your morning sun may set at noon,
> Oh do not grieve fore me in vain,
> In heaven so soon shall meet again.

Walk or drive to the Markillie monument in the adjoining section, surrounded by third and second streets. Lucy's marker, low to the ground, states that hers was the first burial here.

OTHER CEMETERIES NEARBY: Chapel Street/Olde Hudson Burying Ground, *p. 181*

# Mound Hill Cemetery

ADDRESS: East Main St. ~ LOCATION: Seville ~ PHONE: None
ACREAGE: Approx. 20 acres ~ CARETAKER: City of Seville and Guilford Township
Trustees
ACCESS: Grounds open daily dawn–dusk. Records at Seville Historical Society
(330-769-4056), Medina County Library (330-772-2490), and Medina County Historical Society (330-722-1341)
NUMBER OF BURIALS: Approx. 5,200 ~ OLDEST/FIRST GRAVE: First: 1821
RELIGIOUS AFFILIATION: Nondenominational ~ ETHNIC AFFILIATION: Canadian, Scottish
DIRECTIONS: I-71 to Exit 209 for I-76; east on I-76 to Exit 2 for SR 3; south on SR 3; left
(east) on Main St.; on left.

**HISTORY AND SURROUNDINGS:** This is the only Indian mound in Medina County with a cemetery on it. The family that deeded the land stipulated that the mound could not be excavated, was to be used only for graves.

## A TALL TALE

**YOUR VISIT:** About 100 yards from the eastern entrance to the cemetery you'll see the Bates graves. A sign refers to them as the "Giants" graves. It's hard to miss the tall female figure, a statue made in France, on Anna's grave.

Martin Van Buren Bates (1845–1919) was born in Kentucky, the youngest boy in a family of six boys and five girls. By the time he was 15, Bates was six feet tall. When he was 16, the Civil War broke out and he enlisted as a private in the 5th Kentucky Infantry. He was promoted to captain and joined the 7th Confederate Calvary under Colonel Clarence Prentis. Bates was still growing.

He continued to grow until he was 28 years old

*Left: Confederate insignia marks grave of Captain Bates*

*Right: Marker for Anna Bates. The tall figure of a young woman came from France*

and seven feet, eight inches tall, weighing 470 pounds. He received an honorable discharge from the army because they had so much difficulty finding uniforms to fit him. He appeared in various shows and exhibits and eventually went on a European tour.

Anna Swan (1848–1889) was born in Nova Scotia and weighed more than 18 pounds at birth. By the age of six she was taller than her five-foot-three mother. At 15 years she was seven feet tall, and to her embarrassment, people gawked at her wherever she went.

An agent from P. T. Barnum came to woo her into the circus. Her family agreed she could go on tour under the condition that her schooling continue with a private tutor and that her mother accompany her.

In 1862 Swan went to Europe and was presented to Queen Victoria in England.

*Captain Bates (weighing 308 pounds) with friend Frank Bowman (weighing 96 pounds)*

Later, when Barnum's museum burned down, the showman made a big to-do about how he had to get a giant crane to rescue the giantess from the building. But this was only a publicity stunt—Anna had safely left the museum and was never in any danger.

While visiting the New Jersey home of General Winfield Scott, Anna met Captain Martin Van Buren Bates, who was known as "The Kentucky Giant." Anna was seven feet, eleven inches tall at the time and weighed 413 pounds.

Anna and Captain Bates began touring together. On the tour, they attended receptions, mingling with people who paid to see them. In England they were presented once again to the queen, who was so pleased she gave them each a gift—a wedding ring for Anna, and a watch and chain for Martin, which he wore at his wedding.

The pair was married June 17, 1871, in London and settled in England. On May 19,1872, Mrs. Bates gave birth to a baby girl. Sadly, the infant, who weighed 18 pounds and was 27 inches long, was stillborn.

The couple went into semi-retirement and traveled back to the U.S. On a trip to the western United States they bought a farm in Ohio. After the death of her first child, Anna had been advised to live near a large body of water. This, combined with Mr. Bates's desire to farm and the fact that a friend of Barnum's lived nearby, brought them to Seville, Ohio.

Captain Bates built a house with 14-foot ceilings and 8-foot-tall doors. Actually, the house had two parts to it: the front had the larger size rooms for Mr. and Mrs. Bates; the back, where the servants lived or worked, was built lower. Similarly, the back stairway was narrow but the front one was wide enough to accommodate the unusual girth of its owners. A custom-ordered piano for Mrs. Bates was on stilts 36 inches off the floor. Cost overruns on the house led the couple to go on tour again, this time with the W. W. Cole Circus.

On Jan 19, 1879, Anna gave birth to their second child, this time a boy. Until this time, most known giants had been born to normal parents. But here were two giants producing offspring. When Anna's water broke, the doctor estimated six gallons gushed out. The baby weighed 23 ½ pounds but lived only 11 hours.

The 1932 Chicago World's Fair had an exhibit called "Story of Life"

that depicted the giant baby next to its parents. The Cleveland Health Museum used to show plaster models of the baby next to that of a normal-size infant and a premature baby. The *Guinness Book of World Records* has an entry for the Seville Giants and their baby.

The Bateses finally settled down to life in Seville, where they were very much a part of

*Oversized crib of baby giant*

the business and social scene. To accommodate them, the First Baptist Church made their pews four inches higher. Once at a party a floor broke while they were dancing. Another time Captain Bates walked into the back of a store and heard the proprietor comment that if the giant was strong enough to lift a barrel of sugar, he could have it. Bates walked home with the barrel (weighing 200–300 pounds) and returned to the store to ask the owner if he had any more sugar to give away.

When Anna died, Captain Bates sent a telegraph to Cleveland giving the exact specifications for her coffin. The coffin that arrived was built to normal specifications—the coffin maker assumed there was a mistake in the dimensions given. Three days later a coffin of the appropriate size arrived. When Bates ordered Anna's second coffin, he also ordered one for himself and kept it in the barn.

Captain Bates remarried, to a woman only five feet tall.

Look to the left of Captain Bates's monument for a mound. Walk toward the crest of the mound, cross the drive and look for the SAR marker by the grave of William Hosmer (1741–1839). He was the father of the founder of Seville and a soldier in the Revolutionary War.

Nearby there are other Revolutionary War soldiers: Ben Cotton, who died in 1816 at the age of 88; David Nichols, who was a drummer boy from Massachusetts; and, according to SAR records, John Thompson, who also fought in the Revolutionary War, is buried here.

From the Hosmer grave, walk to the newer crossroad and find the Noyes family monument. The monument indicates that some family members were missionaries in China in the early 1900s.

**MORE TO KNOW:** The Seville Historical Society has wonderful exhibits and detailed information on the Seville Giants. The Society is open the first Sunday of the month from March through December. To get there, turn right upon leaving the cemetery, after the stoplight go straight for about 0.3 mile. At the triangular park stay on West Main (SR 3 bears left) to the museum at number 70.

**NOTABLE:**

*About 100 yards from the eastern entrance to the cemetery you'll see the Bates graves. A sign refers to them as the "Giants" graves. It's hard to miss the tall female figure, a statue made in France, on Anna's grave.*

Although their original home was torn down, the Bateses' barn still stands. The roof tiles spell out "Captain M. V. Bates." The Bates barn is 0.5 mile to the left as you exit the cemetery.

~ SUPERSTITIONS ~

# Thunder following a funeral means that the dead person's soul has reached heaven.

# Mt. Peace Cemetery

ADDRESS: 183 Aqueduct Rd. ~ LOCATION: Akron ~ PHONE: (330) 253-4551
ACREAGE: 115 acres ~ CARETAKER: On site
ACCESS: Grounds open daily dawn–dusk; office open Mon–Fri 8:30 a.m.–4:30 p.m.,
Sat 8:30 a.m.–noon. Records at cemetery office; related materials at the Summit
County Library (330-643-9010)
NUMBER OF BURIALS: 37,000 ~ OLDEST/FIRST GRAVE: Oldest and first: August 6, 1880
RELIGIOUS AFFILIATION: Nondenominational
ETHNIC AFFILIATION: African-American, English
DIRECTIONS: I-271 to Exit 18 for SR 8; south on SR 8 to Perkins St.; west on Perkins;
left (south) on Union St.; right (west) on East Market St.; right (north) on Aqueduct
Rd.; on right.

**HISTORY AND SURROUNDINGS:** In 1880, members of the German
Reformed Church organized Mt. Peace Cemetery. The First Grace Unit-
ed Church of Christ now administers it. This is a huge cemetery in west
Akron, populated with trees and shrubs throughout.

**YOUR VISIT:** Drive to the office for section maps to help you find your
way through this large, spread-out cemetery. From the office, drive into
the grounds, keeping the new mausoleums on the
right. Section 20 is in front of you; section 21 bor-

**TWELVE STEPS** ders Aqueduct Street.
"Wells" is a two-tone gray marker about five
feet tall, located toward the center of section 20.
Addie Wells (1883–1954) booked passage for herself and her two young children on the
Oceanic bound for America in April 1912.
Wells was to meet her husband Arthur in
Akron, where he had been working at
Goodrich Tire. But the Oceanic's trip was
canceled due to a coal strike, so Wells purchased second-class tickets on the Titanic.
Addie, her seven-year-old daughter Joan
(1905–1933), and three-year-old son Ralph
(1910–1972), were lucky enough to make it
to a lifeboat, which was so crowded that

*Joan Wells survived the Titanic disaster at age seven*

Wells had to stand with her children in her skirts. The next morning, the lifeboat was rescued by the *Carpathia*; Wells chose to sleep on deck rather than go below.

Look now in section 21 for "Smith," about two rows behind the tall "Kurner" monument. It is a double stone shared by husband and wife. Dr. Robert Holbrook Smith (1879–1950) was the co-founder of Alcoholics Anonymous. The day we visited, the stone had several mementos on it: some buckeyes, a few sobriety stones, and some medals with the serenity prayer on them. Dr. Bob's home, at 855 Ardmore Street, is open to visitors. It has 12 steps leading up to its entrance.

**NOTABLE:**
You'll notice a mausoleum with "Mt. Peace" written across it. No one is buried here. A family purchased the monument but decided not to use it. Because of its location it was made into the Mt. Peace monument.

Proceed to the back part of section 26 and look for "Prade." Dr. Margo Prade (1956–1997), a much-beloved Akron doctor, was murdered in November 1997. Her ex-husband, former Akron police officer Doug Prade, was convicted of killing her. He is appealing that decision.

Follow the map to section 25, lot 92, and look for a flat stone with a bronze marker. Alvin Smith (1844–1948) was the last Civil War veteran in Summit County when he died at the age of 103. Smith, like his mother, was a slave; he was sold for $760.50 when he was 19 years old. He escaped across the river from Kentucky, walked 30 miles north to Hillsboro, Ohio, and enlisted in the Union army. Smith was in the 27th U. S. Colored Infantry, one of only two black regiments from Ohio. The regiment fought in many battles and was commended for gallantry at Petersburg, Virginia. Eight soldiers were killed in action and 149 died in the hospital. Smith always wondered why he survived.

After the war Smith came to Akron and worked as a plasterer. It took him two years to find his family—they were hiding in Kentucky, unaware that they were free. He brought them to live with him in Akron. Thanks to Akron history teacher and Civil War aficionado John Gurnish, Smith's grave now has an official bronze government marker noting his contributions.

**OTHER CEMETERIES NEARBY:**
Glendale Cemetery, *p. 186*

*Mementos found on stone of
Alcoholics Anonymous co-founder*

# Parma Heights Cemetery

**ADDRESS:** Reservoir Rd.  ~  **LOCATION:** Parma Heights  ~  **PHONE:** None
**ACREAGE:** Unknown  ~  **CARETAKER:** City of Parma Heights (not on site)
**ACCESS:** Grounds open daily dawn–dusk. Records at Parma Area Historical
Society (440-845-9770), Parma Heights Historical Society (216-524-3079),
and Western Reserve Historical Society (216-721-5722)
**NUMBER OF BURIALS:** 630  ~  **OLDEST/FIRST GRAVE:** Unknown
**RELIGIOUS AFFILIATION:** Nondenominational  ~  **ETHNIC AFFILIATION:** French
**DIRECTIONS:** I-480 to Exit 15 for Ridge Rd.; south on Ridge; right (west) on US 42
(Pearl Rd.); left (south) on Reservoir Dr. after Snow Rd.

**HISTORY AND SURROUNDINGS:** Not a lot is known about the beginnings
of this burial ground. The date on the receiving vault at the west end of
the plot is 1892. Toward the back of the cemetery, closest to the water
plant, once stood a house where 4-H club meetings were held. Parma
Heights Cemetery is located on a major thoroughfare
near a water treatment plant. Obviously the city grew
up around this site.

## CHURCH BANS SPIRIT SELLER

**YOUR VISIT:** As you turn onto Reservoir Drive, park in
the small culvert on the right next to the cemetery.
Walk in and locate the veterans' marker by standing
near the stairs from Pearl Road and walking several
feet to the left.

Behind (east) and to the left (north) of the veterans' marker lie the
Fays, who offer us the typical legacy of the early settlers—children
dying at young ages, yet some adults living to 90 years or more.

Benajah Fay (1785–1860) and Ruth Fay (1781–1831) came to Parma
in 1816 with 10 children aged nine months to 16 years. Ruth Fay gave
birth to three more children in
Ohio: Mabel Truman Fay,
born 1820, who was the first
white child born in Parma,
and twins Jeremiah and Ruth,
who were born two years later.

In 1819 Benajah opened "B.

*Jeremiah Fay, (youngest son of
Benajah and Ruth Fay) with his wife Mary
Ann at their Parma homestead*

Courtesy Ruth Fay

Fay's Inn" located on the old stage road, where the water was believed to have medicinal qualities. Benajah was denied church membership because he handled spirits at his inn. Fay Junior High School, which is now part of Parma Community Hospital's Health Education Center, was named for Benajah Fay.

Return to the veterans' marker, but go behind (east) and to the right of it (south). About two rows in front of the ball monument for "Whitney," you'll see the curved, aging white stone of Pelatiah Bliss.  Bliss arrived in 1818 having walked all the way from Connecticut. He bought 50 acres, built a shack, and then worked the land. A few years later, he walked back to Connecticut and married his fiancée. On the return trip, Bliss exchanged his services as ox-team driver for transportation for himself and his new bride. His stone is difficult to read but can be found.

Walk to the vault—it's the only building on the site—and peek in. This was used as a receiving vault—a place to hold bodies when the ground was too frozen to permit hand digging of graves. Continue back toward the veterans' marker and farther north looking for a boulder between two large bushes. It is in the northern section of the cemetery. The plaque on the boulder reads: "On this site in 1826 was built a log house that served as Parma's first school building, church and public meeting place. It stood here until 1841."

As you walk throughout the cemetery, you'll find several markers from the last 20 years.

**MORE TO KNOW:** The home of Amos Denison, located at 6037 Pearl Road, was known as a stop on the Underground Railroad. Denison hid slaves in the barn and drove them to the next stop in his specially designed wagon—the sides were built up to hide the slaves, and the wheels were wrapped in cloth to make less noise at night. The home is privately owned, but you can drive past it. Take a left onto Pearl Road from Reservoir Drive and look for the address. An RTA shelter is in front of it.

OTHER CEMETERIES NEARBY: Immanuel Evangelical Cemetery, *p. 46*

# Strongsville Cemetery

**ADDRESS:** 13123 Pearl Rd. (no sign)  ~  **LOCATION:** Stongsville  ~  **PHONE:** None

**ACREAGE:** 5.9 acres  ~  **CARETAKER:** Not on site; no restrooms on site

**ACCESS:** Grounds open daily dawn–dusk. Records at the Strongsville Historical Society (440-572-0057), and Western Reserve Historical Society (216-721-5722)

**NUMBER OF BURIALS:** 3,100  ~  **OLDEST/FIRST GRAVE:** Unknown

**RELIGIOUS AFFILIATION:** Nondenominational  ~  **ETHNIC AFFILIATION:** English, German

**DIRECTIONS:** I-71 to Exit 231 for SR 82 (Royalton Rd.); west on SR 82 (Royalton); right (north) on US 42 (Pearl Rd.); on right.

**HISTORY AND SURROUNDINGS:** In 1822 John S. Strong transferred land to establish a cemetery for the inhabitants of Strongsville. The land was to be used as a "burying yard so long as wood grows and water runs, provided the inhabitants keep the same fenced with a good and lawful fence reserving to me the said John S. Strong the privilege of feeding the same with small cattle or sheep . . ." (Deed book 4D, pages 375–76 Cuyahoga County Recorder's Office). The flat narrow cemetery is without even a sign to distinguish it.

## COUNTING SHEEP, NOT CROWS, WAS PIONEER SKILL

**YOUR VISIT:** Enter on North Drive, the road farthest from Route 82, and park about halfway between the entrance and the turn in the road. The two sidewalks in the center section are labeled "A" (near North Drive) and "B" (near South Drive).

Find the Myrick grave between Sidewalk A and North Drive. Joseph Myrick (1756–1842), a native of Greenfield, Massachusetts, was a minuteman under Captain John Black and Colonel Jonathan Brewer, having enlisted on April 29, 1775, and served until January 1, 1776. He was also at the Battle of Bunker Hill, having enlisted again in the summer of 1777 under Captain Smith and Colonel Cushing in the Massachusetts Infantry. Myrick then reenlisted

*Tree stump monument symbolizes life cut short*

from July 7, 1780, until Jan 7, 1781.

Myrick and his wife, Ruth, moved to Strongsville in 1830 when he was 75. His son, Justus, and his family joined them as well. Ruth Myrick died May 14, 1846.

Walk straight toward Pearl Road, stopping about three rows before the end. A few feet to the north is James Nichols (1755–1829), a native of Canterbury, Connecticut. He married Lydia Herrington on March 9, 1774, and they had eight children. From July 1775 until December of that year, Nichols was with the Connecticut Line under Captain Daniel Lynn's company and Colonel Jedediah Huntington. He enlisted again in February 1776, in the Rhode Island Troops under Captain Samuel Phillip and Colonel Richards. At this time Nichols was sent aboard the *Providence*, a ship commanded by Captain Abraham Whipple. The last six months of his service were as a sergeant in the marines.

Nichols applied for his pension in 1818 and 1820 but lost it for a time because the war department found out he owned land, which he promptly placed in his son's name in order to qualify for the pension. After area residents came to his aid, among them John Strong, Nichols's pension was reinstated.

Nichols was elected justice of the peace in 1818. He was a scribe in the First Temperance Society in Strongsville, made up of members of the First Congregational Church. Nichols died in Rockport Township and was brought to Strongsville for burial. He is buried beside his wife, who predeceased him. Nichols's crumbling marker was recently replaced by a newer one.

From "Nichols," walk toward North Drive. About halfway down you'll see the gray obelisk of Pomeroy. Two early families in the area were the Popes and the Pomeroys. Jonathan Pope and his wife Kezia and seven of their eight children came to Strongsville from New Bedford, Massachusetts, in 1819. Ebeneezer and Violaty Pomeroy came to Strongsville in 1822 from Northampton, Massachusetts, via New York.

Though they attended different churches, the children of these families did meet at singing school and Alanson Pomeroy ended up marrying Kezia Pope. They were active in the community, with Alanson as postmaster and supporter of the abolitionist movement. His office was

*Metal escutcheon (shield) beside the Nichols grave denotes Revolutionary War service*

connected to his general store and adjacent to the Congregational Church. Alanson's youngest son, Harlan, was aware that his father used the office as a station on the Underground Railroad. Harlan later told of seeing his mother take trays of food down the cellar stairs. Only in later years did Alanson tell his son that the slaves were brought in at night from Oberlin, hidden in wagons filled with hay, then hidden in their cellar, before finally being put on a boat in the Rocky River, headed for Canada.

As the proprietor of a general store, Alanson had a lot of contact with the local citizens. His son, Harlan, recalled a customer who came weekly offering to sell butter she had made. Alanson would buy the butter, offering in return groceries from his store. No matter what she chose he always told her that the butter covered the cost of her "purchases." When the woman left the store, Alanson threw away the butter because he didn't feel it was good quality. Alanson Pomeroy died Jan 4, 1877, at the age of 72.

Behind Pomeroy (away from Pearl Road) and toward Sidewalk A is "Whitney." Benjamin Whitney (1741–1833) fought in the Battle of Bunker Hill, having enlisted in April 1775 with Captain John Cole's company and Colonel Woodbridge's regiment. He served with them for less than 10 months and then enlisted for one year in Captain Ballarad's company, Colonel Whitcomb's regiment, Massachusetts Line. He returned to Massachusetts and enlisted again with Captain Samuel Cook and the regiment of Colonel Woodbridge. Whitney was also in the Battle of Burgoyne in 1777 and in July 1779 served nine months with Captain Smith's company, Colonel Thaddeus Marshall's regiment. He married Delana Boyer in 1813, and they moved to Strongsville in 1821. Seven years after Whitney died, his wife moved to Michigan.

Between the two sidewalks, about 10 stones before the vault, is "Hudson." Joshua Hudson (1760–1842), the son of Nathaniel and Martha Hudson, was born in Grafton, Massachusetts. He first enlisted in Connecticut, June 1, 1776, serving under Colonel Wolcott. He also served with Colonel Webb for three months starting in January 1777, and then with Colonel Walbridge for eight months from May of 1777. Mention is made of his being in the Pennsylvania Line as well as with the Connecticut Militia at New London and at Norwich.

After the war, Hudson moved to Massachusetts. He married Celia Smith on June 11, 1789, and they had three children. He continued to move around, living in Cambridge, New York, and Wilmington, Vermont. In Wilmington, where he stayed 20 years, Hudson's neighbors were the Hayes family, parents of Rutherford B. Hayes. Hudson finally moved to the Cleveland area in 1831. His wife, Celia, died two years after he did. Although no stone can be found for Celia, it is assumed she too is buried here.

Walk back to Sidewalk A. On the south side of the walk about six feet from the Pearl Road entrance is the faded white marker for John Strong. The dates 1771–1863 are visible. John Stoughton Strong, the founder of Strongsville, had a legendary reputation in the community. He used his booming voice to round up his livestock and to improvise songs. Seated on horseback, he would offer a running verbal commentary directed at the townspeople or toward the cattle. His ability to accurately count sheep was well known.

> **NOTABLE:**
> *There are five Revolutionary War soldiers buried here and possibly a sixth.*

In his biography of John Strong, Frederick Strong (John's grandson) recounts an occasion when, while traveling east, John stayed overnight at an inn but had to awaken at midnight to take the stagecoach. Upon receiving his lodging bill, Strong said, "I am glad you called me up when you did; if I had slept till morning I wouldn't have had enough money to pay my bill."

The biographer also recounts the time when a much older Strong climbed a tree with a good view of Lake Erie. Being partially blind as well as aged, Strong needed the assistance of a worker on his farm. Strong climbed the chestnut tree but could not see the lake. Having torn his clothes as he descended he said, "What did I climb that tree for? I can't see four rods when I am on the ground."

Strong's son, George B. Strong, is buried at Spring Grove in Medina, but his grandson, also named John Strong, is buried here.

Walk or drive toward the back of the cemetery. Two roads past the vault is the grave of John Bosworth (1760–1865), who was born in Rehoboth, Massachusetts. His parents were Ichabod and Bethia Bosworth. His mother was Ichabod's second wife; she died when John was six months old and he was raised by his uncle, Seth Wood.

Bosworth enlisted with Captain Pelege Peck's company, in Colonel John Dagget's regiment in January 1778, at the age of 17 ½. Records indicate he was discharged three months later.

Bosworth married Rosanna Blackman on March 18, 1784. Of the seven children born to them, only four lived to maturity. He and his second wife, Hannah Luther, had seven more children. The family lived in New York before finally moving to Strongsville with nine children.

John Bosworth was called Reverend, but though he preached throughout his life it is unclear if he was ordained. Bosworth died Christmas Day and was buried in Albion Cemetery, and later reinterred here. His wife, Hannah Luther, died January 7, 1847.

**STORY BUT NO STONE FOUND:** William Fuller lived in Strongsville and died in Cuyahoga County, but his exact place of burial is unknown. His wife died while they were living in Strongsville, so it is quite possible they are both buried here. Fuller enlisted in Wrentham, Massachusetts in 1778. He enlisted again in Captain Monroe's company, Colonel Jackson's Massachusetts Regiment, then was transferred to Captain Hoskins's company in August 1778, serving until December of the same year. In July 1779 he served under Captain Stoddard in Colonel Joseph Vose's Massachusetts Regiment, and later served in the Rhode Island militia. Fuller was a prisoner on the prison ship *Jersey* but was released once peace was declared.

William Pierce, an Englishman who served in the Revolutionary War, is also buried here. Pierce was in the British army for seven years. He served under Wellington in the Battle of Waterloo. His company of 80 men was reduced to a mere eight by battle's end. Pierce is thought to have been the last survivor. When he died in Strongsville on October 7, 1875, the 83-year-old Pierce was receiving a pension from the British government. He is buried in Section B, lot 21, grave D, but his marker is unreadable.

OTHER CEMETERIES NEARBY: North Royalton Cemetery, *p. 155*
Pritchard Cemetery, *p. 158*

~ SUPERSTITIONS ~

**Dogs howling in the dark of night**
**howl for death before daylight.**

# Tinker's Creek / Pilgerruh Cemetery

ADDRESS: Canal Rd.  ~  LOCATION: Valley View  ~  PHONE: None
ACREAGE: 0.3 acres  ~  CARETAKER: None
ACCESS: Grounds open daily dawn–dusk. Records at Bedford Historical Society (440-232-0407), and Western Reserve Historical Society (216-721-5722)
NUMBER OF BURIALS: Unknown
OLDEST/FIRST GRAVE: Oldest and first: Fitch Comstock, 1810
RELIGIOUS AFFILIATION: Nondenominational  ~  ETHNIC AFFILIATION: N/A
DIRECTIONS: I-77 to Exit 155 for Rockside Rd.; east on Rockside; right (south) on Canal Rd.; left (east) on Tinker's Creek Rd.; on left.

**HISTORY AND SURROUNDINGS:** This early pioneer cemetery is known by many names. Pilgerruh, meaning "Pilgrim's Rest," refers to the original settlers in this area. In 1786 Moravian missionaries established a settlement nearby but abandoned it 10 months later. Their leaving was precipitated by discord with both local Indians and hostile white inhabitants. As pacifists they found this an intolerable situation, and so in April, 1787 the group moved out.

> **NOTHING IS LEFT BUT SILENCE, ITSELF**

Just finding this unmarked, secluded cemetery makes you feel like a pioneer, filling you with the sense of discovery. Within this one small plot of land are many remnants of our country's early history, from the *Mayflower* to the Revolutionary War and, finally, the building of the Ohio and Erie Canal.

**YOUR VISIT:** The markers, some no longer upright, can be found randomly arranged throughout the small plot. Two are for descendants of Revolutionary War veteran Peter Comstock. Captain Comstock served in Colonel Lattimer's Regiment, 13th Company, 3rd Connecticut Militia. He was stationed at Fort Trumbull, Connecticut, when General Benedict Arnold burned New London. Comstock and

*Broken stone for Zephania Hathaway*

his wife Elizabeth had 18 children. Two of those children, Fitch and George, are buried here.

Fitch Comstock, though born in Connecticut, moved here from Charlemont, Massachusetts, in 1810. In November of that year he died. His is one of the oldest known graves in Cuyahoga County. His brother George's grave is next to his. George died in 1824.

*Fragmented marker for Fitch Comstock is still legible*

The marker of Zephania Hathaway, husband of Silence Hathaway (see below), is here and attests to his long life of 93 years. Nearby Hathaway Road is named for this family.

Several workers on the Ohio and Erie Canal who died from malaria are also buried here. Some history books mention the graves of Revolutionary War soldiers being here, but in actuality they were veterans of the War of 1812.

The last burial was in 1925 in an unmarked grave.

**NOTABLE:**

*Finding this unmarked, secluded cemetery makes you feel like a pioneer reveling in the sense of discovery. On this small plot of land are remnants of our country's early history from the* Mayflower *to the Revolutionary War to the building of the Ohio and Erie Canal.*

**STORY BUT NO STONE FOUND:** "The Courtship of Miles Standish," a poem by Henry Wadsworth Longfellow, tells of the marriage of John and Priscilla Alden, who came over on the *Mayflower.* Their great-great-granddaughter, Silence Hathaway, is buried here, but her marker can no longer be found. Fortunately, in 1977 Robert Allen Burns made a list of the gravestones and inscriptions at this site. His manuscript collection at the Bedford Historical Society lists the inscription on Silence Hathaway's grave. It read:

Remember me as you pass by, For as you are so once was I, And as I am so must you be, Therefore prepare to follow me.

OTHER CEMETERIES NEARBY: West Family Cemetery, *p. 217*
Darrow Cemetery, *p. 185*
Crossview Cemetery, *p. 184*

# West Family Cemetery

ADDRESS: Rockside Park Dr. ~ LOCATION: Independence ~ PHONE: None

ACREAGE: Unknown ~ CARETAKER: Unknown

ACCESS: Grounds always open. Records at Western Reserve Historical Society (216-721-5722)

NUMBER OF BURIALS: approx. 5 ~ OLDEST/FIRST GRAVE: Unknown

RELIGIOUS AFFILIATION: Nondenominational ~ ETHNIC AFFILIATION: N/A

DIRECTIONS: I-77 to Exit 155 for Rockside Rd.; east on Rockside; left (north) on Rockside Park Dr.; on left.

**HISTORY AND SURROUNDINGS:** This is an excellent example of how the early settlers buried their dead right on the family homestead. Located in what is now the middle of a busy commercial development, West Family Cemetery is a reminder of pioneer times. Fortunately, someone cared enough to preserve this important part of our history.

**YOUR VISIT:** While you may only spend a few minutes reading what's legible on the markers, you'll marvel at the fact that this spot has been preserved.

### THE REST WENT WEST

There were five markers when I last visited here. One is for Thomas West, who died in 1869. Another is for Susan West, wife of Thomas West. Another has the name John West on it. Nearby West Creek Drive is named for this family.

OTHER CEMETERIES NEARBY:
Darrow Cemetery, *p. 184*
Crossview Cemetery, *p. 185*

*19th century family graveyard meets 20th century corporate America*

# Single Marker

**NAME:** Benjamin Waite

**LOCATION:** 9367 Brecksville Rd. (south of Royalton Rd., north of Oakes Rd.)

Details: Benjamin Waite came from Massachusetts to the Western Reserve because of the promise of land to those who would settle here. He was a private in the Revolutionary War, serving in Mosely's Massachusetts Regiment. With his son Charles he built the third log cabin in Brecksville. Waite died in 1814, shortly after moving here, and is buried on land that belonged to his family. He was the first adult buried in Brecksville. To see his grave, park at the Brecksville Historical Society building and walk across the footbridge into the park. There is a bench nearby.

OTHER CEMETERIES NEARBY:  Highland Drive Cemetery, *p. 194*
North Royalton Cemetery, *p. 155*

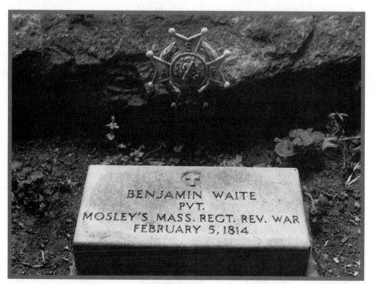

*Benjamin Waite died soon after moving to Brecksville*

# BIBLIOGRAPHY

**For general information:**

Arbeiter, Jean, and Linda D. Cirino. *Permanent Addresses: A Guide to the Resting Places of Famous Americans*. New York: M. Evans & Co., 1983.

Bay Village Historical Society. *Bay Village: A Way of Life*. compiled by Mrs. Raymond F. Menning Jr., and Mr. Dale F. Harter. Bay Village, Oh.: The Society, 1974.

Bellamy, John Stark II. *They Died Crawling and Other Tales of Cleveland Woe*. Cleveland, Oh.: Gray & Co., 1995.

Benton, Elbert J. *Cultural Story of an American City, Cleveland*. Cleveland, Oh.: Western Reserve Historical Society, 1943–1946.

Blum, Shirley Tanzer, ed. *The Ratner House*. Portland, Ore.: Max and Betty Wohlvert Ratner, 1988.

Breen, Donald J. *Johnson's Island Civil War Prison: Sandusky, Ohio, 1862–1963*. monograph.

Brown, John Gary. *Soul in the Stone*. Lawrence, Kans.: University Press of Kansas, 1994.

Bunnen, Lucinda, and Virginia Warren Smith. *Scoring In Heaven*. New York: Aperture Foundation Inc., 1991.

Burrows Bros. Company, The. *The Book of Clevelanders: A Biographical Dictionary of Living Men of the City of Cleveland*. Cleveland, Oh.: The Burrows Bros. Co., 1914.

*Burial and Removal at Erie Street, 1840–1918*. Cleveland, Oh.: Western Reserve Historical Society. microfilm.

Butler, Margaret M. *The Lakewood Story*. New York: Stratford House, 1949.

Cahoon, Ida M. *History of the Cahoon Family*. Cleveland, Oh.: 1911.

Calvin, Lee. *There Were Giants on the Earth*. Seville, Oh.: Seville Chronicle Press, 1969.

Cleveland Jewish Genealogical Society. *Fir Street Cemetery Necrology: A Project of the Cleveland Jewish Genealogical Society*. 1989.

Coates, William R. *Cuyahoga County and the City of Cleveland*. Chicago: American Historical Society, 1924.

Cuyahoga West Chapter of the Ohio Genealogical Society. *Cuyahoga County, Ohio, Genealogical Research Guide*. 2nd Ed. Mansfield, Oh.: The Ohio Genealogical Society, 1998.

Davis, Russell H. *Black Americans in Cleveland From George Peake to Carl B. Stokes, 1796–1969*. Washington: Associated Publishers, 1972.

Davis, Russell H. *Memorable Negroes in Cleveland's Past*. Cleveland, Oh.: Western Reserve Historical Society, 1969.

Dooner, Vincetta DiRocco, and Jean Marie Bossu. *Seasons of Life and Learning: Lake View Cemetery, An Educator's Handbook*. Cleveland, Oh.: Lake View Cemetery Foundation. 1990.

Downer, Edward T. *Johnson's Island*.

Ellis, William Donahue. *Early Settlers of Cleveland*. Cleveland, Oh.: Cleveland State University, 1976.

Franz, Minnie Weston. *Revolutionary Soldiers of Summit County*. Akron, Oh.: The Commercial Printing Co., 1911.

*Gamut Looks at Cleveland, The*. sp. ed. Cleveland, Oh.: Cleveland State University, 1986.

Gartner, Lloyd P. *History of the Jews of Cleveland*. Cleveland, Oh.: Western Reserve Historical Society and Jewish Theological Seminary of America, 1978.

Grismer, Karl H. *Akron and Summit County*. Akron, Oh.: Summit County Historical Society, 1952.

Grosvenor, Jeanette. *The Raccoon Brigade: Soldiers of the Revolution in Geauga County, Ohio*. Cullman, Al.: Gregath Co., 1990.

Harper, Robert. *Ohio Handbook of the Civil War*. Columbus, Oh.: Ohio Historical Society. 1961.

Hatcher, Harlan, and Fran Durham. *Giant from the Wilderness*. Cleveland, Oh.: World Publishing Co., 1955.

Holzworth, Walter F. *Men of Grit and Greatness*. Berea, Oh., 1970.

Ingham, Mary Bigelow. *Women of Cleveland and Their Work*. Cleveland, Oh.: W.A. Ingham, 1893.

Jacobs, G. Walker. *Stranger Stop and Cast An Eye: A Guide to Gravestones & Gravestone Rubbing*. Brattleboro, Vt.: S. Greene Press, 1973.

Johnson, Crisfield. *History of Cuyahoga County*.

Philadelphia: D.W. Ensign, 1879.

Kelly, Thomas. *The Cleveland 200: The Most Noted, Notable and Notorious in the First 200 Years of a Great American City*. Cleveland, Oh.: Archives Press, Inc., 1996.

Kelley, Thomas *Catholic Cemeteries .. A History, .. A Tradition,* ed. Rev. Ralph E. Wiatrowski. monograph.

Kennedy, James Harrison. *A History of Cleveland 1796-1876*. Cleveland, Oh.: Cleveland Imperial Press, 1896.

Kusmer, Kenneth L. *A Ghetto Takes Shape: Black Cleveland, 1870–1930*. Urbana: University of Illinois Press, 1976.

Marion, John Francis. *Famous and Curious Cemeteries*. New York: Crown Publishers, 1977.

Miller, Carol Poh and Wheeler, Robert. *Cleveland, A Concise History 1796–1990*. Bloomington: Indiana University Press, 1990.

Morton, Marian J. *Women in Cleveland: An Illustrated History*. Bloomington: Indiana Univesity Press, 1995.

North Royalton Historical Society, The. *History of North Royalton: 1811–1992*. North Royalton, Oh.: North Royalton Historical Society.

Oberlin Historical and Improvement Association. *Westwood: A Historical and Interpretive View of Oberlin's Cemetery*. Oberlin, Oh.: Oberlin Historical and Improvement Association, 1997.

*Official Souvenir of the 35th National Encampment of the Grand Army of the Republic*. 1901.

Ohio Genealogical Society. *Ohio, The Cross Road of Our Nation: Records and Pioneer Families*. Mansfield, Oh.: The Ohio Genealogical Society, 1960.

Ohio Genealogical Society, Southwest Cuyahoga Chapter. *Strongsville Cemetery 1816–1994: Memories in Stone*. Strongsville, Oh.: The Chapter, 1995.

Orth, Samuel P. *A History of Cleveland, Ohio; with Numerous Chapters by Special Contributors* (3 vols.). Chicago: S. J. Clarke Publishing, 1910.

Page, Tim. *Dawn Powell, A Biography*. New York: Henry Holt, 1998.

Porter, Roderick Boyd, ed. *Sacred Landmarks: a Selected Exhibit of Existing Ecclesiastical Structures in Cuyahoga County*. Cleveland, Oh.: Board of Cuyahoga County Commissioners, Cuyahoga County Archives, 1979.

Post, Charles Asa. *Doan's Corners and the City Four Miles West*. Cleveland, Oh.: The Caxton Co., 1930.

Rose, William Ganson. *Cleveland: The Making of a City*. 1950. reprint. Kent, Oh.: Kent State University Press, 1990.

Smith, Maxine Hartman, ed. *Ohio Cemeteries*. Mansfield, Oh.: The Ohio Genealogical Society, 1978.

Squire, Dick. *Bedford Vignettes*. Bedford, Oh.: Bedford Historical Society, 1982.

Stanton, Scott. *The Tombstone Tourist*. Portland, Ore.: Musicians 3T Publishing, 1998.

T.R. Koba & Company. *Rebel Fire Yankee Ice*. Berlin Hts., Oh.: T.R. Koba & Company in association with Butternut & Blue Film and Video. 1995. video.

Turner, James. *Heritage of Parma Heights*. Parma Heights, Oh.: The Heritage of Parma Heights Committee, 1969.

Upton, Harriet Taylor. *History of the Western Reserve*. Chicago: Lewis Publishing Co., 1910.

Uran, Clara. *A Centennial History of Cleveland*. Cleveland, Oh.: J.B. Savage, 1898.

Van Tassel, David D., and John J. Grabowski, eds. *The Dictionary of Cleveland Biography*. Bloomington: Indiana University Press, 1996.

Van Tassel, David D., and John J. Grabowski, eds. *The Encyclopedia of Cleveland History*. Bloomington: Indiana University Press in association with Case Western Reserve University and the Western reserve Historical Society, 1996.

Vincent, Sidney Z., and Judah Rubenstein. *Merging Traditions: Jewish Life in Cleveland*. Cleveland, Oh.: Western Reserve Historical Society. 1978

Wallen, James. *Cleveland's Golden Story*. Cleveland, Oh.: Taylor, 1920.

Warren, Violet, and Jeanette Grosvenor. *A Monumental Work: Inscriptions and Interments in Geauga County Through 1983*. Evansville, In.: Whipporwhill Publications, 1985.

Western Reserve Historical Society. *The Simon Perkins Papers*.

Whittlesey, Col. Charles. *Early History of Cleveland with Biographical Notices of the Pioneers and Surveyors*. Cleveland, Oh.: Higgins Book Co., 1867.

Wickham, Gertrude Van Rensselaer. *Pioneer Families of Cleveland, 1796–1840*. Salem, Mass.: Higginson Book Co., 1993.

Williams, Cornelia Bartow. *Descendants of John Williams.*

Wilmer, Kathryn Gasior. *Old Brooklyn New, Book II: A Portrait of Old Brooklyn.* Cleveland, Oh.: Old Brooklyn Community Development Corp., 198-.

Wilson, Craig, Samuel Lane, and Betty Fleming, *Fifty Years and Over of Akron and Summit County.* Akron, Oh.: Summit County Chapter, Ohio Genealogical Society, [1986 or 1987].

**For information on specific cemeteries:**

Adams Street Cemetery
> *Men of Grit and Greatness,* by Walter F. Holzworth; *Berea Enterprise,* various articles.

Alger Cemetery
> Lakewood DAR book, 1978; *The Lakewood Story* by Margaret Butler; *The Plain Dealer,* 8/30/90.

Bedford Cemetery
> *Bedford Vignettes* by Dick Squire; *Bedford Times-Register,* 7/8/55; *Sun Press,* 3/12/98.

Bet Olam Cemetery
> *The Ratner House,* by Shirley Blum Tanzer.

Brainard/Broadview Cemetery
> *Old Brooklyn New* by Kathryn Gasior Wilmer; *Cleveland Press,* 9/12/30, 8/14/37; *West Side Sun,* 7/15/71.

Brookmere Cemetery
> *Old Brooklyn New, Book II,* by Kathryn Gasior Wilmer; *Cleveland Press,* 2/25/60.

Butternut Ridge Cemetery
> *Dawn Powell, A Biography,* by Tim Page; *Cleveland Press* 8/18/69; "The Resurrection of Dawn Powell," by John Stark Bellamy II, *Cleveland Press,* 8/18/69; *The Plain Dealer,* 8/24/97.

Calvary Cemetery
> *Catholic Cemeteries .. A History, .. A Tradition,* by Thomas Kelley; *They Died Crawling and Other Tales of Cleveland Woe,* John Stark Bellamy II; *The Plain Dealer,* 8/18/74, 5/11/97, 5/2/98, 10/15/98; *The Sun Journal* 10/22/98.

Cathedral of St. John the Evangelist
> "History of the Diocese of Cleveland" (pamphlet); "The Cathedral of St. John the Evangelist" (pamphlet).

Chapel Street/Olde Hudson Township Burying Ground
> *Hudson Times,* 2/21/79; *The Plain Dealer,*

1/17/31.

Crossview Cemetery
> *The Plain Dealer,* 9/23/66, 4/27/92, 5/25/92.

Denison Cemetery
> "Burial Records of the Denison Street Cemetery," from DAR Ohio, Western Reserve Chapter, 1959; *Cleveland Press,* 3/4/70; *The Plain Dealer,* 5/27/39.

East Cleveland Cemetery
> Inscriptions at East Cleveland Cemetery and Presbyterian Cemetery; *Cleveland: The Making of the City,* by William Ganson Rose; *Northern Ohio Live,* 9/24/98; *The Call & Post,* 10/20/94; *Cleveland Press,* 4/18/08, 10/2/56; *The Plain Dealer,* 6/23/32, 7/21/35, 7/24/35, 7/6/88, 6/5/90.

Erie Street Cemetery
> *Cleveland's Golden Story,* by James Wallen; *Early Settlers of Cleveland,* by William Donohue Ellis; *A Ghetto Takes Shape: Black Cleveland, 1870-1930,* by Kenneth L. Kusmer; *History of Cleveland,* by James Harrison Kennedy; *The Cleveland News,* 7/28/54; *The Plain Dealer,* 3/18/34, 5/31/38, 7/22/40, 5/30/67, 5/26/83, 11/15/83, 7/22/87, 10/13/85, 4/28/90, 11/15/97, 5/10/98; *Cleveland Press,* 6/26/40, 6/12/54, 6/11/77.

Euclid Cemetery
> *Euclid Sun Journal,* 11/6/86; *Cleveland News,* 7/17/57; *Cleveland Press,* 5/1/29.

Evergreen Cemetery
> *The Lake County News-Herald,* 8/7/83, 9/14/98; *The Plain Dealer,* 1/26/91, 4/3/91, 5/5/91.

Fir Street Cemetery
> *Fir Street Cemetery Necrology,* by the Cleveland Jewish Genealogical Society: *The Jewish Independent,* 12/6/07, 8/30/12.

Glendale Cemetery
> *Akron and Summit County,* by Karl H. Grismer; *Revolutionary Soldiers of Summit County,* by Minnie Weston Franz; *Akron Beacon Journal,* 4/15/14, 4/27/55, 1/21/98, 11/8/98; *The Plain Dealer,* 8/9/98.

Harvard Grove Cemetery
> *Descendants of John Williams,* by Cornelia Bartow Williams; *History of the Cahoon Family,* by Ida M. Cahoon; *The Simon Perkins Papers,* from Western Reserve Historical Society; *Pioneer Families of Cleveland, 1796–1840,* by

Gertrude Van Rensselaer Wickham; *Cleveland Press*, 7/4/63; *The Plain Dealer*, 3/28/44, 7/17/97, 8/17/98; *The Neighborhood News*, 7/23/97.

Highland Drive Cemetery
*Cleveland Press*, 8/11/37.

Highland Park Cemetery
*The Cleveland News*, 3/48.

Hillcrest Cemetery
*Cleveland Magazine*, 4/77.

Immanuel Evangelical Cemetery
*Cleveland Press*, 6/10/81; *The Plain Dealer*, 3/12/59.

Jackson Burial Plot
*The Plain Dealer*, 9/27/65.

Johnson's Island Confederate Cemetery
*Johnson's Island*, by Edward T. Downer; *Johnson's Island: Civil War Prison Sandusky, Ohio, 1862–1863*, by Donald J. Breen; "Johnson's Island Prison," by Roger Long, *Blue and Gray* (March 1987); *Rebel Fire, Yankee Ice* by T.R. Koba & Co.; *Cleveland Press*, 5/18/32, 8/11/37; *The Plain Dealer*, 9/11/67, 4/5/91.

Knollwood Cemetery
*The Plain Dealer*, 9/15/97, 9/18/97, 7/26/98, 12/27/98.

Lake Side Cemetery
*Bay Village: A Way of Life*, from the Bay Village Historical Society.

Lake View Cemetery
*Seasons of Life and Learning*, by Vincetta DiRocco Dooner and Jean Marie Bossu; *CWRU*, 11/91; *The Heritage* Fall 1997, Spring 1997; *People Weekly*, 9/29/97; *The Plain Dealer*, 9/17/97, 8/9/98.

Lakewood Historical Society
"The Oldest Stone House Museum" (brochure).

Lakewood Park Cemetery
*Cleveland Press*, 8/23/56; *The Plain Dealer*, 8/29/57, 9/19/92, 1/24/94, 6/4/98.

Lower Cemetery
*1880 Township History of Geauga County; A Monumental Work*, by Violet Warren and Jeanette Grosvenor; *The Raccoon Brigade*, by Jeanette Grosvenor; *The Plain Dealer*, 11/29/70.

Lutheran Cemetery
"A Walk Through The Past," *Old Brooklyn New,*

*Book II*, by Kathryn Gasior Wilmer.

Markillie Cemetery
*Hudson Times*, 2/21/79; *The Plain Dealer*, 1/17/31.

Mayfield Cemetery
*The Book of Clevelanders*, by The Burrows Bros. Company; *Merging Traditions*, by Sidney Z. Vincent and Judah Rubinstein; *The Cleveland Jewish News*, 11/21/97.

Monroe Street Cemetery
*Memorable Negroes in Cleveland's Past*, by Russell H. Davis; "Annals of Cleveland," *The Cleveland Press*, 4/3/67; *The Plain Dealer*, 4/8/89, 1/21/96.

Mound Hill Cemetery
*Medina County Cemeteries; There Were Giants on the Earth*, by Lee Cavin.

Mt. Peace Cemetery
*Fifty Years and Over of Akron and Summit County*, by Craig Wilson, Samuel Lane, and Betty Fleming; *Akron Beacon Journal*, 5/29/54, 1/21/98.

North Royalton Cemetery
*History of North Royalton: 1811–1992*, from the North Royalton Historical Society; *Cleveland Press*, 5/29/40.

Parma Heights Cemetery
*Heritage of Parma Heights*, by James Turner.

Pritchard Cemetery
*History of North Royalton: 1811-1992*, from the North Royalton Historical Society.

Riverside Cemetery
*Claud Foste:r A Capsule Biography*, by Genevieve E. Maurer; *Mr. Jones' Home: A Westside Story*, by Richard W. Cochran; "Take a New Look at Riverside" (pamphlet); *The Tradition*, a publication of Riverside Cemetery; *The Plain Dealer*, 9/29/90, 4/2/95.

Riverside Golf Club Cemetery
*The Plain Dealer*, 10/2/32, 10/24/32, 12/18/40.

Scranton Road Cemetery
*Cleveland: The Making of the City*, by William Ganson Rose; *Cleveland News* 6/1/45.

St. John Cemetery
*The Plain Dealer*, 11/13/94.

St. Joseph Cemetery
*Catholic Cemeteries … A History, … A Tradition*, by Thomas Kelley.

St. Mary Cemetery
*The Plain Dealer*, 6/6/85.

St. Theodosius Cemetery
*The Plain Dealer*, 10/29/32, 1/10/37, 7/23/40.

Strongsville Cemetery
*Men of Grit and Greatness*, by Walter F. Holzworth; *Strongsville Cemetery 1816–1994*,
from the Ohio Genealogical Society, Southwest Cuyahoga Chapter.

Sunset Memorial Park
"Hungarian Monument," published by Sunset
Memorial Park, 1998; *The Plain Dealer*,
8/25/94, 10/23/89.

Tinkers Creek/Pilgerruh Cemetery
*Cleveland Press*, 9/28/70; *The Plain Dealer*,
9/22/64, 4/1/92.

Warrensville West Cemetery
Notes from "Bus Talks" found at Shaker His-
torical Society; *Shaker Magazine*, 1/85; *Sun
Press*, 8/14/58.

Westwood Cemetery
*Westwood: A Historical and Interpretive View
of Oberlin's Cemetery*, from Oberlin Historical
and Improvement Organization; *The Plain
Dealer*, 5/25/92.

Willoughby Cemetery
*The Lake County News-Herald*, 9/6/69,
12/19/93.

Woodland Cemetery
*The Call and Post*, 8/23/90; *Cleveland Press*,
8/11/37; *The Plain Dealer*, 2/23/81, 5/26/96.

Woodvale Cemetery
"Berea Back When," *The Berea Enterprise*,
12/5/41; *The Plain Dealer*, 5/30/56.

# Index

## If you enjoyed this book, try one of these other great books about Cleveland ...

**They Died Crawling and Other Tales**
**The Maniac in the Bushes**
**The Corpse in the Cellar** / Three collections of gripping true tales about Cleveland crimes and disasters. Include spine-chilling photos. *John Stark Bellamy* / $13.95 softcover (each)

**Bed & Breakfast Getaways from Cleveland** / 80 charming small inns perfect for an easy weekend or evening away from home. *Doris Larson* / $13.95 softcover

**The Cleveland Orchestra Story** / How a midwestern orchestra became a titan in the world of classical music. With 102 rare photographs. *Donald Rosenberg* / $40.00 hardcover

**Neil Zurcher's Favorite One Tank Trips** (Book 1)

**More of Neil Zurcher's One Tank Trips** (Book 2)
**One Tank Trips Road Food** (Book 3)
Hundreds of unusual nearby getaway ideas in three books by Northeast Ohio's favorite TV travel reporter. / $13.95 softcover (each)

**Dick Goddard's Weather Guide for Northeast Ohio** / Seasonal facts, folklore, storm tips, and weather wit from Cleveland's top meteorologist. / $13.95 softcover

**Cleveland Family Fun** / Great ideas for places to go and things to do with kids of all ages. Written by parents, for parents. *Jennifer Stoffel* / $13.95 softcover

**Cleveland Golfer's Bible** / All of Greater Cleveland's golf courses and driving ranges are described in this essential guide for any golfer. *John Tidyman* / $13.95 softcover

**365 Ways to Meet People in Cleveland** / Friendship, romance, and networking ideas for singles, couples, and families. *Miriam Carey* / $8.95 softcover

**52 Romantic Outings in Greater Cleveland** / Easy-to-follow "recipes" for romance, for a lunch hour, an evening, or a full day together. *Miriam Carey* / $13.95 softcover

**What's So Big About Cleveland, Ohio?** / What does a well-traveled 10-year-old think about her first visit to Cleveland? "B-o-o-o-ring". Until, that is, she discovers a very special little secret ... *Sara Holbrook & Ennis McNulty* / $17.95 hardcover

**Cleveland Ethnic Eats** / Discover Cleveland's authentic ethnic restaurants and markets and taste the exotic flavors of the world without leaving town! *Laura Taxel* / $13.95 softcover

**Cleveland Fishing Guide** / Best public fishing spots in Northeast Ohio, what kind of fish you'll find, and how to catch them. Directory of fishing resources. *John Barbo* / $13.95 softcover

**Cleveland On Foot**
**Beyond Cleveland On Foot** / Two books of self-guided walking tours: first, through Greater Cleveland's neighborhoods, suburbs, and metroparks; then, through parks and small towns of 7 neighboring counties. *Patience Cameron Hoskins* / $14.95 softcover

**Continued ...**

**Cleveland Garden Handbook** / Local experts tell how to grow a beautiful garden in Northeast Ohio. Filled with practical tips. *Susan McClure* / $12.95

**Cleveland: A Portrait** / 105 color photographs capture Greater Cleveland's landmarks and hidden details in all seasons. *Jonathan Wayne* / $35.00 hardcover *(photo above is from this book.)*

**Ghoulardi** / The behind-the-scenes story of Cleveland's wildest TV legend. Rare photos, interviews, show transcripts, and Ghoulardi trivia. *Tom Feran & R. D. Heldenfels* / $17.95 softcover

**The Ghoul Scrapbook** / Rare photos, show transcripts, and video captures from "The Main Maniac" of Cleveland late-night TV. *Ron Sweed & Mike Olszewski* / $17.95 softcover

**Feagler's Cleveland** / The best from three decades of commentary by Cleveland's top columnist, Dick Feagler. Witty, insightful, opinionated, thoughtful. / $13.95 softcover

**"Did You Read Feagler Today?"** / The most talked about recent columns by Cleveland's most outspoken columnist. / $13.95 softcover

**On Being Brown** / Thoughtful essays and interviews exploring what it means to be a true fan of the Cleveland Browns. *Scott Huler* / $18.95 hardcover, $10.95 softcover

**Indians Memories** / A nostalgic roller coaster ride including laughably bad seasons and two exciting eras of championship baseball. *Tim Long* / $5.95 softcover

**Indians on the Game** / Quotations from favorite Cleveland ballplayers give an insider's look at the game of baseball. *Wayne Stewart* / $9.95 softcover

**Barnaby and Me** / Linn Sheldon, a Cleveland TV legend as "Barnaby", tells the fascinating story of his own extraordinary life. / $20.00 hardcover

**The Great Indoors** / The first decade of Eric Broder's hilarious weekly "Great Indoors" column. Reread favorites, or get caught up with the ongoing saga. / $13.95 softcover

**Cleveland Sports Trivia Quiz** / Test your knowledge with these 500 brain-teasing questions and answers on all kinds of Cleveland sports. *Tim Long* / $6.95 softcover

**Cleveland TV Memories** / Remember when TV was local? A nostalgic collection of 365 favorite local shows, hosts, jingles, bloopers, stunts, and more. *Feran & Heldenfels* / $6.95 softcover

## Available at your local bookstore.

These books are stocked at Northeast Ohio bookstores, are available from most online book retailers, and can be ordered at any bookstore in the U.S.

Need help finding a retailer near you? Call us toll-free: **1-800-915-3609**.

### Gray & Company, Publishers

1588 E. 40th St., Cleveland, OH 44103 / 216-431-2665

for more information, visit: **www.grayco.com**